Don't Look Back

Don't Look Back

KEITH MORLEY

Troubador Publishing Ltd
Unit E2 Airfield Business Park,
Harrison Road, Market Harborough,
Leicestershire LE16 7UL
Tel: 0116 279 2299
Email: books@troubador.co.uk
Web: www.troubador.co.uk/matador

ISBN 978 1 80514 163 1

British Library Cataloguing in Publication Data.
A catalogue record for this book is available from the British Library.

Printed byPrinted and bound in Great Britain by 4edge Limited
Typeset in 11pt Aldine401 BT by Troubador Publishing Ltd, Leicester, UK

Matador is an imprint of Troubador Publishing Ltd

In fond remembrance of Denis Vanoystaeyen

INTRODUCTION

Nazi expansion in Europe had reached its height by 1942. The majority of countries west of the Soviet Union were either under German occupation or in the control of Hitler's allies, co-belligerents and puppet states. But 1943 saw a bombing campaign begin against Germany at a level and intensity never seen before. The RAF hit German targets at night and the American Eighth Air Force raided from England by day. Large numbers of casualties were predicted as the aircrews faced a formidable opposition of Luftwaffe fighter aircraft, concentrated air defence systems, searchlights and flak barrages. In addition, the airmen also battled intense cold, fatigue, icy conditions and mechanical problems with the overworked aircraft.

The average life expectancy of a new crew on RAF Bomber Command was six weeks and over 55,500 men died. The American Eighth Air Force suffered one half of the total U.S. Army Air Force casualties in World War II (more than 47,000, of which in excess of 26,000 were deaths). Many crews never finished a tour of operations; their aircraft being either shot down or destroyed in mid-air. Those lucky enough to bale out and land safely were mostly taken prisoner by a hostile enemy. Others faced a frightened population or the danger of Nazi sympathisers and collaborators. Such was the death and destruction on the ground from Allied bombing raids, any airmen landing in Germany ran the risk of being attacked or even killed by civilians. The prospect of evading capture was remote but some did defy the odds and get home. This would not have been possible without the escape lines and patriots in countries under Nazi occupation. The *Abwehr* and Gestapo made persistent efforts to penetrate these lines and, in the face of great danger, people risked not only their own lives to help complete strangers but the lives of their families. Many paid the ultimate price.

I was seven when my father first mentioned his wartime escape* (as he always termed it). In late 1943 he was close to completing his tour of operations as a wireless operator in an RAF Lancaster crew when his aircraft was shot down. In spite of attempts spanning almost forty years, I managed to reach beyond his initial brief words only in rare and sometimes unexpected moments. This had seemed a mystery to a boy awash with stories of the Second World War. My junior years were spent with the heroes in *War Picture Library* and *Commando* books, the weekly war stories in the *Victor* comic, and viewing TV programmes *The Valiant Years* and *Victory at Sea* which my father always watched with me. To discover the story of what happened after he baled out of his aircraft was a boyhood dream which remained out of reach until he agreed to tell me, two months before his death.

Time had misted some of the memories, but his deeper thoughts and emotions emerged. The night of 3rd November 1943 and weeks on the run had left their scars and a raft of unanswered questions. Only limited official documents were accessible to the public until much later when some of the embargoed papers became available, which helped to fill in the story. Assistance from expert researchers, interviews and correspondence with veterans and escape line helpers, memoirs of the immediate timeframe and a physical retracing of sections in my father's journey have enabled me to write this account. What began as a record for family history purposes grew into a human story to be preserved and read by a wider audience.

His deep, frank thoughts and the close-up feel in this book may well transcend a reserve and modest underplay present in many personal accounts of the period, but they formed the backbone of what I was told. Descriptions of some locations and characters were expanded later using photographs and my visits to the actual places. Given the passing of the years, any dialogue has been written as accurately as possible. In addition, the level of spoken English amongst certain helpers was not always known, so some words have been adapted.

Sadly, so many of these amazing people have now passed into history and if by writing this memoir I can help preserve their memory and convey what it was like out there for airmen on the run and their helpers, then it will have been worthwhile. We must never forget them.

*According to the British Directorate of Military Intelligence (MI9) in WW2: an escaper had managed to get away from the secure custody of the enemy. This was usually from a POW camp, prison or under the charge of guards. An evader had not fallen into enemy hands and remained at large.

ACKNOWLEDGEMENTS

My thanks extend to a legion of people and there are too many to name everyone. You all have an important place in this work.

During the research and writing of these memoirs, it was an honour and privilege to meet and correspond with veteran helpers, evaders and their families. Without their memories I could not have written this account with the same level of detail or perception. The courage and quiet modesty shown by the helpers in the face of great danger still shone through even with the passing of the years and was a truly humbling experience for me. The evaders had also lived a precarious existence in the air from the moment they approached an enemy coast. Once they found themselves alone in occupied territory with its own set of challenges, this added to their ordeal, yet their accounts often had a matter-of-factness and *'c'est la guerre'* acceptance. Their bravery and fortitude was astounding and their memory lives on.

I am indebted to:

Denis and Maria Vanoystaeyen and family for their help, kindness and wonderful hospitality. Retracing with Denis the first part of Ronald's evasion route, visiting the locations and meeting some of the people involved was an emotional and unforgettable experience.

Henriette 'Monique' Hanotte, who welcomed me into her home in Nivelles and shared so many stories and photographs connected with her work in the Comet Escape Line. On a subsequent occasion with the aid of another family member and his car, she retraced the route with me from Rumes to Bachy that she used on the night Ronald crossed into France with the other evaders. We also visited the Bricout and Houdart homes in Bachy.

Amanda 'Dianne' Stassart, who I met in her Brussels apartment, along with Monique. Amanda brought out the champagne for us.

Her memories of Comet work, the helpers and her time on the Rumes to Bachy route were both remarkable and essential to this memoir.

Aline Dumon, 'Michou', who in her correspondence still remembered my father and recounted the evening he arrived in Brussels.

George Ward, who answered so many of my questions and relayed the account of his own evasion by audio tape and email.

Special thanks are also due to:

Philippe Connart, Edward Renière, Michael Moores LeBlanc and Bruce Bolinger for their expert help, guidance and amazing encyclopaedic knowledge of the Comet Escape Line. I couldn't have written this without you, boys.

Brigitte d'Oultrement, President, *Ligne Comète Remembrance* who made the meets with Monique and Amanda possible and looked after my wife and I so well on the day.

Cheryl Padgham for her work and photographs on the Larressore crossings.

Frédéric Haldimann for the weather information and synoptic charts of Western Europe, November to December 1943.

Gene Buck, John Clinch, Geoff Cooper, Jean Erkes, Matty Evans, Wim Govaerts, Michael Hanotte, Murielle Hanotte, Keith Janes, Martine LeGrelle, Jack McAvoy, Victor Schutters and Margaret Pope.

My writing groups past and present – Just Write Workshop, Phoenix Writers, Friday's People and Grace Dieu Writers for their critique and insightful comments.

Author, Dianne Noble for her re-read of the manuscript and her perceptive thoughts and valued comments.

Finally, to my dear wife, Anne, whose help, patience, encouragement and constant support kept me going. You always believed.

Lancaster 111 No　'U' Uncle　　　　　　　　　　**467 RAAF Squadron**
JB121

3 November 1943　**Take off: Bottesford 17.03**　　**Target:**　　**Dusseldorf**

Captain and Pilot	Squadron Leader W. J. Lewis D.F.C.	'Bill'	24th Op
Navigator	Flight Sergeant K. Garvey	'Ken'	24th Op
Flight Engineer	Sergeant C. E. Stead	'Eddie'	22nd Op
Wireless Operator	Sergeant R. C. Morley	'Ron'	22nd Op
Bomb Aimer	Sergeant A. J. Scott	'Scotty'	22nd Op
Mid Upper Gunner	Sergeant G. P. Baylis	'Curly'	22nd Op
Rear Gunner	Flight Sergeant J. H. Mallin D.F.M.	'Jimmy'	22nd Op
Second Pilot	Flight Sergeant J. W. Evans	'Evans'	1st Op

Briefed Outward Route: Base – 5215N 0300E-5149N 0353E-5103N 0518E-5100N 0617E-Target

PART ONE

Belgium

1

'Five minutes to enemy coast, skipper.'

'Thank you, navigator. Five minutes.'

My stomach dropped. It always did. Ken's words hung there like a huge lead weight. I switched from intercom back to my wireless set. The same fear twisted my insides when the rocket signal went up for us to board the Lancaster and start engines. It burrowed deeper as I entered the dark fuselage and hit a smell of oil, aircraft dope and chemicals from the Elsan toilet. I never spoke about it, none of us did. If any aircrew reckoned they weren't scared, they were liars.

The threat was always there when crossing the enemy coast and all hell would let loose as we neared the target: enemy night fighters and flak lying in wait, red and crimson flash bursts closing around the bomber stream, searchlights coning an aircraft with their long white fingers before enemy gunners encircled the plane with swarms of exploding shells. Our gunners called out any stricken aircraft and parachutes over the intercom and I had seen the carnage for myself from the astrodome. The black silhouette above us at two o'clock, rising up for an instant before a flash and orange explosion instantly turned everything to fire, a Lancaster diving down off our starboard wing with flames streaking from the fuselage and before its glow had disappeared, the Halifax on our port side veering off ablaze.

I was spared from seeing much of that nightmare until we neared the target; there was more than enough to occupy a wireless operator. Decode and log Group broadcasts every quarter to the hour and every quarter past, send Morse acknowledgements and half-hour wind readings to base, take bearings and fixed position reports, tune in to German fighter control transmissions and attempt to jam them. The battle with controlling our aircraft's heating outlet near my feet came after other peripheral jobs. I sweltered in the heat while the rest of the aircraft went down to minus forty degrees. Amongst the din from our engines, my mind immersed itself in each immediate moment, so I never looked too far forward. It was a strange kind of sanctuary.

I switched back to intercom. Scotty's voice.

'Hello, skipper, bombardier here. Enemy coast ahead. No flak or searchlights.'

'OK bombardier. Hello, mid-upper. Can you see anything?'

'Not much, skipper. Searchlights to port further down the coast. Cloud's about five-tenths. No aircraft sighted.'

I couldn't recall a visit to Happy Valley when we hadn't spotted our own bombers for over half an hour or the reports of friendly aircraft from the Monica radar system had been so infrequent. The light above my wireless set flickered. Enemy night fighters picked off stragglers, the navigator kept us in the bomber stream for safety in numbers and better chances. Ken was the best, but for once, the worries slipped into my mind.

'Hello, navigator, bombardier here. Crossing enemy coast… now.'

I glanced at my watch. Just after nineteen hundred hours. Ken would see us right, he always did.

'Navigator to skipper. On track.'

'On track. Thank you, navigator.'

Time to take the wind readings before the next half-hourly group message.

'Wireless op here, skipper.'

'Go ahead, wireless op.'

'Switching to group broadcast.'

'OK, wireless op.'

The signal whistled and drifted in my headphones I strained

2

to listen through the static. Operational flying was fear: the first thing you did each morning was look outside at the weather to see if you were working that night. Clear skies meant different things now. Some men went outside and were physically sick after they saw their name listed on battle orders. An imminent op invaded your thoughts all day. The strain grew, despite equipment checks, a night flying test and briefings to keep you busy. You pushed it down behind the immediate moment. Everyone handled things their own way. Some cracked jokes and blustered bravado, others were quiet and withdrew into themselves. I needed something to do, or too much to do. The last hour at our dispersal pad before take-off was the worst: the sombre silence and the waiting.

A blinding white flash came before the explosion. The aircraft lifted and bucked, whiplashing me forward against the wall of radio equipment. Floor and fuselage on the starboard side burst inwards with flying red-hot metal splinters and balls of flame. The air was thick with sparks, smoke and a sour smell of cordite. The navigator's curtains were open. Flames devoured the maps and charts on Ken's table – the floor suddenly ignited near his feet. I switched back to intercom and stood up.

The skipper's urgent voice. 'We're on fire, get the extinguishers.'

Ken emptied one into the flames on his table then tried to put out the fires by beating, pressing and stamping on them. Smoke rose from his gloves.

'Skipper here. Prepare to abandon aircraft.'

The Lanc was listing and losing height. Breath caught in my throat and a hot choking terror hit me. Pieces of burning debris littered the fuselage; the bomb bay was directly underneath.

'Pilot to crew. Abandon aircraft. Abandon aircraft.'

My parachute pack? I clambered back over the main spar and pulled it out. No burn marks or outer damage. Through a jagged mass of shadow and flashes, Ken frantically brushed at his smouldering gloves as he battled to get his chute on. The engines groaned, raced – settled again. I clipped my parachute to the harness, unplugged my flying helmet and waited – we had a set order to exit the aircraft.

Ken was ready. My oxygen mask came off and I followed him forward, stooping and twisting down the narrow fuselage. Wind buffeted through holes in the side and more flak blasts sparred with the aircraft as I passed the empty flight engineer's position. Bill was still in control in the pilot's seat – Eddie, Scotty and the second pilot had already baled out. Neither of the gunners was behind me – I'd heard nothing from Curly or Jimmy over the intercom. Cold air blasted up through the open forward escape hatch in the bomb aimer's position. Ken climbed down into the well, removed his helmet and fell out headfirst. Bill gave me the thumbs-up sign. I sat on the edge, drew back my helmet and jumped feet first into the screaming air.

Trailing flames licked at the bomb bay and the slipstream buffeted me about. Flak was still bursting all around. Clicks and pops sounded in my ears as I plummeted down. Count to five and pull the D ring. I yanked it hard with my right hand. The crackle of unfurling silk rippled through the air, a sudden jerk snagging at my shoulders and groin, crushing the breath from my body as the parachute burst open. I grabbed a line on either side of the canopy, pulling at them to stop the pendulum swing. Flak guns kept firing, each shell another orange burst in the sky. The air beat against me at every explosion and became clouded with evil-smelling smoke. One metal chunk tearing into my body or a hot fragment of shrapnel on the parachute silk and it would be over. I waited for the pain or full horror of plunging through the night.

Wind rippled under the canopy. Flashes and explosions grew more distant. A half-moon poked low through thinning cloud. The landscape appeared below: the black cube of a farmhouse, hedges and trees bordering fields. I drifted over a railway track and wide canal. The guns opened up briefly again. My mind raced through the hazards – the Germans had seen my parachute by now. Get down safely, no broken ankles, no hitting trees or buildings. What happened to the boys? Jimmy, Curly and Bill – did they get out? What about the others, had anyone landed yet?

A dog barked. I caught the damp, winter scent of countryside as a field rushed up to meet me. Knees slightly bent, feet pushed together, I hit the ground hard and rolled over amongst the leaves and furrows. Silence. I slowly moved my legs and feet. No pain. Adrenaline and relief coursed through me – a safe landing. The parachute suddenly billowed in the wind, dragging me across the field. I managed to scramble up, pull on the risers, move towards the canopy and collapse it before unbuckling my harness and twisting the lines as I drew them in. Something dropped close to me – a dull thudding sound. More of them, as if someone were throwing stones into the field. Shell splinters were still falling from the guns. I half gathered, half dragged the parachute and harness and ran to a hedge for cover.

The turnip field disappeared in shadow at the corners. I crouched amongst the earthy smell of hedge and thickets. A beech tree creaked on the far side and wind gently fanned the swathes of leaves around me. All quiet. No lights or houses. Past nineteen-thirty hours by my watch – plenty of night left for me to get away. The soldiers would be searching now and again at first light. I felt in the front pocket of my battledress trousers for the escape kit. It was missing.

2

Where the hell was it? I took off my Mae West and knelt by the hedge, tearing at my pockets: side pockets, flap pockets, button pockets – the back one with a seam which always caught against my fingernail. The Merlin engines still drummed in my head. I saw the flash again, felt the blast and rock from the explosion. My fingers rode over the pleated pocket on the front of my trousers. The button was undone. A clockwork search started through my clothes. I had a place for everything. Right-hand trouser pocket – the handkerchief was still there. Cigarette case, lighter and coins were inside my locker back in the crew room. Regulation items only in the battledress, I always checked twice before the trip down to our dispersal pad.

Aids to escape must be carried in a safe position, preferably in a battledress pocket. The instructor's voice niggled in my ear. The escape box had been safe and fitted perfectly. Everything was in that box: compass, rations, rubber water bottle. Horlicks tablets, waterproof matches, and glucose sweets were in there. It must have fallen out of my pocket when I jumped from the aircraft, or maybe during the four-mile descent. Or when I hit the ground? I staggered to the centre of the field near my landing point and scrabbled amongst the turnip leaves and darkness.

A flattened circle had formed around me in the patchy moonlight shadow. I stayed on my knees and took deep breaths, there was never panic in the aircraft and it made no sense now. A ghostly quiet lingered behind the breeze – no dogs, no shouts or vehicles. My parachute began to rustle and flap next to the hedge. I crept back, bundled up the canopy and harness, dropped in my flying helmet and whistle then knelt down to dig out a hole with my hands.

A mound of dead leaves under the hedge was easy to spot, easy to see if you were searching. I should have grubbed out more earth before adding my gloves and Mae West. No more time. I turned up my battledress collar and hurried along the field's edge. The boys must have landed close by. We would run into each other soon – stick together, get help. I needed to find them, find north in the sky and head southwest for Spain and Gibraltar.

How had I managed to land in one piece? The training for baling out was practising how to fall on landing, half an hour in a hangar swinging about in a parachute harness and occasional exit drills from our aircraft whilst it was parked at the dispersal pad. I must have taken a quarter of an hour to reach the ground. Fifteen minutes was an eternity. Eyes always scanned the skies at the drone of a bomber stream: locals slipping out from their homes to stand in the shadows, sentries observing the slow, angled descent of parachutes. The place would be crawling with Germans within minutes if they found my chute. Stars winked through skims of cloud, the cold hung around my head and shoulders. I reached the next field. Was it Belgian or Dutch? Holland meant one more border to cross.

The cardboard map wallet? It was in my battledress before we drove out to the aircraft. Someone at the escape lecture had said there was another compass in the purse. I always knew it as a wallet with maps and foreign paper money inside. A ridge of stiff card in my top pocket caught against my fingers. How had I missed it? Heart thumping, hand shaking, I pulled out a small envelope shape and opened the flap. A tiny metal object rolled into my hand. I held it up to my face. Two luminous dots on the compass needle pointed north. The sky was clear enough to pick out the Pole star, which should stay at my right shoulder. I slid the wallet back in my battledress and turned around, keeping close to the hedge. Short steps, long steps, each one ploughed a hole through the quiet. I ran up to a gap in the bushes, stumbled into the next field and fell onto wet grass. Only the wind whispered above my rapid breathing.

The air was thick with leaf mould and a mushroom smell of late autumn. I lay still, hanging on every sound and listening out for

Jimmy's friendly whistle or Scotty's long legs scissoring through the grass. My fingers tightened around the compass. The curfew blackness we'd flown through so many times, stretched back over endless grey miles of North Sea to home.

I needed to remove the insignia from my battledress and look something like a worker in overalls, at least from a distance. I squeezed between some bushes and crouched under a chestnut tree. My breath formed white plumes in the night air as I picked at the stitching around the wings and sparks patches. They came away. The sergeant stripes took longer. All such a vagrant act, like some self-inflicted court martial and there was something terribly simple about it all.

The cold had wormed its way inside me and my battledress trousers were soaking wet around the knees. Voices told me to stay put until morning but the landing site was still too close. I had no choice. Bury the insignia, check my compass and set off southwest.

The half-moon seemed to move across the night sky behind wisps of thin cloud. *Never walk in the centre of fields. Stay close to hedges and keep away from roads and paths.* The instructor's words had skimmed over my head at the time. *Pay attention, gentlemen. At least five of you in this room will be shot down over enemy territory.* Me, who would never be shot down – me who would always return for his bacon and egg. *Keep eyes and ears wide open. Watch the behaviour of birds and cattle ahead. Any noise, then lie low and listen.* I remembered a chap gazing out of the class window, chewing his pencil, and the round-faced lad with wavy, fair hair who looked at me as if I was some oddity. How much did they remember now, sitting drinking by a warm fire in some RAF Mess or bar?

I kept close to the field edges, ducking behind bushes and thickets, quickening past gaps and trying to decipher the shadows amongst shadows. Dry leaves became creeping feet around me – every twig snapped like the click of a rifle bolt. No patrols or lights yet, only cattle, the wind and dark corridors in my imagination.

A dim, conical shape came into view. The haystack had rounded sides with the top half shaped like an ice cream in a cornet. I could shelter from the cold. Best keep moving and forge more distance from the landing point before dawn. No. The clouds showed signs of thickening; it would be easy to miss a farm or barn in the dark. Thoughts pounded in my head like drumbeats. I circled the haystack. It felt temptingly dry. Something tumbled out and ran over my feet. I burrowed into the straw with a plan to leave at first light.

A breeze nosed around the haystack. There had been no sleep, only cold, a bank of thoughts towards home and this huge clot of fear. Every joint felt stiff and my mouth tasted like ash. I crawled out into a grey dawn. Ploughed fields, pastureland and trees – the flat countryside was a wash of hazy green and brown with a low milky ground mist. Only a smudge of trees broke the blurred horizon. I knelt down low on the grass. The dew felt cold and sweet against my face.

The black flying boots were a giveaway with their fur-lined insides and zippers. The right one had a hidden pocket for a knife, ready to cut away the calf-length section above the lace-up shoes. No knife. I never put one in. Serious walking would be a struggle now with the battle dress trousers tucked in. I tugged them out and forced the bottoms down over the boots.

The cloth map from my wallet covered Belgium, France and Germany. Its cartography was too small and until I knew my location there was no starting point. The vastness of it all began to overwhelm me. I stared across an abstract landscape and felt my misery rise. South lay beyond the far corner of the meadow. In the middle distance a faint line of figures on bicycles ghosted along open ground. Maybe it wasn't an enemy patrol, maybe farm labourers going to work, perhaps? They disappeared from sight before I took a compass check. The ground mist would give me temporary cover. Best to make a move and keep away from lanes and open fields as once the low haze lifted it would only be a matter of time before someone saw me.

Over half an hour passed. I hadn't advanced my watch: we had come off Double Summer Time in August, and occupied Western Europe was aligned with Britain at Greenwich Mean Time, plus one hour. Farm buildings came into view at the end of a furrowed track. I approached on the flank and hid behind a wattle fence away from the house. The brown tiled roof sagged in the middle and was crusted with lichen. A stooped old man in a black jacket picked his way through the muddy yard. *Watch isolated farms in the day, check traffic in and out of the house before approaching.* The instructor's voice echoed like an angry parent. A flap of feathers and chickens squabbling came from the other side of the fence. I raised my head slowly. A white-haired woman in a green dress looked straight at me from an upstairs window.

3

My brain was a storm. *You should delay approach until dusk.* I stood up, forcing a way through the bushes. The woman disappeared from the window when I reached the yard. Next to some ramshackle outbuildings, the old man was struggling to tip feed from a sack into a bucket. My boots squelched in the mud. A horrified expression filled his face.

'RAF,' I said.

He dropped the sack, his gaze never leaving mine – big eyes with puffy bags underneath. Barking came from inside the farmhouse and the door creaked open. A woman stood holding onto a yapping mongrel – the woman from the window. She yelled and the dog sat down quietly on the step. The man stepped back, looking past me towards the meadow. I pointed to the house.

'Belgium? Is this Belgium?'

The man nodded, revealing a row of blackened teeth. *'Belgie.'* He caught the woman's stern expression before she disappeared inside the house with the dog.

I pointed to the sky. 'English airman... *Anglais.* Can you help me?'

He scanned the fields again then fussed me across the yard into a musty-smelling kitchen with a grey flagstone floor. The door closed, instantly dulling the light. A single window looked out across the track and countryside and the man took up position, scratching at the dirty glass with his finger. The couple bickered in loud, edgy voices until the woman motioned me to a scrubbed table with two wooden chairs. She picked up a grey shawl, draping it around her shoulders. Deep in the house the dog whined incessantly.

I sat down slowly. The woman placed a bowl of milk in front of me and I gulped it down, spilling a trail down my battledress.

11

'Can you help me?' My voice sounded weak and brittle. 'Resistance?'

Colour drained from the woman's lined face. The couple were terrified, yet I'd thought of nothing beyond help or capture. Soldiers could be near – searchers, a patrol or daily call for eggs and milk. The dog might give me a warning – buy some time? The other door from the kitchen would lead deeper into the house. I dabbed my handkerchief on my battledress, trying to decide what to do.

The dog quietened. Only a rhythmic wheeze in the woman's breathing punctuated the silence. She brought bread on a plate and drew out the other chair to sit opposite me. Whilst I ate, her gaze strayed to a framed photograph on the wall. It was difficult to make out any detail in the dull light.

'Your family?' I pointed to the picture.

She turned away as if that simple act would make her worst thoughts disappear. I stuffed the last crust into my mouth and stood up.

'My thanks, Madam. I must go. This is too dangerous for you.'

The man slipped outside, leaving the woman to take his place at the window. He muttered his way back inside within seconds, speaking in a meaningless stew of foreign words. When he proffered his hand, I shook it and hoped to God he was wishing me luck.

4

Less than twenty minutes had passed since the woman saw me from the window. A few crows pecked between the cart tracks. I walked away from the farm; the couple huddled together in the doorway, honest patriots afraid for their family. They would wait until I was out sight before the woman cleaned up my bowl and plate then swilled the floor while the man got rid of my boot prints in the yard. What would happen if the soldiers came?

The cloud hung steel grey and heavy. It was after nine when I headed for the table-top quilt of fields and meadows. The ground mist would clear soon. Somewhere across the farmland, a wide line of men and dogs would be closing in. I set off for woodland to the southwest. *Make for the trees. Hide in the day, travel at night.* The instructor's voice oscillated like a drifting wireless signal. *Approach someone who is alone – find another house – look out for enemy patrols.* Thoughts of help came in simple pictures: a barn loft, a log fire, the man with a beret and sub machine gun shifting me to another remote hideout. I walked along the side of open beet fields, through empty meadows and past haystacks. This land had no farm gates, continuous hedges or straight-line borders.

The Bottesford crews would be waking after last night's op. Was it the Ruhr or Nottingham Palais tonight? The absurdity of that live and die world hit me: the two sets of chat and laughter, one for beer, one for bravado. I could hear the men's matter-of-fact talk around the previous night's missing aircraft. *'Any news about the Lewis crew?'* They were numb and faraway words. I was part of the Squadron's past now, like a spirit watching the group from a distance. The treadmill had moved on: telegram to next of kin, letter from CO to follow and the removal of my possessions. I'd seen the trappings of young men's lives emptied from lockers, but the ghouls usually waited until we had left the hut for breakfast or went to the aircraft. The job was done before our return, beds stripped and ready for more cheery new faces. I pictured the adjutant rifling through my suitcase, the one an aunt bought me as a twenty-first birthday present. Handkerchiefs, photographs and Mary's letters – the same chill cut through my body as years ago when I returned home from the cinema to discover our front door open. The house had been burgled.

Mary. For the briefest of moments I saw her in absolute clarity outside the phone box on Granby Place, her fire-red hair, the navy raincoat and a spread of coins in her hand in case my six o'clock call from the aerodrome was cut off. She wouldn't know what had happened. No call from me simply meant the base was sealed and ops were on. Today was Thursday. Dad would get the telegram. Mum would go and tell her.

Wreaths of mist still hung about in sheltered places. I reached the woods via a cabbage field with long grass around the edges. Moisture dripped from big oaks and beeches as they creaked in the wind. There must have been fresh animal-like senses in my head as I was already dropping into the grass when two men walked from the trees and pushed on to the next field. At least five minutes passed before I dared move. My forehead and cheeks were sore and crusty to the touch so I spat on the handkerchief and wiped my face. There was dirt and dried blood.

The wood was too dense to hide in but had a track alongside the edge. I squelched through the mud and reached an earth road cutting through two large open fields. Workers were busy. Women dug up beets and tossed them onto a pile near three men with shovels clearing out a dyke. The tallest man looked up. No one was close to me or alone, so I pressed on. The others were watching now. My legs felt like they were treading water. The urge to hurry overwhelmed me. I turned south onto a lane just as a cart rounded the bend. A man in a cap and long brown coat spoke to me above the clop of hooves. I half raised a hand to stop him and did nothing as the wheels rattled past.

The lane rose sharply, obscuring any view ahead. *Keep away from roads and paths.* A ploughed field to the right looked empty except for a thin screen of bushes running up to the gravel. I barged through the undergrowth and stopped dead.

5

The concrete bridge spanned a wide canal where open ground ran down to a towpath. The bushes only half screened me from the lane. I crouched down and wriggled into a snarl of brambles which snagged my battledress.

No sign of life at the near end. Sentries might be on the far side. It was quiet – too quiet. *Travel at night in the countryside, there is less chance of discovery.* The bridge would be guarded after dark. Voices came from the fields. I should go back and approach the workers. Someone must have recognised me. Was that good or bad? What about informers and quislings? My mind ran around on its own hamster wheel. Was everyone blind or too afraid to help? Was that how it was going to be – workers, heads down tilling the land, or men scuttling away as if they had seen some sort of plague? The instructor's words were only a guide, a basic lesson for survival. I was right not to go back. If the locals wanted to help, they would have done it by now, or at least tracked me.

The far end of the bridge was about a hundred yards away. Grey water lapped against the opposite bank. Fields and trees on the other side were a mirror image of the land behind me. I shouldered my way out through the bushes and walked straight onto the bridge. A tight, gnawing sensation grew in my stomach – something was not right. I reached the centre. The noise came from behind, distant at first, then louder on the wind, bringing a low puttering sound across the water. A motor cycle. The lane only led one way: to the bridge. My skin crawled. This would be no civilian.

I ran towards the far side, legs flying like a madman. My feet slid around inside the boots – the putter from the engine grew louder. I shuddered with every running step, praying no one would appear from the opposite direction. The final yards were a frantic sprint and dive into thick undergrowth, my breath blowing out in huge, agonised gusts. The rider was close. I pivoted around on my elbows and lay still, heart hammering behind my ribs.

Blood pounded in my ears. He was on the bridge now, a sinister figure in black jackboots with a field grey trench coat flapping at the edges in the wind. The engine fired across the water, goggles below his helmet stared straight ahead. Cold sweat stuck to my face, I started to tremble. He looked straight through me then blurred past in a cloud of exhaust. I could taste the fumes and shut my eyes, willing the sound to throttle away down the lane.

Silence except for wind sifting through long grass opposite. I waited a few minutes before setting off. Time enough for the wet to soak through my battledress. The lane veered southwest towards a church spire in the distance. I moved slowly across fields and pastureland to each hiding point. None of the spots was sheltered enough. My route stayed away from groups of workers but it was a certainty I had been seen. The time was well after midday. Thirst burned again, my feet chafed inside the boots and a ragged sense of inevitability crept in. At least discovery meant no more choices. Was that such a bad thing? I snapped the thought from my head.

A line of trees bordered one side of the next field. A rhythmic, shuffling sound came from behind the hedge. I inched closer. Through the foliage, a slim, fair-haired boy wearing a brown outdoor jacket poked his hoe between rows of turnips. He was alone.

6

The boy still looked young enough for school. He stopped to lean on his hoe, glancing absently in my direction. I walked between a break in the hedge, treading over rows of turnips. He had the same brittle expression as the old man at the farm, the same trembling hands. I prodded my battledress and pointed to the sky again.

'Can you help? I'm RAF.'

He tugged at the top of his collarless shirt, looking about the field with anxious birdlike glances. A riddle of foreign words spewed out, his finger pointing to trees in the corner.

Do you want me to leave? I could have said it; the left side of the field was open and merged into an empty meadow – I could have gestured into the distance and walked away to take my chances elsewhere. Why risk the life of a lad? The thought vanished, because it was never there. We stared at one another. He waved me towards the trees again then tapped the back of his wrist. I showed him my watch. He placed a grimy finger on the number seven.

I held up seven fingers. 'I hide until then?'

He looked nervously around again.

'Thank you,' I said, trying to shake his hand.

I charged into undergrowth about twenty yards in front of the trees. Part of an old drainage ditch ran parallel behind long grass. I jumped in. The boy dropped his hoe and walked towards the top of the field – exactly what he would do if moving to alert the Germans. But why indicate seven o'clock on my watch? My mind raced through the scenarios: the precise time seemed to ring true, except that was only the beginning. If the boy was genuine he would have to tell someone – it might be the wrong person. What had I done? What responsibility had I put on his young shoulders? My earlier rush of adrenaline and relief faded into guilt and creeping doubts. The boy picked up a bicycle lying near the field entrance and disappeared from view.

The ditch offered some cover and shelter from the wind. I knelt down low enough to keep out of sight and still see all sides of the field. Our bomber stream would pass over again tonight. The people listened out for us, waited in their farms and houses for the growing drone of our aircraft. They drew strength from that sound to get through another day and prayed for liberation. We all needed hope. Surely the boy had friends: he would bring help.

A biting cold cut through my battledress, numbing my legs and feet. The afternoon dragged – still three hours until teatime at home. Mum, hundreds of miles away, busy in the kitchen – remote and unreachable. Dad, all cap and overcoat, arriving home on his bicycle, hand on the front fence for a split second before he flicked up the gate latch and rode down the path at the side of our house. Those memories were stencilled in my head, yet I couldn't picture them. The cold draught of isolation and loneliness chilled every thought.

The boy returned around an hour later. I watched him for a few minutes through the leaning grasses, the patterned sound of his hoeing drifting on the wind again. A young man approached the field from the meadow on the left side. He stepped carefully over the turnip rows and spoke to the boy. They looked urgently in my direction before the man made straight for the land ditch, reaching me in seconds.

'*Eng-erls?*' he said, tousling his thatch of thick fair hair.

I managed to stand. 'Yes, I'm English. Can you help me?'

'*Ya.*'

I began to rub my legs hard. He gripped my arm, hauling me up and pointing to the trees.

'*Als-ter-bleef.* Boche here.' His eyes were wide and dark with fear. I said nothing until we were in the trees and he let go of my arm.

'Do you speak English?'

'*Ya.*'

'I crossed a canal and walked all day. I saw a—'

'*Ik-be-grayp het neat.*' He shrugged his shoulders. '*Ex-koos-ear me.*'

'I hide here until seven?'

'*Zay-ver. Zay-ver.*'

I pointed to my watch. Seven?

He nodded. '*Ya.*'

We shook hands. I watched him walk across the meadow until he vanished behind a large oak tree and hedgerow in the distance.

In the fading light, a silhouette whistled from the top corner of the field. The boy shouted back, hitched up his trousers then hurried away resting the hoe 'rifle style' on his shoulder. Evening came with a loaded hush. The wind had dropped to a breeze and cloud was too dense for moonlight. Almost seven-thirty now. I blew into my hands, scanning the dark with a growing helplessness at the waiting. If some of my crew were already in the bag (or worse), or broke down under interrogation, the Germans would account for our numbers. An extra pilot had been on board, eight men instead of seven – maybe that would stymie their sums. Other aircraft might be down in the area? The night was so cold. I rubbed my legs and arms and shuffled along the same few yards in the trees. Another spell of leave had been close. I lived for those days. We all did, each of us keeping our own silent thoughts until the last minute – no one presuming, no one tempting fate until we could escape to that other world. The world of smoky bars and beer-soaked pianos, or halls pulsing to the sound of dance bands. Or maybe straight home to parents, wives and sweethearts where every second got squeezed out before racing for a last train back to the aerodrome. Planning convoluted railway journeys, which swindled an extra few hours at home, became a science. My last forty-eight-hour pass got Mary sacked from her job at Taylor Hobson. Her request for time off work was turned down, so she took it anyway: sweethearts lived for the day. I couldn't comprehend the thought of not seeing her for years or worse.

The distant rumble of a train beat its way through the night. I moved to the edge of the trees. At first, it sounded like a distortion in the wind: voices and whispers, then footsteps rustling across the field. Two dim shapes were beginning to reveal themselves.

7

I recognised the boy's gait. A figure in a short coat and cap followed him – the young man from earlier. The boy came forward and we shook hands properly this time. He stepped back as if expecting the man to take charge. I waited like some mute, lost soul for something to happen. The man stayed completely still; there was no arm around my shoulder and 'follow me, Monsieur' moment. The space between us seemed to widen. Every simple fidget of my body had an edge, each sound an intrusion. I'd searched for this moment since landing and it was slipping away.

The man's behaviour made me uneasy given his earlier actions when guiding me to the trees. He finally whispered to the boy, who tugged at my sleeve. I stumbled after them over the muddy ground, the boy always waiting for me to catch up, before hastening away again. We joined a narrow path heading into the thick black of a copse. Dry leaves crinkled underfoot, an earthy smell of decaying vegetation filled the air. I groped about for a trunk or branch and tiptoed on through the void, watching for tell-tale flashes of torchlight. Surely, a foot patrol or search party would never pass through this dense and impenetrable place, not at this hour. A loud snap cut through the night – we all trod on twigs, it was impossible to avoid them. The man's boots stopped ahead. A small hand gently gripped my arm until the boots moved off again. We halted where the path ended abruptly at a wide track cutting the copse in two. The man's thin shape waited at the edge of the trees.

'Steff,' he murmured.

The boy let go of my arm and went up to him. Whispers passed between them. The man waved me forward.

'*Boche,*' he said, pointing up and down the track. He checked both ways again before running to the trees on the opposite side.

Steff felt closer to me with a name, the right-sounding name, something to hang on to. He spoke softly as if thinking out aloud. We waited for the man's footsteps to fade in the windy uneasy night then hurried across. Steff took a diagonal route away from the path. The wood gradually thinned out and he picked up pace, crossing wide stretches of grass and meadow without using cover. The landscape had a blank, dead look at night, yet it still saw my every move and fed the growing anxiety in my mind. A snatched check of the compass showed south–southeast – we had beaten the patrols so far.

Steff halted, merging in with some thickets and undergrowth. A rustling came from behind us. His companion crept out from the side, cap now pulled low over his forehead. I doubted he would reveal a name, so I decided on Victor. A clock chimed on the wind – six, seven, eight. Steff led us towards the sound. A dark geometry of buildings loomed into view – solid shapes with sharp angles as if they were cast from black metal. I stayed close through a field with haystacks until we reached a back lane. A low barn was on the opposite side. Victor leaned full in my face, a finger to his lips. He pointed ahead. A house stood set back from the lane and away from other buildings. Steff had already moved off. When he approached the house and disappeared around the back, I was marshalled forward. We reached the side wall where I almost collided with him wheeling out his bicycle. He nodded to Victor as he passed us. No knock at the rear door, I was rushed straight inside through a darkened room to a dimly lit parlour and a smell of wood smoke. A woman with long, greying hair and flushed cheeks stood near the fire, next to a slim girl of around eleven. The man sitting near them in an easy chair had a familiar look, the resemblance to Steff etched in his round face, thin nose and high angled eyebrows. Victor took off his cap and spoke with them. A wide parting split his hair and the short grey-green coat hung more like an oversized jacket. He signalled me to an armchair near the door. I fell into it, drawing in the warmth, but with a nervous edge I hadn't recalled since childhood when sitting in a stranger's home for the first time.

The heavy curtains were closed and a large carpet covered most of the floor. My weary mind absorbed no more detail except another door. The woman left the room and returned with a basin of hot water. She began to bathe my cheeks and forehead. I'd seen the expression on her face before; the same one my mum gave me when I picked up my kit bag to return to ops after a week's leave at home. The young girl came to kneel beside me. Her bright, inquisitive eyes and copper-tinted hair shone in the firelight as she grinned and passed me a small hand mirror. My face had a corpse-like pallor and scatter of tiny cuts. At least it felt soft and clean now.

I must have dozed because the woman woke me when she brought in a bowl of milk. The girl glanced up from her book and smiled. I barely had time to guzzle the drink down before the back door banged shut. Footsteps stomped across the next room. The woman moved past the fireplace and the girl rose from her seat when Victor blustered in, rain shining on his coat. He helped me up from the chair and across the room. As I entered the kitchen the woman grabbed my hand, pressing something small and metallic into the palm. The parlour door closed, leaving a memory of how a little girl's smile had made a complete stranger feel like a friend.

The metal object went into my trouser pocket as we hit the cold night air. A thin mist of drizzle soaked my face. Victor stayed in front and we turned a corner on to a street with brick houses on both sides. I heard nothing except our own hasty footsteps. Left, down a street and past the side of a church, we stopped by a gabled building with dark windows. Victor guided me through a gap. A sooty smell hung about the air. The back door opened, spilling yellow light across the space. Underneath a canopy in the corner, a forge and anvil were visible amongst the shadows. A broad-shouldered man filled the doorway, trying to speak between coughs. He escorted us into an unheated kitchen where I was shown to a chair at a varnished table. White shirt, sleeves rolled up above his hairy forearms, the man was likely the village blacksmith. He appeared impervious to the cold and thumped his chest when the coughing started again. Victor closed the outside door and stood close behind my back. The blacksmith sat at the opposite side of the table and peered at me with studied interest.

'So… RAF. What is your name?'

'You speak English. Are you Resistance?'

His chair creaked. 'English, a little. The Tommies. Yes, many years ago. *La Guerre Mondial.*'

He shook his head and gave another cough. 'But Resistance? No.'

The words hit me like a punch in the stomach. Every muscle in my body already ached. Exhaustion was pulling me down and the weary circles around his eyes likely mirrored my own. He glanced doubtfully at Victor.

'My father fought at Ypres and Passchendaele,' I said. It was the first thing which came into my head.

'And now *you* are an English pilot.' There was an edge to his voice.

He sat forward, elbows on the table, hands cupped under his chin.

'I'm English,' I said trying to hold his stare. 'But I'm no pilot. I landed north of here. Have you seen any other fliers?'

My words had dropped out, tired and flat.

'I understand you a little. No one has visited.'

A thickening silence filled the room. I pictured him outside, silhouetted against a hot orange glow, moving from forge to anvil as he heated and hammered the metal against the breathing bellows and roar from the forge fire. Victor spoke and the blacksmith's face reddened. I placed my compass on the table.

'My name is Ronald. I'm RAF. I can't say any more. Please… look at my uniform.' I pulled a sleeve up so they could see my watch. 'I've walked for hours… tried to get help. There was a boy working in a field. He helped me and came back at night with this man here. I don't know their names.'

The two men talked across me. I turned to Victor, then back to the blacksmith.

'Are the Boche in this village, sir?'

The blacksmith nodded. 'The Boche is everywhere. But you are with friends now.'

8

I recovered my compass and moved the chair around so I could face both men. The blacksmith stretched his hand out across the table. It was ice cold.

'We find more friends, Ronald.' He nodded in Victor's direction. 'He helps. I will speak with him.'

'Where are we? What village is this? I've seen no signposts.'

The blacksmith shook his head. 'I understand not everything you say.'

His grey eyes tarried for an instant before he took Victor outside. Their hasty conversation ended when a single set of footsteps scurried away. The blacksmith coughed and shuffled about in the dark. My hand caught against the metal object in my trouser pocket. It came out easily. The woman with the sad eyes had given me a small crucifix. I ran a finger over the cross and Christ figure. Thoughts turned to my parents: Mum would pray for me, Dad would hope. He went to the Great War a Christian and returned as an atheist. The woman had given me the crucifix with faith and from her heart. I replaced it carefully in my pocket.

A jaundiced light shone from the yellow lampshade. The sink, table and stove made up a small kitchen, but any woman's touch had been invaded by the man's work. Glass jars competed with papers on the shelving. Hand hammers, metal tongs and pincers lay on top of a wooden cabinet, invading the neat areas as if the room couldn't decide on its state. The instructor's voice was a distant scramble of words now. I would put my trust in the blacksmith and take the risk.

'We wait here,' he said, closing the door behind him.

While the water heated up for coffee, he sat down opposite me again.

'You say your father, he fight at the Ypres and Passchendaele.'

'Yes. But he hasn't talked much about that war.'

'I do not speak of it. What regiment was he in?'

'The Suffolk. He was a stretcher bearer and volunteered later for the Machine Gun Corps. That's all I know.'

He walked to the stove. 'And he did not speak why he is with the machine gun men?'

'Yes. It was a new corps and there was some training back in Blighty... the chance to get away from the trenches for a few weeks.'

'Ah yes. Blighty.' He placed two cups of a steaming, nutty-smelling liquid on the table. His grasp of English was better than he made out.

'So what happens next, sir?'

'We drink and we wait.'

The temperature inside the room had dropped. I cradled the cup in my hands and heard the church clock strike nine.

Victor returned twenty minutes later with a fawn raincoat draped over his arm. He tossed it to the blacksmith who examined it suspiciously.

'Please be wearing this, Ronald.'

I forced the raincoat on over my battledress and joined him at the door when he turned off the light. Victor had already stepped into the darkness. I felt the blacksmith's hand on my shoulder.

'Go with him and good luck.'

By instinct and touch I found the forge and anvil. A few seconds passed before Victor's shape became clearer, edging slowly nearer the street. He waited at the end of the side wall. A thin slit of light appeared at an upstairs window in the next building as we stepped into the grainy night together. It had stopped raining. I hurried across the cobbles and past the church towards the corner we had turned earlier to reach the blacksmith's. Victor retraced our steps. It was no surprise when I stood at the back door to Steff's house.

From their startled looks when we walked in the parlour, the man and woman had not expected me back. Steff and the girl were absent, likely asleep at that late hour. Victor spoke in short bursts animated with an orchestra of hand gestures. The man always looked to the woman before replying. Their thoughtful nods and worried expressions only increased the conflict in my head. The risks they were taking far outweighed any of my own.

After Victor left I sat in the same armchair as before. The urgent voice of hunger roared in my stomach, but that was the last thing on my mind. The hour passed with forced smiles and a heavy silence. I closed my eyes. They had nowhere to look without catching someone's stare. The padre's words from one of his sermons popped into my head. *We're never alone in our moments of despair.* If there was any solace in that, I didn't find it.

Time never stood still. At that precise moment I wished it had. The back door closed and a muffled conversation came from the kitchen. Victor walked in with another man behind him. I looked straight at the uniform of a Belgian policeman.

9

Instinct was to break free and run. Victor blocked my route to the door. The policeman's gaze swept over me, patterns of light and shadow quarrying his sharp features. He looked late thirties, blue uniform with red piping: a Belgian gendarme with a square jaw. I waited for the inevitable revolver and a march to somewhere in the house until the Germans arrived. The blacksmith had spoken of finding more friends. Why bring me all the way here for this? It made no sense.

The gendarme stepped forward. 'I will help you, but it is not safe here.'

His level of English took me aback. I gathered my thoughts as we shook hands. Victor slipped from the room with a smile and self-conscious wave.

'There are some clothes in the kitchen,' the gendarme said. 'We have not the time for you to be wearing them now. We must leave.'

It was just short of ten twenty-five by my watch when I cycled close behind the gendarme onto the deserted main street. Was there a curfew? I should have asked. How much influence did he carry around here – enough to make him conspicuous – enough for people to remember us – enough for the soldiers not to stop him? Creeping across fields had got me this far and now I was following a policeman straight through a village full of Germans. Maybe the Boche were in their beds and the locals had boarded themselves in for the night? I pedalled hard and hoped.

The village ended when the lane sheered away. We dismounted after a few minutes to wheel our bicycles along a track across open fields. Anyone nearby would hear us in an instant or pick out our profiles against the flat landscape – even in the dark. The short cut, if that's what it was, led to another lane. My fear and the determination not to be afraid had merged into a simple dread. I tried to narrow every thought and not speculate beyond the immediate moment.

We passed a barn on the bend approaching a crossroads. The gendarme juddered to a stop and dismounted.

'Quiet. Someone is close.'

He laid down his bicycle, vigorously waving me to do the same. We retreated into the shadow of the barn. Men's voices came from the left: no footfall, only the rhythmic tick of bicycles freewheeling across the junction ahead.

I didn't stand up until he returned from scouting in front. 'Boche?' I whispered.

'Perhaps? The main road crosses here and there are patrols.' He looked into the darkness behind me. 'The curfew is soon. No one is outside after midnight unless they have special papers. We must hurry.'

He righted my bicycle and spun the front wheel, giving the frame a cursory jolt against the ground. 'You must stay with my friend. I will return before midnight.'

We rode in single file over the crossroads, stopping outside a house further down the lane.

'Follow me.' He leaned his bicycle near the front door and entered without knocking. I crept into the house. The room was in half darkness and I had to push hard against the door to close it. A thin, gnarled figure of a man leaned on his stick in front of a wood fire, the flames casting a goblin-like shadow on the wall. The two men talked across me as if I wasn't there. I tried to make sense of their body language and any words spoken in my direction. It only added to a growing apprehension.

'He is deaf,' the gendarme said when he passed me, as if that explained everything.

An orange light grew inside the room. The old man shone his oil lamp towards the door as it scraped shut and a bicycle clanked away.

'Do you speak English?' I asked.

His large gimlet eyes stared through a curtain of straggly white hair. He prodded me towards two armchairs by the fire and we sat down in a glow of uncertainty. I strained to catch noises outside, listened for the door and willed the gendarme to reach his destination and return safely. The old man's eyelids drooped. His breathing slowed to a faint wheeze. One solitary German sighted in over thirty-one hours – had I just been lucky? To a background of snores, I rose from my armchair and paced the floor near the window.

The fire had almost burned out when the gendarme returned. He gave me a sidelong glance, his face set in disconcerted lines. Midnight had passed over twenty minutes earlier.

'I apologise for my delay. If we are stopped, you say nothing. I will speak.'

The old man stirred in his armchair, coughing thickly. We left while he was still asleep. The gendarme pedalled down the lane, casting urgent glances over his shoulder. I leaned left with the curve as it narrowed into a cobbled village street. He dismounted, running his bicycle down by the side of a brick house. We parked up against a wet wall, the spat-spat of water dripping close to my feet. I saw him disappear around the back but he didn't open the door until I rounded the corner. I was eased through the kitchen onto a narrow flight of wooden stairs and his tread came close behind me. We clumped up the last two steps to a narrow landing.

'Please wait in there.'

The room opposite was the only one with its door open. The gendarme switched on the light and pointed at an iron bedstead. I perched on the edge of a bare mattress at the same moment a woman called up from downstairs. The gendarme closed in on me.

'Please rest on this bed and do not walk near the window.'

An oblong of dark navy material nailed to a wooden frame covered the glass.

'You wish for the drink?'

'No thank you.'

The blacksmith had given me coffee. Was it bad manners to refuse now? How little I knew about life in other countries. The gendarme backed away. I half expected a lock to click after the bedroom door closed. Only his descending steps and the creaking stair boards sounded.

The room looked empty except for the bed and a large mirror propped against a trunk. I caught sight of my own wild-eyed reflection, the face tired and sucked dry. All strength had ebbed away in the strain of the day, so I lay back on the mattress. A quiet pounding drummed inside my head: listen and be ready, listen and be ready. Downstairs, the conversations always began with the woman's voice first. A door closed. Footsteps walked across the quarry-tile kitchen floor. My world had been reduced to this room and existed on noises.

A tap came later on the bedroom door. The gendarme entered, carrying the bundle of clothes from the kitchen at Steff's home. A pair of faded brown shoes with the laces tied together dangled over his right arm. He wore the uniform without his hat; revealing brown hair, cut and parted like a soldier's. The clothes were speedily laid out on the bed.

'Do you want me to put those on now?' I started to unbutton my raincoat.

'Yes.'

'What about my uniform?'

'You leave it here.'

The fabric covering the window rippled as he shut me in again. I inspected the outfit: a rough charcoal grey jacket and trousers, braces, white shirt, collar and scuffed shoes. The raincoat came off. I rummaged through my battledress pockets. Compass, map, handkerchief and crucifix formed a line on the mattress along with French and Belgian franc notes and my escape photographs from the cardboard wallet. Dutch paper money was in there and some which I didn't recognise. I removed my battledress, tie, collar, braces and RAF shirt. The long-sleeved silk vest would have to come off as my replacement shirt looked too small.

The trousers fitted a shorter man, but would pass muster. I sat shivering in my singlet, fiddling with the two identity discs around my neck. The small red one was fire resistant with a single hole for the string to pass through. *RAF* was indented into one side with my surname and service number punched around the circumference. The octagonal grey disc was liquid resistant with a string of numbers and letters around the edges. The reverse side read *'Do Not Remove'*. Marvellous: burn to death or drown and still be identified. Both discs stayed around my neck, I could be shot as a spy without them. Photographs went back inside the wallet along with the folded money. The shirt and jacket might not fit and what about the shoes? I stalled but not for that reason. This was a moment when the flimsy protection of a uniform disappeared and I became someone else in an occupied country.

Even with a top button undone the shirt was tight across my back. Shoes felt soft and loose – they might stay on with a stiffer lace-up. The jacket fitted and the braces were more comfortable than my RAF ones which had no stretch at the shoulders. I managed to shove the wallet and other items into my jacket pockets before the gendarme bustled in. He ignored my uniform on the bed.

'Wear your coat again. When we are outside, walk with me.'

We crept down the stairs and out the back way. I never saw the woman. The gendarme walked nearest the road, a bulky overcoat covering his uniform. With no warning he steered me between two houses. I followed him to the rear of the left building. A man in a white shirt without the collar waited in the kitchen. He might have been middle-aged, but his strained expression and leathery skin made him look older. He guided us up the carpeted stairs – it was almost a replay from earlier. I entered a box room with whitewashed walls and lino on the floor. The ceiling sloped down in line with the roof to the foot of a single bed. A chair and cabinet were close to a bucket near the blind which covered a small side window. The gendarme pointed to the blind.

'I understand. Keep away from the window,' I said.

We stumbled through the farewell. The man in the white shirt nodded each time the gendarme spoke to him. He reminded me of Maurice who lived down the road at home. The gendarme turned out the light when they left and his distinctive tread soon passed along the gap between the houses.

I lay on the bed mentally rehearsing my steps to the bucket. Hours had passed since the pubs and dance halls shut at home, the time when footfall sounded through the blackout more than voices. I pictured my home. The council house would look the same as any other in the road, but that telegram had left a shroud of waiting grief hanging above the door. I saw my parents' ruined faces and their endless days stretching ahead. The not knowing would torture them.

The noise from our aircraft worked its way into my head. I pictured the boys again with their Mae Wests, the jangle of a loose parachute harness, Jimmy's heated flying suit ballooning his small figure. They walked past me in single file, 'eyes right' – the graveyard look, gaunt, grey faces which knew me yet didn't know me at all. My limbs twitched with the shudders from the aircraft, the twist and groan in its final dive, a mass of mechanical agony and orange flame as it hit the ground. I should have tried harder to find them, at least discover what happened: Scotty just married, Jimmy a father and Bill left at the helm when I baled out. What about Eddie, Ken and Curly? They all mattered. We stuck together, went out together, put our lives on the line together. What more could I have done? But why assume the worst? They might be on the run, or still in hiding. I pushed the thoughts away.

Floorboards creaked outside the door. A head and shoulders peered around in an oblong of light: the same ghostly portrait from childhood when my sweat-soaked body lay ravaged with scarlet fever – Mum checking during the day and Dad after dark. I'd become conscious then of the night-time sounds in a house and noises outside. There was no refuge and morning always seemed an eternity away.

I sat up suddenly in the dark, still wearing the raincoat. The bedroom door opened. Maurice flicked on the light. He wore the same clothes as the previous day. A white towel was draped over his arm and he held a basin of steaming water.

'*Goeiemorgen.*' I answered him. He placed the basin carefully on the floor, laid the towel on my bed and fetched soap and razor from another room. My first real wash and shave in two days, except all I could think about was food. He glanced at the bucket before leaving me in private.

Breakfast was two thin bread rolls and a hot coffee with the same nutty taste as at the blacksmith's. I got up and killed the light. Traces of morning showed in dots and ladders through the worn window blind. The village twitched into life outside: a bicycle, sluggish footsteps – men's voices. They likely worked in the fields or slaved away in some town factory. It was after seven-thirty. How long before the Germans came and searched the street?

Maurice moved about the house. I put on the shoes and lay back in bed, fingers laced behind my head. No cigarette since leaving the hut for ops two days ago. The craving had crept up unnoticed. Players Navy Cut; my best friend helping to pass time and wade through the hours before take-off. A ciggy in the briefing room, pub, billet, or on the train – I longed for the tang of freshly lit tobacco with a mild Virginia bite, yet slightly sweet to the taste. A packet of twenty, wide enough to fit my outstretched fingers, and the branding with its lighthouse and sailing ship on the horizon, the concentric rope-edged circles in the foreground, where the head and shoulders of a bearded sailor in uniform looked away from two tall ships.

Smoking was an art. A skill to avoid the puffing clouds of

novices. I played out the automatic actions, my left palm upturned, smacking the packet into it twice to push the tobacco tight at the end of the cigarettes and then opening the flap ready for a rich aroma beneath the soft foil. A cigarette from the middle was best, tapped once against the side of the packet for perfect, settled tobacco, the clipped end moving gently up to my lips. I could flick the lighter, watch a yellow flame beckon the tip and take in that first velvet draw. Time to ask Maurice if he had any smokes.

Around six o'clock a bicycle crunched to a halt outside. A jostle of noise came from below then two sets of footsteps coming up the stairs. I swung my legs off the bed. A young fair-haired man walked in, cheeks fresh and mulberry from the evening air. Maurice stayed outside the room as if not wanting to intrude. The young man nodded to him and closed the door. He lugged the chair across, his gaze darting around until it settled on my face.

'Hello,' he said, sitting down and unbuttoning his jacket.

His left hand went to the inside pocket. I saw the cold gleam from a revolver.

10

My stomach cramped. All sensation drained from my legs. The young man took out a small notebook and pencil.

'It is cold and windy tonight,' he said, parking the pencil behind his ear. 'You are comfortable here, yes?'

The revolver image flickered in my head. 'You speak English too.'

He puffed out his cheeks and nodded.

My lips quivered. 'Are you Resistance? Can you help me?'

He crossed his legs then perched the open notebook on one knee.

'Perhaps? First I must ask you some questions. You say that you are an English aviator.'

There were jottings on the page. My thoughts took off in a huge rambling circle. The instructor told us to cooperate with helpers – try to prove our identity. The man was a helper, he had to be. What if he was a quisling? What if all this was some elaborate deception and the Germans were waiting? He would get my answers then turn me in. The Germans could masquerade as *me*. This was madness. Such scrambled thinking didn't belong here.

He sat, pencil poised. 'What is duff gen?'

The words startled me. I groped for an answer.

'It's… it is incorrect information, the wrong facts. On ops we used to get it with the weather forecast when—'

'I understand you.'

I waited for him to start writing in the notebook. He stared at me with no sign of life except the blink of his eyes. The silence lingered.

'And what is your position in the aircraft?'

'I can't tell you that.'

The feeling was returning to my legs. I fidgeted on the edge of the bed.

'We will begin, please, with your name and aviator number,' he said, eying the notebook. A noise in the street distracted him. He cocked an ear before settling again.

'All of your names.' He licked the pencil.

I stalled, trying to work things through for one last time. All reasoned thinking slipped away like a trail of smoke. From the second I buried my parachute the focus was on reaching this point, yet once the young man had all my information, I would belong to others.

His eyes were deep and hard to read. He tossed the pencil and notebook on the bed.

'If we are going to help you, we must trust each other, yes?'

He held out his hand. 'My name is Denise.'

'Dennis?' I went through the motions of a handshake, an automatic action with so many strangers since the war started.

He picked up the notebook and pencil again. 'No, it is Denise. Now we must begin your answers.'

Denise was no more than twenty. I gave him my full name. 'My RAF number is…' It came out in clots. I straightened up and repeated it.

'Please check this carefully,' he said holding up the notebook. 'We must be sure there are no mistakes.'

His notes at the top were not in English.

'The spelling of my name is correct and also the number,' I said.

'Good. Tell me the date and place where you were born.'

We laboured through a string of questions and answers, the pauses in between separated by the scribble of his pencil and a page turning. I listened for noises outside and in the house. He always reacted to them first.

'You have told me the names of your crew. So we—'

'Denise, what has happened to them? Do you know if they are OK?'

'I am sorry. I have heard no words. Can you give more facts which might help us?'

A lump thickened in my throat. I looked away to the door. 'Nothing more than I've told you.'

'It is difficult. They are your friends, I understand this.'

'You haven't got a cigarette, have you?' I sucked in my breath as if rehearsing. 'It's been days.'

'The man who lives in this house is alone and does not smoke the cigarettes. The people who visit will know this. *Voila*, it is easy to be sure someone is in a room up here. We will smoke later, perhaps.'

He checked back over his notes. I thought about my answers: home address, parents' names, squadron number, target, date, time and place of take-off. A sick feeling grew in my stomach, his list was a questionnaire and I'd committed too much intelligence to a stranger.

'I must leave soon,' he said. The pencil appeared to have a mind of its own as it passed through his fingers into his jacket.

'So what happens next?'

'I bicycle a long way to visit you. I bicycle a long way back again. We check what you say. *Voila*. I may return soon.'

'Do you know when?'

He held up his hands in mock surrender. 'So many questions, and there is one more. The photographs... do you have the small photographs of yourself?'

They were next to the fold of money in my cardboard wallet. I handed them over.

'For your papers,' he said.

He got to his feet, looking at me with an amused expression.

'I am sorry that the clothes do not fit. They are from many places. Goodnight, Ronald. Perhaps we will meet again?'

A rattle came from outside as he cycled away. I kept the light on and lay down exhausted on the bed, trying to think how my information would be checked. I imagined him palming his notes across to some shadowy figure in a doorway, or crouching over the radio in a remote barn and frantically tapping out messages before his location could be tracked. I wished he was still here – wished we could talk again, talk about anything: the weather, Belgium, England, anything except this war – just talk.

I must have dozed for a while. Maurice was calling from deep in the house. Someone raced up the stairs. I leapt to my feet. Denise hurried in, gasping.

'Excuse please. We will leave directly.'

He tugged at the fabric covering the window and squinted into the street. I sat on the bed and bent down to put on my shoes.

'Now, Ronald. We must leave now. Quickly... the Boche.'

11

I fumbled with my shoelaces.

'There is no time. Follow me.' Denise threw open the bedroom door and bounded down the stairs.

I clattered after him, trying to pull on the raincoat. Maurice waited near the bottom with a shattered expression on his face. A nightmare filled my head: army trucks, brakes squealing, our street blocked off. I listened for shouts, running jackboots and a hammering on the doors.

'The Boche is near. They already visit where you were hiding yesterday,' Denise said, as we left via the back door.

'Did you check my gen?'

'No. Do you ride the bicycle?'

'Yes.'

'I pedal. You sit on the seat behind me. No more English unless I say.'

The cold night air took my breath away. A vague shape of handlebars stuck out from the house wall. I sat astride the saddle, legs dangling down. Denise balanced on the crossbar, croggy-style, forcing down the pedals. The back wheel slipped and spun before we careered off down the deserted street on to a lane away from the village. A light wind had moved some of the cloud and the moon cast a whitish glow across the landscape. We picked up speed, the masked cycle lamp creating dim, shaky lines on the ground. In the broken shadows, a spread of black trees ahead looked familiar. A light winked in the fields. I bent forward trying to hold on. Denise dug his heels into the gravel and the bicycle juddered to a halt by an open ditch. My breath clouded around his face in the cold air as I dismounted.

'We rest for a short minute,' he gasped. 'I forget... please take off your watch.'

'I can see a small light over there?' I said.

'Not every farmer remembers to cover all their windows.'

'We haven't seen anyone either.'

'It is very late. And now please… your watch.'

I slipped it inside my jacket. He wheeled the bicycle several yards forward. 'It is dangerous here. We leave now.'

'I still don't know where I am.'

'We speak of this later. Please listen.' He stepped nearer. 'Soon we cross the *Kanaal*. In one kilometre… a bridge. Sometimes there are the guards, Belgian traitors in the Boche army.'

'But they're already searching for me and I have no documents.'

There was a hard, glassy shine in his eyes as he turned back to the road.

'We have no choices. If there is a guard I will do the speaking.' He swung his leg over the crossbar. 'Soon we see some houses. After this, you must be ready.'

I climbed onto the saddle and the bicycle moved off through loose stone. We took another road, freewheeling past a small hamlet. The wind dropped and I sensed a thickening in the air. A raised concrete section loomed ahead with steps at the side and a sentry box. A dull circle of torchlight moved into the road. Two figures blocked our way. Soldiers. An icy shiver coursed through my body. Denise glanced behind.

'They have seen us. If there are troubles I have a revolver. I take the first man. You take the second.'

A cry sat behind my lips – the pounding in my chest felt like a jackhammer. I locked my fingers under the saddle and the bicycle picked up speed.

12

Denise sat forward on the crossbar, shouting and pedalling straight for the guards. Flemish words cut the night air – the bicycle veered across the lane. He waved his arm and called out. A rusty voice spoke back. Both sentries carried rifles. We slowed. The skin tightened over my cheekbones, I struggled for breath and my jaw locked. Denise called out again in aggravated, urgent tones. The torch lowered in a pendulum swing as the guards waved us through.

Beads of sweat ran down my neck, a sharp pain swelled in my chest. Black water lay below both sides of the bridge – the road skimmed by under my feet. I felt the guards' eyes rivet onto me. Every rattle and creak from the bicycle tempted fate, each twist as I tried to hang on made me seem awkward and shifty. The end of the bridge was an eternity away and my head screamed for the night to fold in around us.

Two figures stood at the far parapet. They looked up from their conversation – more soldiers. Denise pedalled faster. We freewheeled past them, hurtling off the bridge and down a shallow incline on to the lane. I heard nothing except a clip in their voices and the terrified whisper of my own breath. Somewhere in the depths of my senses, I felt metal under the saddle cutting into my fingers.

Ditches bordered the lane on both sides – a smell of stagnant water made me heave. Maybe the guard had changed? Maybe there were sentries at both ends? The ground rode more even now and my grip on the saddle relaxed. Flashes of white light and shadows flickered in my head: the bridge and soldier's silhouette – the swing of his torch. I focused on anything to blot out a rising tide of fear. The sky arched above me in a patchwork of pin prick stars. How did we get through without being challenged? What had Denise said?

We crossed over a junction near a group of houses and barns. Denise stopped once the buildings were out of sight.

'The riding on the bicycle is difficult, yes?'

'Yes.' I dismounted and walked around, flexing my legs. 'How much further?'

'We are near. No one is following. Soon… a rest.'

'Where are we?'

'No more questions. We visit a house, directly.'

'On the bridge… how did you do that? What did you say to the guards?'

'I speak later.'

The lane angled away, straightening up before the approach to a village. Houses lined a deserted street on both sides to the point where a railway crossed and the village ended abruptly. Around twenty paces before the tracks, Denise swung the bicycle into a sharp left turn along the side of a house. We stopped. Both of us were leaning heavily against the wall when I almost fell off the saddle into a standing position. Denise pushed the bicycle out of sight in the corner.

'Our room is there,' he whispered, pointing upwards.

I followed him back onto the street keeping close to the front wall. We crept past two narrow windows and he tapped on the door twice. Movement came from inside the house. The door cracked open. Denise hurried me through the narrow gap into a hallway. A broad-shouldered man with a smiling full-moon face rolled down his shirt sleeves while Denise spoke to him. I heard my name amongst a wash of Flemish.

The man called out up the stairs. He shouted again. 'Dinah.'

A girl answered.

'Jos,' he said, shaking my hand.

'Papa.' The girl had crept down unnoticed.

'Hello,' I said. 'Are you Dinah?'

Her thick black hair almost touched her shoulders. She smiled, turning her head away from the banter between Jos and Denise.

A woman in a blue twin set and woollen skirt entered the hallway from another room and greeted me. Her voice was a whisper, her face warm and thoughtful. Jos's wife, I guessed, as the couple were both in their early fifties. She took hold of my right hand and pressed a small silver pendant into the palm. I didn't need to understand her words.

Denise gave me an assertive nod. 'We go to our room now.'

He led me up to a narrow bedroom under the sloping roof.

'It is late, Ronald. Soon we have food.'

'What was Jos saying?'

He peeped out through a small gap in the curtains. 'He is saying to Dinah, there is a surprise. Denise is here and they have another guest. He is an Englishman.'

'So he had no idea we were coming.'

'He does not know when I visit. Nobody knows when I will visit them.' He sat on the bed, patting the sheets. 'You will sleep here tonight, I sleep on the floor.'

I took off my raincoat, threw it on a chair next to the window and sat beside him.

'Now,' he said. 'You ask what I say to the soldiers on Sasse Bridge. Well, I was speaking in Flemish and sometimes swearing. I say we are late for our work, because you have a worn-out bicycle and it has broken.'

'But if they had stopped us. If they—'

'It does not matter. They did not stop us.' He smiled. 'Never show the Boche you are afraid. They stop me many times. I am talking and smoking with them. I am their friend.'

The chatter and whistle from a distant train cut across the night.

'Later, we sleep a little. Tomorrow when the clock is early, we walk to the railway station. It is very near. There are checks, but not many. We travel to a safer place. I know a friend who will help.'

'Is it safe here?'

'For tonight. Perhaps?'

'Have you stopped here much?'

'Yes, but I do not stay in any place for more than one night. Sometimes I arrive very late.' He grinned. 'I throw the stones at Dinah's window so I do not make a noise at the door.'

The longing for a hot meal roared inside me and it wasn't long before I caught the smell of meat cooking, no mistake. Sunday dinners at home in the old days: a joint sizzling in the oven, juices rolling off and spitting in the fat. Roast potatoes, vegetables, simmering greens and stock.

Denise clicked the chambers around his revolver. He slid it inside his jacket.

'We have the luck tonight. It is very late, but soon we eat some small meat… and potatoes.' The grin stayed on his face. 'I hope you are liking potatoes in Belgium? You will eat many.'

'What happens about food? Are there ration books?'

'We have the tickets every month. Many times there is nothing to buy with them. In the country we hide a little food, the Boche take the rest. If you are caught, there are bad punishments. In the towns and cities it is difficult. To get some things, this is possible but they cost much. Some sell the eggs, butter and meats for large money.'

The clatter of dishes sounded below.

'You mean black market?'

'If they are the English words, then yes.'

He took out a crumple of paper money and tossed it on the bed.

'Many times these are not Belgian francs. German Reich Mark is here for two years now. It is not only money that changes when your country is taken. People who were your friends, they are not friends, now. Some are afraid for their families.'

He eyed me carefully. 'The Boche offer money and food for information. There are bad things. Also it is easy to look away and see nothing.'

This would not have happened at home. I thought of summer days and powder-blue skies after Dunkirk when we waited behind the beaches and barbed wire, listening for the drone of enemy bombers and scanning the skies for German parachutists. Families crowded around a wireless for news. I drilled and marched in the LDV, learned to fire a Lee Enfield, guarded factories and strategic points at night. We stood together, men and women shoulder to shoulder, accepting what had to be done, never dwelling on the unthinkable, not even in the dark hours. As my mind strayed, I did remember people who shut themselves away and prayed for the church bells not to ring, and men who took jobs in reserved occupations once war clouds began to gather. I thought about the black market, the spivs and takers, Black Shirts, conchies and sympathisers. How many would have courted favour with the enemy or kept their heads down if Britain had fallen?

The money still lay on the bed. I searched for the right words. Nothing came. Denise looked at me with an empty expression.

'Here, it was Friday morning. The hour is just before five. I do not forget May fourteen, it is three years now. We hear the aircraft and think they fly over to bomb England. This time it is different. In the distance we hear explosions and many guns firing. The wireless says Germany has invaded Belgium, Holland and Luxembourg in the night and we are at war.'

'We heard about it too,' I said. 'Then it was in the newspapers and cinemas.' I stopped. My trite words and picture memories did not belong in this moment.

The money disappeared into his pocket. 'The next night we do not hear the bombs, it is the guns from the Boche. Their army is near Antwerp and they come through the dawn. They are nowhere… and then they are everywhere.' His voice faded. 'Two weeks and it is finished.'

He took out two cigarettes from his jacket. 'We speak no more of this. I have something for us. Black market.' He smiled and we laughed together for the first time.

I struggled through the meal of potato and meatballs. How much of their ration had the family given up for me? Denise had mentioned Jos was the local cattle dealer. That didn't make me feel any easier.

'I must go to speak with the family for some minutes,' Denise said, rising from the bedroom chair. 'Please stay in this room and rest. Also, I say one more thing.' He picked up the plates. 'When friends give you food, always eat. They wish to help you return to England. It is their way of fighting back.'

The time was well after midnight. I waited until he reached the downstairs before examining the silver pendant. It was no bigger than a farthing coin. The front had a Christ-like portrait, and on the back, two figures knelt in prayer next to a shrine. Lettering in Flemish bordered three-quarters of the circumference. I lay back on the bed thinking about what Denise said – and what he hadn't said. Facing the unknown without him unsettled me, yet as I slipped towards sleep, some of my jaded thoughts had been replaced with a cautious glimmer of hope.

13

The room was black and cold. I looked through sleepy eyes at a hazy, whispering shape.

'Ronald. Wake up. It is time for leaving.' Denise struck a match. His face contorted in the eerie glow. 'Sometimes there is no electricity. Please follow me, carefully.'

I found my raincoat and groped a way down the stairs. Every creak broke into the sleeping quiet of the house. He lit a lamp in the kitchen. Wind rattled the back door latch, the flame wavered and our shadows danced on the wall. Jug and glasses were on a wooden table next to a small bread loaf, part-wrapped in paper. The bucket from our room was next to the back door, covered with a cloth. Denise picked it up.

'The toilet is near.' He passed me a box of matches. 'You will take these. Please walk behind me and wait.'

I didn't have to stay long in the passage. Afterwards, I lit another match and found my way back to the kitchen. He was seated at the table, arranging the jug and two glasses.

'We drink the milk. I speak of our journey, but first there is something important.' He produced four elastic bands, laying them on the table.

'From Dinah. They will help your shoes to fit.'

I sat down to stretch the bands around my shoes and tighten the laces. Rain spattered against the window.

'We take my bicycle to the railway station. There is a space on the train,' he said.

I gulped down the cold milk. He handed me a brown scarf.

'Please put this over the mouth before we leave. When anyone speaks to you, I tell them you are ill and it is the throat, so you cannot talk. If I am not there, move the head and say *ya*.'

The scarf wrapped snugly around my neck.

'Only people who go to their work sit early in the carriages,' he said. 'If there is a seat, you must sit by the window. It is best to close the eyes and be asleep. Soon, our train is at the station… if the track has not been blown up again.'

'I wanted to thank Jos and his family.'

'They know.' He pushed the bread inside his jacket and blew out the lamp.

It was still dark outside. The wind blustered in our faces. I turned away from a cold fling of drizzle, pulling the scarf tight against my mouth. The railway crossed the street about twenty yards ahead. Denise leaned across me as he spoke then wheeled his bicycle away in a half turn to the left. I couldn't hear anything above the squall.

The small brick station had a gable roof and line of blacked-out windows. We entered a cramped booking hall. A faint light shone from inside the ticket window and about a dozen men wearing overalls and caps waited around in small groups away from a set of double doors. Denise went to buy our tickets while I held on to his bicycle. My hot breath stoked up under the scarf. A hush settled around the hall. Nobody ventured outside.

As if by a prearranged signal, the doors opened and everyone moved towards the platform. The dark shape of a steam loco rumbled past, a dim orange glow escaping from inside the shielded cab. A ticket was pressed into my hand – not much larger than a tram ticket at home. The blacked-out carriages squealed to a stop. Denise took his bicycle and merged into the queue. We walked onto a low platform. Figures clambered aboard, doors banged and shouts were lost in an upward hiss of escaping steam. I followed through the rain to the last carriage. He climbed the steps. I passed him his bicycle then pulled myself up while he lodged it in a space at the back. The inside had no compartments or partitions, only simple bench seats with an aisle along one side. Window blinds were down and the unheated interior carried a fusty smell of wet clothes. Men sat clutching their tool bags and lunch boxes. I made for the nearest window seat and Denise slumped down next to me as the train jolted forward. A youth opposite with a clamour of acne around his mouth stared at my shoes and the elastic bands. Every time we stopped my heart raced. When each new set of footsteps entered the carriage I tried not to look at the faces. Part of me was desperate to be on my way, the rest hankered to be back in Jos's house, curtained off from the world. If there were identity checks now, my war was finished.

The train crawled along. Our carriage light went out as the youth opposite raised the blind on my window. He wiped a porthole in the condensation. Dawn mist and drizzle soaked the flat countryside. The railway cut through lanes and cart tracks but there were no bridges. We neared a town. Two and three-storey narrow brick houses crowded the cobbled streets, and larger buildings showed touches of ornate architecture on their stonework. The spotty youth joined a queue in the aisle. *Lier Lierre* was in large letters on the side of a white-walled station building. Two soldiers lounged against a German Renault truck parked in a cobbled square outside the station. Our carriage stopped under the platform canopy where a crowd milled around. Denise stretched across to wipe our side of the window. Three German soldiers stared in at him from the platform. A railway porter in a grey uniform and short peaked cap pushed a trolley past them. When I looked again the soldiers had left.

Blasts of steam misted by the window. We slid past the signals and Lier's suburbs vanished into the green fields and trees. I soon felt a nudge against my arm and followed Denise to the back when the train stopped. The carriage door swung open, he pulled out the bicycle, hoisting it tight against his shoulder on the descent down the steps. I climbed down to the platform as he made a show of searching for his ticket. It had stopped raining. Passengers hurried past, crossing the tracks behind our carriage. Supervised by a railway worker, we took the same route to the opposite platform. Like Lier, Boechout station was a brown brick building signed in white paint on the end wall. A collector dressed in a grey, military-style uniform with large pockets and silver buttons waited by the door. Denise let me approach first. The train was pulling away when I handed in my ticket. I took several more steps before the collector called out to me in a pressing voice. He shouted again, his words bulleting into the back of my head.

'Ya,' I mumbled from underneath the scarf.

A man ahead of me stopped and turned around. He spoke above the clatter of carriages.

'Ya,' I said, nodding my head. 'Ya... ya.'

He frowned. Denise said something to him and the man replied giving me an acid look as he walked onto the street. Denise wheeled his bicycle out of the station, with the merest flick of his head that I should get moving.

The platform was still visible from behind wicket fencing stretching down the cobbled street. Brick or plaster-fronted business buildings lined the opposite side and were single level or had an upper floor. A woman watched me from a doorway – every window would have a face behind the glass. At the end of the street a man struggled to turn a handcart around.

The main village lay on the other side of the railway line. We turned the opposite way to where houses were more scattered. I waited until we reached an empty stretch of road.

'I'm sorry about what happened back there. I didn't know what to do.'

Denise stuck out his lower lip and blew. 'The man is taking the tickets, yes? You give him your ticket. He was trying to give you the ticket back. I tell you this before.'

That must have been what he had said to me after we left Jos's house. We stopped beside a ditch and he rested against his bicycle. 'We are two men who journey on a train, yes? The train leaves early for the workers. We are also the workers. Why would we buy the tickets which are not for the returning?'

He fiddled with the handlebars, pivoting them from side to

53

side. 'I buy them, even if we will not be returning. I do this so no one will ask the questions and no one remembers us.'

'I'm sorry. I didn't check my ticket properly.'

'We must be careful. Now it is two people who remember us at the station.' He shook his head. 'You answer the man who speaks to you and after this he asks me a question. He says, what is wrong with him?'

He grinned. 'Well, I tell him what is wrong. I tell him you are drunk.'

'What about the ticket collector?'

'I think he collects the tickets,' he replied, with a false briskness.

They were stupid mistakes. A black cloud hung over me as we walked past a cattle shed and turned on to another cobbled road. When Denise tapped quietly at the back door of a semi-detached house, the first of a string of cramps ripped through my stomach.

I had steadied myself by the time a petite woman in her late twenties with long fair hair let us in. The sleeves on her white blouse were pushed up past her elbows and an apron slewed to one side of her black skirt. A smell like baked bread scented the hallway. We stood next to the stairs where I clung on to the wooden banister spindles. If the woman noticed, she didn't show it. We exchanged nods and pleasantries and she led us to the kitchen. Four dining chairs with leather upholstery and light carvings on the back rests were at a square wooden table. A baby lay asleep in a rocking cradle and a child aged about four sat staring at us from the rug. The woman scooped up the figure.

'They have another infant,' Denise said. 'At the school.'

My insides clenched again. I knew what would happen soon.

A man wearing a blue corduroy work jacket entered through the back door. Cropped hair and low angled eyebrows gave him a naturally severe look. He chatted briefly to Denise, who introduced me. The man's face was reddened from the weather, his hand rough and calloused when it gripped mine in a strong handshake. The woman joined us and from the ring on her finger she must have been his wife. The man's name might have been Petr, Petru or something similar, as the woman had used it when she spoke to him. I decided on Peter. We sat at the kitchen table while the baby slept. Denise tried to include me with small talk which prompted nods and smiles. I listened to a conversation with little idea of what was said.

The kitchen had no clock and it wasn't appropriate to take out my watch. At least half an hour must have passed before I followed the two men up to another attic bedroom with a similar angled ceiling and wind whistling under the roof tiles. A small skylight at head height looked out over a back garden and sporadic farm buildings before fields and trees stretched out to a misty horizon. The two men spoke at the door. I turned around when Peter left us.

'The man will tell his children that a friend stays for a small time,' Denise said. 'Again, you must not leave this room.'

A sandbag weight pulled at my gut. I felt the first worrying slip of my bowels.

'Ronald, I must leave soon. We may not meet again, so it is better to wish you the goodbye now.'

I'd expected this – prepared myself for it. What mattered was saying the right words to Denise. If it was to be our last time together, he would have something which came from my heart. It might sound hackneyed, yet I wagered he would understand.

'I don't know how to thank you, Denise. What you've done... what would have happened. You risked everything for me. If there is any way I can help you... a message I can take?'

'This is not necessary. We fight the Boche together.'

His hand slipped inside his jacket. 'First, I must see my friend for some minutes. You may write a message in my *poche* book, if you wish?'

He handed me a pencil and small brown leather notebook, opening up a double blank page. It wasn't the book from before. In the quiet I wrote a short letter without looking at the other pages and placed it on the bed alongside his pencil. He returned, handed

55

me his last two cigarettes and a box of matches. We shook hands and wished each other luck. The rest was left unsaid.

The next two days fell into a blur of shivers and half sleep. Night merged into day through the skylight. I recalled little apart from the wrench of my insides and a chamber pot near the bed. Peter's voice was absent whenever I woke. Children's whispers sounded near my room and scrambled steps always followed after the woman's voice called out from below. I remembered her troubled face at the bedroom door and the sips of water I took. My mind scrubbed out the rest until late on the second day when I managed to eat some bread and weak potato broth.

It was still dark when the bedroom door creaked open later. I sat up. Two figures stepped into the room. The smallest one shone a light in my face.

'We must leave. It is not far to travel to my friends. Can you walk?'

It was Denise. I would have crawled out of bed to get there with him.

14

Peter shone a light on the stairs. I pressed my hand hard against the wall for balance as Denise guided me down.

'What time is it?'

'It is one hour and then the daylight,' he said. 'My friends are waiting. You will meet them soon. The journey is eight kilometres. You can walk this?'

'I'm alright.'

Peter shook my hand. I tried to apologise. It turned into untidy thanks and a goodbye when he marshalled us to the back door. I drew the scarf up around my face and stuck close to Denise on the empty cobbled street. He let me take a turn pushing his bicycle which helped focus my mind and stop the shaking. The same griping ache rolled around my gut. Life had shrunk to an instant when all I could think about was reaching the next place before I needed to be excused. My bowels cramped again. What had Denise been told? Peter must have known what was wrong, however discreet my issues around the chamber pot might have been. The whole rotten circle felt embarrassing and unsavoury. I worried that my apologies had been lost in the language barrier.

Denise said nothing; it was hardly the time. His stride quickened once he reached a straight country lane leading away from Boechout. We stopped outside a single-level farm house with pinned-back shutters. He gently threw small stones at a window until the curtains parted and a shadowy portrait filled the space. It was a girl with long hair. He gave an exaggerated wave and she waved back when he wheeled his bicycle around to move off.

'My fiancée,' he said after a long moment. 'Do you have the special girl, Ronald?'

'Yes.'

Silence returned. I found myself counting our steps, a march to time over the noise from bicycle wheels on a lane. We had placed a foot in each other's private world.

An outline of trees and thickets was visible nearby. Another spasm cut into my gut. I staggered into the open field. Uncontrollable bouts of shaking hit me as I fumbled in the bushes with my clothing.

Low whistles from Denise guided me back across the field to a sheltered spot further down the lane.

'You still have the illness?' His question came as if he knew the answer. I told him what happened after arriving at Peter's home.

'You can sit on the bicycle if the walking is difficult.'

'No thanks. Sitting on that saddle is the last thing I want to do right now. How far is it to where we are going?'

He checked in both directions and stepped on to the lane.

'We will not be arriving directly. First, there are some kilometres. Then it is the daylight. It is four days since you fall into the field. I do not hear any bombers after this, so the Boche will not be searching there now, but they may still be looking. We must have the eyes and ears.'

Dawn light appeared on the horizon. Several men passed by from the opposite direction, greeting us with a *goedemorgen*. With no warning my insides dropped again.

'Denise, I've got to disappear for a minute.'

This time my legs buckled. I staggered to a sheltered spot inside the field. He was looking anxiously up and down the lane when I re-joined him.

'I'm sorry,' I said, 'I can't stop it. Been like this for two days.' I put my hand against my stomach. The instinctive gesture felt ridiculous. Something between a smile and grimace flickered on his face.

'We rest, only for some short minutes. After this, we walk and, later perhaps, the bicycle?'

We took cover further along the lane under a tree near the

end of a ploughed field. The furrows stretched back in straight lines into the gloom. Spots of rain began to fall with a patter on the leaves. Denise laid down his bicycle and turned away from the elements. He leaned against my shoulder and struck a match. Smoke puffed out around his head and was snatched away in the wind. A smell of freshly lit tobacco blew across. He passed me a cigarette. We hunched into our coats, watching a diagonal curtain of hail sweep over the landscape. When he offered me a piece of bread I shook my head. Behind his chewing expressions, a serious look had stamped itself on his face. How far to go? Where were we heading? Had my details been checked yet? The ragged state of my innards only reminded me of what Mum used to say. *'When you're ill, you just want to be in your own bed.'*

The rain began to ease. Rooks cawed in the distant trees.

'Listen,' Denise said.

The whine from a vehicle drifted between gusts of wind.

'Quickly, behind the bushes. We can see from there.'

Two yellow spots moved down the lane. With a crash of gears, a truck emerged, canvas flapping, a squint of light showing through its masked headlamps. The tailgate chain rattled when it passed. Soldiers in steel helmets looked out from the back, rifles between their knees. The engine faded into the distance.

'We do not see trucks. There is no petrol here. And the soldiers?' Denise shook his head. He raised himself slowly and righted the bicycle.

'I will speak with my friends.'

I followed him to the lane, trying to wipe a film of water off the saddle.

'Please pull the scarf over your mouth again,' he said, raising his coat collar. 'Can you sit on the bicycle now?'

'Yes. I'll be OK.'

I noticed workers in the fields and pedestrians passed us carrying a hoe or spade. In the dull morning light to the northeast, a church spire pointed up through a cluster of buildings.

'Not there,' he said. 'The next village is for us.'

My clothes were damp and heavy – water on the saddle shimmied under the raincoat, soaking the seat of my trousers. The village buildings sharpened from a grey smudge to deeper, textured shades. Our route ran close enough to make out houses on a street leading up to the church. I should have felt relieved, yet the quiet and absence of people whispered around my head. Denise pedalled faster. I was glad to see the back of the place. We decided to dismount and walk. Open fields butted up to the lane or ended where the drainage ditches ran parallel alongside. I scanned the flat landscape. It was just killing time until the next uneasy minute. He walked alongside me, guiding the bicycle with his hand holding the saddle. A smile often interrupted his subtle glances around, or head cocked at a listening angle.

We neared a narrow crossroads. There was no cover for miles.

'Our friends will be ready. First, we must...' He broke off.

On the left, a line of distant figures cycled down a lane towards the junction.

'Soldiers... seven. A patrol.' I heard a click in the back of his throat.

15

The soldiers rode in perfect symmetry: helmets, field grey greatcoats, rifles slung on their backs, jackboots pedalling and freewheeling together. Maybe they would go straight over the crossroads or turn the other way? The knot tightened inside my stomach. What would happen to Denise because of me?

'We can split up at the junction,' I said. 'It'll give you a better chance.'

He kept moving. 'No. We must walk together. We see the soldiers, so they will be seeing us also. They arrive before we reach where the roads join. You must be taking the scarf away from the mouth.'

I tugged it down, trying to plaster a deadpan expression on my face. Someone dressed in a raincoat, walking through the countryside with a man pushing his bicycle was way out of place. We reached the crossroads at the same time as the soldiers turned in our direction. Denise rattled away in Flemish to me. My lips trembled and my heart crawled up into my throat again.

'*Goedemorgen,*' he called.

There might have been a reply – I didn't hear it. My legs had stiffened and assumed a will of their own. Hairs prickled on my neck and arms – I forgot everything except a desperate pleading in my head, *keep going, please keep going.* Wheels splashed through puddles in the road, with no time for ripples before the tyres came again and again. The last bicycle passed and I tried to steady myself, willing the sounds to fade in the breeze.

We took the route the soldiers had used. For a while I absorbed only the quiet. Denise glanced back down the empty thread of lane. A wry smile crept across his face.

'We have the good luck before at Sasse Bridge. Now we have the luck again.'

Shivers came with more tightening in my bowels. Nothing could have prepared me for any of this. He stopped and pointed ahead to a misty blur of buildings.

'We walk through the fields to the village. It is best not to be on the road. Also there is more Boche. They stay in the houses.'

'Germans, in the village?'

'Yes. I do not know how many.'

'You mean they are billeted?'

'They live in the houses, yes.'

He hid his bicycle in an overgrown land ditch, covering it with grass. I struggled after him through a muddy field, trying to control the spasms gripping my insides. We were visible for miles in the countryside but it was better than taking chances on an open road.

A thread of wispy smoke rose from the red brick house standing some way from other buildings strung out east in the village. We had crossed the fields in a narrow arc to reach it. Denise trod carefully down the muddy path dividing a garden vegetable patch at the rear. The back door was open.

'Good. It is safe for us to enter. My friend knows someone will be arriving,' he said.

We entered a dreary-looking room with a few sticks of furniture. Half-closed curtains at the front window obscured any view outside. A balding man with a stony face sat in an armchair in the corner. The rounded end of a wooden right leg stuck out through the bottom of his black trousers. What was left of his short black hair had been cropped at the sides. An olive-coloured casual jacket over a striped shirt didn't suit his fifty-something looks. He levered himself up to clump across the stone floor. Denise spoke to him. I heard my name before it was bulldozed aside when the man limped past him, chattering incessantly.

'Louis,' he said, pumping my hand.

Denise took a step back. 'He is pleased to welcome you into his house. He says you can dry your clothes.'

'Does he speak any English?'

'He understands a little.'

I thanked Louis for taking me in and offering to help with my clothes. He nodded energetically, steering me to his empty armchair. When he went to the back door and locked it, I removed my raincoat and eased myself down.

'What about your wet clothes, Denise?'

'They will dry while I ride the bicycle. I return here later.' He looked at the ceiling. 'Please hide up the stairs. The Chief will visit tonight.'

Louis hobbled to the front window, talking and chuckling. He drew back the curtains. I worried about him. In the wrong place at the wrong time, his garrulous bluster would be noticed and draw attention to us. Eventually, he quietened. As the two men talked, his gaze kept shifting back to me. The tightrope between trust and the unknown remained thin here. I still had unanswered questions, but it was not the right moment to speak.

'Until yesterday, the Boche search for more aviators,' Denise said. 'This is all Louis knows.' He paused as if listening to the knock from the wooden leg on the stairs. 'Please leave your wet clothes here and go to the room. Louis will be waiting.'

The bedroom window looked out over fields and meadows we had crossed to reach the house. I stayed out of sight, watching the smoky light of evening absorb the landscape. It was fully dark when Denise returned and called up to me. I went straight downstairs as I'd left only my raincoat there in case we had to leave suddenly. He was stooped close to a wood fire, warming his hands when I entered the room. The curtains were closed and a shabby light came from the ceiling lamp. Louis unlocked the back door and waited there.

'Your health is better?' Denise asked.

'Yes. Louis brought me a bowl of hot water and a towel. I've also eaten soup this afternoon.'

The back door opened.

'It is the Chief,' Denise said.

A tall, slim man in a navy-coloured overcoat entered,

exchanging a greeting with Louis. His piercing blue eyes scanned the room through thin-rimmed spectacles. He sat on the nearest chair, smoothing his blond hair.

'Good evening, Denise. You will please translate for Louis, we do not have much time.'

I aged him at mid-thirties. The sharp features contrasted his pale, smooth complexion. He took out a crumpled sheet of paper and gave me a perfunctory nod.

'And you are?'

I hesitated.

'It is alright,' Denise said, softly.

I gave the man my name. His handshake was firm and brief.

'I am the Chief. Please sit down,' he said with a marked accent.

Louis brought two wooden chairs closer and we joined the group to form a circle. I noticed how dirty my shoes were.

'Ronald Morley,' the Chief said in a low voice. 'And you are an RAF pilot officer.'

'My rank is RAF sergeant… temporary sergeant.'

He took out a pencil and studied his notes. 'Ah yes. What is this temporary? Surely you are a sergeant or you are not?'

I tried to hold his cold stare. He looked the sort of man who could unscrew the top off my head and peer inside anytime he wanted, trawling through my mind, picking out thoughts and tossing them aside until he found the right one. Louis sat forward, elbows on thighs, hands under his chin. I stumbled through an explanation about my rank. The Chief fired more questions about my squadron and take-off time.

I jumped in on a pause. 'Do you know what has happened to my crew?'

'Please answer my questions. Before you joined the RAF, you were working in a factory?'

I tried to recollect what I told Denise when we first met in Maurice's attic bedroom.

'I was an apprentice printing machine minder.'

'Where was this?'

'In Guildhall Lane, Leicester.'

He peered over the top of his spectacles. 'Please continue. What work is this?'

My words poured out in a taut, airy voice. I told him about my job and how we printed the cartons for Colgate toothpaste. It felt easier when Denise was around, but he had no control here. The Chief never asked the firm's name.

'There will be more questions later,' he said.

'I gave the information to Denise.'

'And I am checking it.'

The Chief stood up, slipping the paper and pencil inside his overcoat. 'Denise, please be sure Louis understands what is happening. Ronald, you will leave with me now.'

He walked to the back door. Denise was in conversation with Louis and they gave us a brief wave.

'We will stay away from the road,' the Chief said. 'There is no moon yet, so follow closely. This is only a village, but soldiers are always around. We are stopped for no reason.'

I lost all sense of direction in the night as we hurried through the fields. He took me through a space behind some buildings and on to a deserted street. We entered a large house via a back way. A look-alike with fair hair stood in the kitchen beside a silver-haired man and a woman. The Chief escorted me through to a dimly lit front room where we sat in two leather wing-backed chairs under the blacked-out front window. An oil painting of a country scene hung on the far wall above a walnut-coloured gramophone. Flower-patterned wallpaper and ornaments on the mantelpiece gave me a jolt of home.

'You will meet my family tomorrow,' he said, digging a hand in his overcoat pocket. 'Do you smoke?'

'Yes, I do.'

He would already know this; the Chief would have checked with Denise. His gaze stayed on me as he held out a brown packet with red print. I noticed an eagle. My chest tightened.

'They're German?'

'Better than we have here. Take one.'

He was monitoring and reading me again. I pinched out a cigarette from the packet, trying to keep my hand steady. The match hissed. I teased out a red glow.

'Cigarettes are difficult to buy,' he said. 'Everyone uses the paper and Belgian tobacco. It is like smoking straw.'

'What… they roll their own?' I tried to keep the conversation going.

'Yes.' He tapped the packet and smiled. 'Do not ask me where these came from.'

Conversation murmured in the back room amongst the ceramic clatter of crockery. The Chief took a long draw on his cigarette. 'I am sorry we had to leave Louis so quickly.'

My eyelids kept drooping. I forced them open. 'Will I see Denise again?'

'This is possible. First, I must leave you for a short time.' He smoothed back his hair.

'I will take you to your room. Please stay there, keep away from the windows and there must be no lights unless I say. You will eat some meals with us. If anyone visits the house, hide in the bedroom.'

'Yes. I've been told some of this before.'

His face brightened. 'Good. My name is, Marcel. If the others are here, you will always call me the Chief. This is understood… yes?'

'Yes.'

'Follow me and make the careful steps. Your bed is behind the door and the closet is near.'

Climbing the stairway was a slow, groping progress. A tender, raw sensation burned my insides and my head began to swim. I kept close to him, felt my way along to the open door, hit my knees against the bed and keeled over into a black pit, with no sensation or dreams.

16

A steady, scraping noise worked its way into my half-consciousness. I turned over and winced at the painful response from my body. A nick of daylight filtered in through the curtains. I heaved myself out of bed, slowly peeled off the raincoat and crept to a small gap between the lined curtains and window frame. The grey-haired man in the kitchen the previous evening was hoeing between rows of vegetables in the garden.

I crept back to the metal bedstead. The only other furniture was a wooden chair next to it. A church bell began to toll in steady rings. Days had become a blur. I wrote the letter to Denise on the sixth of November, it could have been Tuesday now, or Monday – maybe it was Sunday? No. I had stayed at Peter's for more than a day.

Sunday mornings were special before the war. In the back garden, helping Dad amongst the banked-up lines of potatoes and an earthy scent of fresh pulled carrots. Beyond our stick and wire fencing, the gardens behind Tailby Avenue's houses stretched across until their rhubarb patches reached the allotments where men in white shirts, braces and rolled-up sleeves were digging, bending or leaning on a spade talking with their neighbour. I tunnelled into those memories; they were easy sunny days.

The past was supposed to be a kind of marker steering our destiny. I heard that somewhere. Was it at school, or in a cinema film? Why had it entered my head now? Whatever life's greater truths and meanings held for the future, that kind of highbrow thinking had held no place in my world; I worked at a printing machine from fourteen until I joined the RAF. Four years had passed since I stood with Dad in the back garden on the same vegetable patch. No potatoes or carrots, only a large hole dug for the Anderson air raid shelter. The living room sash window was up. A gap like an open mouth shouted gruff tones from our wireless inside. Not the done thing on a Sunday; except for that day. Eleven-fourteen. The allotments and gardens were empty as everyone was indoors or within earshot of a wireless. Nature carried on oblivious in the late summer warmth. I stood next to the window with Dad. Our two spades stuck out at opposite angles on a mound of earth at the end of the garden. The Prime Minister would broadcast to the nation in less than a minute: the ultimatum given to Germany had expired at eleven.

Chamberlain sounded tired and despondent, his voice struggling to hide the emotion. We were at war. The words cut through me. I wanted action – wanted us to make a stand. I'd prepared for the inevitable, yet when it finally came I wasn't ready. Chamberlain faded, asking God to bless us all. The wireless went silent. Mum's shadow moved away from the window. Dad walked off down the path. Somewhere at the back a woman was crying. Just before eleven-thirty the air-raid sirens sounded across Leicester.

Marcel tapped on the bedroom door and walked in. 'I am sorry it is so cold in here.'

We wandered through some small talk as he drew back the curtains.

'You must stay in this room today. If you visit the closet, please do not walk near the window, you will be seen from outside.' He gave me a matter-of-fact look and stood away from the window, pointing out a safe route around the room. 'Do not worry. If the Germans are coming, they will not arrive until tonight. They visit just before dawn when the family is at home or in the evening as everyone sits together for their meal.'

He shook his head as if dismissing his own comment. I couldn't decide whether I'd failed another one of his tests, or he was passing me genuine information and making light of it.

'Your health,' he said, patting his stomach. 'It is better this morning?'

I rolled off the bed, excused myself and left the room. He sat on the edge of the mattress when I returned.

'We have something to stop your problem. My brother, Rupert, is here as I must go out today. He does not speak much English, but if anything is wrong he knows what to do.'

Marcel shut the door quietly. I was left looking at faded rose patterns on the wallpaper where the sun had bleached it and wondering what he meant by his last remark.

The day slipped by in limbo. Rupert brought me a white, chalky drink and returned later with hot water, a towel and shaving kit. He placed the cut-throat razor, leather strop and tube of shaving paste carefully on the chair and introduced himself with a reticent smile. His light, fair hair and thinner nose bore a striking resemblance to Marcel and he had similar mannerisms and expressions. My ablutions were the same as in the other houses: everything else felt different. Marcel was in control and unflappable. I felt a sense of being safer from the enemy, yet in a strange paradox he made me uneasy. Days had passed since Denise wrote down my answers to his questions. Marcel was checking the facts, but he might add his own queries in a separate message to London. So many things could go wrong in a process I knew nothing about. He had not answered the question about my crew. It was obvious the Resistance were holding me until they received an answer to their wireless transmission. I could only hope my details were sent correctly and had reached the right people. *Have a little faith, lad.* Dad's words drummed in my head. I lay down, listening to scrubbing sounds and the furniture being moved around below.

Late afternoon was fading when Rupert brought in a tray and placed it on the chair. I stayed seated on the bed. In fifteen minutes, the room would dissolve in black shadow and after another half hour it would be night outside. The place was quiet, except for a woman's voice downstairs. If there was street noise it never reached me in the back bedroom. Steam from the soup thickened in the cold air. Another glass of white drink was on the tray.

'*Goeije'n avend.*'

Rupert's greeting sounded something like good evening. We

both spoke in awkward bursts, treading on each other's words. He gave me a smile and shrugged his shoulders. It was dark when he returned to close the curtains and collect my tray.

Later, a restless conversation started up from downstairs. The man and woman talked above muffled music. One door always closed louder than the rest and I learned to match voices with footsteps tramping the hallway. When I woke during the night, the house carried that low, empty feel of the early hours. Floorboards creaked outside my room. I sat bolt upright in bed.

'Who's there?'

The door opened slowly.

'I apologise for waking you,' Marcel whispered. 'Goodnight. We will speak tomorrow.'

I heard the bedsprings sag in the next room. What had kept him away for so long?

17

A mist hung over the countryside again. All the items from my pockets were on the chair. I sat on the bed making a mental checklist of them.

'Hello, Ronald. Can you be stepping down here please?'

The voice had bounced up the stairs. It sounded like Denise and my mood lifted. Rupert waited in the hallway. He pointed to a back room near the kitchen and followed me inside. Dull afternoon light struggled in through the window. Denise sat in the corner, arms folded. Marcel stood facing me in front of a sideboard, the back of his head and shoulders reflected in the mirror hanging on the wall behind him. The length of an oblong dining table separated us. He walked around the side, no sound on the carpet, his stare a cold sheen behind the spectacles. A rush of panic and confusion hit me when his right hand went to his jacket. I looked at Denise – I turned back. An identity card lay face up on the table. Marcel's hand was outstretched.

'I have good news. Your information has been checked. Now we will move you away from here.'

He was shaking my hand and then the others were. It barely registered. I felt hot and light headed.

'I thought... I thought you were going to—'

'Going to what?' Marcel's hard blue stare fixed on me. His smile vanished as if it had never been there. 'We would have done that already if your words were false.'

He picked up the card. 'I speak of your papers later. Denise, explain to Ronald what happened here.'

Marcel left the room with Rupert. The steady throbbing in my head eased – I wanted a cigarette. Denise sat down with me.

'Yes...' he said. His voice sounded distant. 'Two weeks ago, I ride the bicycle again. I must speak to a man. He is hiding in the house of one of our friends. The man says he is an aviator and has parachuted from an aircraft.'

A frown creased his forehead. 'He spoke very good English… very good English.' Denise kept nodding as if to drive home the point. 'He tells us his name and about the aircraft. Also there are some other words. I ask him more questions. He is not saying everything… We are not sure. Then London says they know nothing of this man.'

He looked towards the window. 'He is buried under a tree in the fields.'

My mouth went dry. Life or death was a single wireless message away.

Marcel and Rupert returned from the kitchen with the man I saw hoeing in the garden. A grey-haired woman came in with them. She was in the hall the night I arrived. After a day and a half in the house it was the first time the parents were introduced to me. I knew them only as the mother and father.

'We sit soon for the meal,' Marcel said.

A meal? My senses had blocked any smell of cooking in the room: vegetable soup with potatoes for sure. He started to remove his jacket then changed his mind.

'So you know about this man. There are many risks. We shoot anyone who is…' He stopped. *'Un imposteur.'*

The four of us sat together, while the parents fussed in and out of the room.

'The Germans have intelligence from crashed aircraft and sometimes the crews,' Marcel said. 'They leave *un imposteur* to find help. The patriots do not see this and try to assist. There have been arrests… torture… executions. We must be careful with our questions and messages to England. My friends must be certain who they can trust. We always wait for information, check it and then we move.'

He drummed his fingers on the table. 'When it is dark, the airman can bury his parachute and leave the landing site before he hides or tries to find help. In the day, the parachute floats down. It is easy to see. Men and women who work in the fields run to reach it before the Germans. Some only want the parachute and anything the airman is carrying. They take it and then they leave. Others try to help. Often there are only small minutes before the soldiers arrive. If anyone tries to help and is discovered, do you know what happens to them and their families?'

'Yes. I think about it most of the time now.'

He stared at me like a schoolmaster but behind the mask I saw the ravages of war in his face.

The father trailed into the room, followed by the mother carrying a large white terrine full of steaming clear soup with small chunks of turnip, onion and potatoes. Hot and salty, it warmed my chilled body. We ate in silence for long periods, apart from the same occasional conversation I had heard at Peter's.

'My mother says you are not eating,' Marcel said. 'She is worried you do not like the food.'

There was too much of it and my insides still felt fragile. As soon as my bowl became half empty, more soup had been ladled in. I had no need to remember what Denise had said to me at Jos's.

'Please tell your mother her soup is excellent. I eat slowly to enjoy it.'

The parents looked unconvinced. After the meal they cleared the pots and shut themselves in the kitchen with Rupert. My sense of guilt lingered. I sat at the table drinking acorn coffee with Marcel and Denise. The vague caramel taste had grown on me, but it was the warm cup and hot liquid which I appreciated most.

Rupert rushed in. 'Boche.'

Marcel's chair crashed back against the sideboard. He flicked his fingers.

'Ronald. Follow me. Now.'

I jumped up and heard the door to the kitchen open. Denise went to the back window, Rupert rushed down the hallway. The parents blundered out through the kitchen doorway. We pushed past them. Marcel pointed to the back door. 'Wait there.'

He shut me in. The kitchen was a clutter of cupboards and shelves. I stepped past the stove and tried the back door: it was unlocked. The hallway became cloistered in whispers – someone was climbing the stairs. My items were still on the bedside chair. I gripped the handle tighter, sweat gathered on my chest and the shirt began to stick against my body. A hush filled the house. I tried to shut out the minutes, or were they only seconds?

Eventually Marcel looked around the kitchen door. 'It is safe to sit again. We continue our business.'

His voice held the same blunt tone. I let go of the handle and tried to steady myself.

'What the dickens happened out there?'

'Soldiers were outside but they have left now. Rupert will be *la sentinelle*... the guard, until later when I leave.'

We returned to the table and empty cups in the other room. Marcel recovered his chair from the floor and sat next to me alongside Denise.

'It is important,' Marcel said, 'that you understand what will happen when we leave and also know the dangers. We will speak of this now.'

'When do we go?'

'I do not know. Again, you ask questions. This must stop. Wait for instructions and follow them. I am certain that the RAF orders you to do this.'

I winced. 'I'm sorry... I just—'

'We only have a small knowledge ourselves. This way, if any of us are arrested...'

I looked in the mirror above the sideboard. Everyone sat on a slant in the reflection, as if we should have been sliding down the floor. Marcel took a deep breath.

'There will be no questions. We know nothing about the people who will help you. I will be given instructions and I follow them exactly.'

'I have to ask you this, my friends,' I said. 'Have you any more news on my aircraft or crew?'

'Please answer him, Denise. He does not listen to what I say.'

Denise gave a polite cough. 'People are afraid to speak about these things. It is dangerous and we cannot be asking too much. After you landed, two burned Lancaster aircraft were found in this area. Next morning three bodies are in an aircraft and one body in another. I am sorry, but this is everything we know.'

My thank you tailed off. I had always convinced myself the boys had got out in time. Our aircraft was on fire, losing height and listing. With flames around the bomb bay, they wouldn't have had long. Maybe neither of those Lancs was mine.

Marcel propped his elbows on the table. 'I can give you some good news about the war. The Americans are only a hundred miles from Rome and the British Army is moving northwest from Foggia. In the east the Russians have recaptured Kiev.'

Bickering rose in the kitchen above a noisy shift of pots and pans. He gave a disapproving glance towards the sound.

'Denise and I will leave soon, so you and I must continue our talk now.'

He took my identity card. 'We will check this document in a moment.'

Cigarettes were offered. We all lit from a single match and the room was soon thick with smoke. A twinge of hot tobacco hit the back of my throat.

'This may be your last one of these,' Marcel said, talking through the corner of his mouth. 'Smoke it to the bottom and *never...*' he hung onto the word, 'throw the end away.'

His head was at a slant as if waiting for my response. He drew on his cigarette.

'You know that tobacco is precious here. Anyone throwing a cigarette away will be noticed. In the cities it is busy with many people, but the police and Germans are always looking for anything unusual. They are very good at spotting details. The simple things make people suspicious. How you walk, how you act, this is very important.'

He drew himself tighter to the table. 'Your hands are never in your pockets. People do not do this. In the streets, please walk as if you know where you are going. If you can be with the crowds, this is good.'

Denise nodded, giving me a reassuring smile. Marcel picked up the cigarette packet and matchbox, placing them apart on the table.

'Others may give different instructions. I can only speak of what we do. This is Ronald,' he said, touching the identity card. 'My cigarette packet is your guide. You travel with them, but will not walk together. In the street they are a hundred or certainly fifty metres ahead. There are some differences. On the trams or trains, they do not stand or sit near you and will act as if they are alone.'

He moved the props about on the table to illustrate his points around walking, queuing and travelling on public transport.

'Be certain you can see your guide. They are also in danger. If they stop, you must not walk or speak with them unless you have been given the directives to do this. They may pass you to another *convoyeur* during the journey, but you will be given instructions before.'

The end of his cigarette grew a hanging grey ash. He tapped it onto the saucer.

'Always be ready. Things happen.'

I sensed him sifting through my thoughts again.

'Do you speak any French words?' He asked in a tone as if he already knew my answer.

'No. We were given a card with words and phrases on. I've not read it.'

'Feldgendarmerie and Gestapo checks are at railway stations and on trams or other places. When you are asked for your papers they will speak in French or Flemish. *Cartes d'identité s'il vous plait,* or *vos papiers, s'il vous plait.* Look what the guide does and what others do. Hold out the card. If you are asked questions the guide may try to help, but you are on your own.'

He stood up. 'I think this is everything for now. Do you understand it?'

'Yes. May we talk again?'

'We speak later. But I must leave with Denise now. Please learn the information on the identity card. You are a student and your name is Pierre Willems. It is easy to say.'

He left the room then returned wearing his overcoat.

'Write the signature in the space near your photograph.' He handed me a pen and hovered impatiently while I opened up the card. One of the photographs I gave to Denise had been used.

'Now, I wish you the good evening,' Marcel said, recovering his pen. 'Tonight, I will try to be quiet.'

He turned around at the door. 'The card will help, but if the Germans stop you in the street, they may already know who you are.'

18

I went to my room and examined the card. A circular German stamp was imprinted on the inside page across one corner of my photograph. The light was too dull to read other details. Items on the chair went straight back inside my jacket and trousers. Only the crucifix stayed in my hand. Every time I touched it I pictured the old woman at Steff's house, with her sad eyes and gentle voice as she bathed the cuts on my face.

The night spooled endlessly ahead: long silences, sudden noises which always made me start, doors closing, voices from the rooms below. The bedroom curtains were still open – they were closed on my first two nights. There would be a reason for that. I lay awake and tried to think of other things, folding and refolding my card to make it appear well-used. Time passed like the restless toothache darkness I endured as a boy.

Some of the old memories were misty. Was that the legacy of war? I could have been in the Navy instead of Belgium. Mum's stern face stared through the blackness – the only time she had looked at me that way. In early 1938 I went to the Navy recruitment office on London Road, opposite Saxby Street. When I arrived home, all she had to do was sign the papers. That scene was dim now, yet her tone still echoed in my ears.

'A sixteen-year-old sick berth attendant… it's not right.'

'I've always loved the sea, Mum.'

She took out a loaf from the bread bin. 'I'm not signing you away. Two years ago, I saw you disappear into the fog on that bike. Starting work at fourteen… poor little devil, I thought… yes I did. And now, Lord knows what else is coming our way. It's for the best. One day you'll realise that.'

Later, I had sat with Dad by the fire. Mum was in the kitchen. A lump of coal crackled and sparks flew up the chimney. He looked up from his newspaper.

'You know what they have to do, don't you?'

'What they have to do?'

'Yes, Ron. What they have to do. Sick berth attendants.'

I thought I knew. Those days had an innocent polish and shine, when only the sparkle showed through. Dad put in some realities, and for the first time spoke about being a stretcher bearer in the trenches. I gave up trying to join the Navy for two years.

Everything changed after Dunkirk. I was used to a distant war before then: air-raid practices, false alarms, blackout and rationing. Cinemas, dance halls and theatres soon reopened in 1939. Life was different, but the fight remained a faraway standoff abroad handled by professionals and reservists. By the end of May 1940, invasion stared at us from across the channel. So much had happened since. Bomber Command and ops changed my thoughts. Dunkirk might have been a miracle, but whatever the papers, wireless and newsreels made of it, we had left our vehicles, weapons and supplies in France. An empty army staggered ashore. Exhausted men in dishevelled uniforms, some wearing plimsolls or borrowed shoes, marched wearily from Leicester railway station up the London Road hill to Victoria Park and rested by the tennis courts near the war memorial. Some of my workmates were in that fight and it was a while before I discovered who made it back. The Dunkirk newsreels showed us giving mugs of tea, sandwiches and cigarettes to the soldiers, and the country pulling together. We just got on with it. I thought about old George's words as we clocked off work the month before Chamberlain's broadcast.

'If the war comes, we'll all have to do our bit. You'll soon know everyone in your street and the next one.'

He was right and when Aunt Harriet asked what I was going to do for the war effort, I told her I would volunteer for the Royal Navy again. I had learned Morse code in the Scouts and attended classes run by a Navy veteran in the basement of the Turkey Café on Granby Street, Leicester, so would try to join up as a wireless telegraphist. It didn't turn out well. A petty officer in the recruitment centre at Ulverscroft Road was part-way through checking the paperwork when he sent me away. Apprentices aged under twenty-one in the printing trade were required to have their firm's permission to join the Armed Forces. Lemuel Bell had already lost apprentices to the British Expeditionary Force in France as the lads were in the Territorial Army. He refused to release me, so I joined the Local Defence Volunteers in the evenings and weekends.

The house stirred. I guessed the routine: floorboards creaking, door opening down the passage, footsteps on the stairs, the mother first then the father coughing his way down in stages with Marcel and Rupert following later. Dawn crept through the window. Was this the day to leave and what would be the route? It was after ten when the mother backed into the bedroom with a cup of coffee and rolls on a tray. Much later, I ventured on to the landing. A gust of baking bread hit me. I could hear Rupert in the hallway talking to the parents. Marcel headed me off.

'I am sorry. You have not yet shaved?'

'No, I haven't. I was about to have a wash first.'

He looked at his watch and sighed. 'When you are ready, please go down to the back room. Denise is here. The meal is this afternoon and I will return later.'

I took a while with my ablutions before venturing down the stairs. Rupert pored over a newspaper on the table.

'Good afternoon, Ronald,' Denise said. A trace of his breath showed in the cold air.

'You must see this. *Le Soir*. It is the largest newspaper in Belgium. We say it is *Le Soir Vole*, the stolen *Soir*. Belgian people shiver in their homes and read stories of many great German victories and how they are winning the war. There are bad things about the Jews also.'

He turned back to the front page. 'This newspaper is from

Brussels. You do not speak the French, but something is different about it… yes?'

The edition was for 17:00 hours on 9 November and cost sixty centimes. The typeset and columns were routine. I guessed at some French words then stopped. On the left near the top of the page was a photograph of a Flying Fortress in action and further down a captioned cartoon of a glum-faced Hitler. Rupert smiled at me.

'Yes,' Denise said. 'It is a different *Le Soir*. We read stories of many victories. The invasion will begin soon.' He placed his finger on a front-page column. 'Berlin says the situation is more serious.'

Rupert flicked through the sheets, pointing out cartoons and articles.

'I've been in the printing trade for six years,' I said. 'Whoever did this used a large press with skilled people to set the type and operate the machinery. They must have taken huge risks. Is it alright to ask where you got this?'

Denise threw up his hands in mock defence. 'It is from Brussels. We hear about much planning. One evening, *Le Soir* arrives early at *les kiosque de nouvelles*.'

'The news-stands?'

'Yes. The people who buy, they see it is different and speak to others. After only some small minutes many are waiting in lines. All are sold before the usual *Le Soir* is delivered. Later the Boche realise what has happened.' He tapped the paper. 'Today, these are sold to others for much more than sixty centimes.'

He gave me a mischievous look. 'As we both say before, it is black market.'

The smile vanished from his face. 'Today, there are twenty-five years after the Boche surrender in Belgium and France. We are told not to remember this, it is *verboten*.'

He gestured to the newspaper. 'This helps to make smiles. Also on one day when it is dawn, the Belgian flag is flying from a grand building in Brussels. We also hear more good news. After the curfew, American flags are on the street lamps and in important places.'

Rupert spoke to me. I couldn't understand him.

'He says there are other newspapers,' Denise said, '*La Libre Belgique* and *La Voix des Belges*. These are not every day or every week, but they are good newspapers. Our friends risk much for us to read the truth.'

'What about our propaganda leaflets? You must have seen those. I've pushed bundles of them out from the flare chute.'

Denise nodded.

'One of the leaflets got stuck and was still in the aircraft when we landed after an Op,' I said. 'The front had a photograph of thousands of German soldiers with back packs in rows at some Nazi rally. A couple of chaps translated the headline: *1939 – Who Wanted Blitzkreig*. On the back, above a photo of British and American Bombers was: *1943 – Who will lose the war?*'

'I have seen many. We also print words like this and put them into the letter boxes of apartments or buildings where the Boche and Black Brigade are living. We try to stop their... their—'

'Spirit?' I said. 'Morale?'

'Yes... morale. We leave them in the cafés, trams and parks, sometimes in the factories. It is dangerous work, but important.'

He wandered to the window, looking out to the fields again. An action carried out with no thought or premeditation in a life of watching and checking, keeping on the move, staying one step ahead. He returned to the table, tapping it lightly with his hand as he took his seat. When Denise was around, things felt safer. I sat beside him.

'You mentioned there are bad things written about the Jews in *Le Soir*. What has really happened here?'

His face looked hollow and drawn in the afternoon light. I instantly regretted my question. He glanced at Rupert. I only wanted to talk, wanted to keep the conversation going.

He took a long moment.

'Last year it begins. They take much time with the Jews. There are many in Antwerp. First they must all wear the yellow Star of David on the clothes. Identity cards are stamped with J or JUIF in the big red letters, and then they cannot work for others who are not Jews. They must walk on the road if there are people in the streets standing or coming the other way. Anyone who does not do this is punished.'

His voice dropped to little more than a whisper. 'In Antwerp, many Jews live close together. The SS and Gestapo go there. They choose some streets. It is very fast. Gestapo and soldiers spread out and visit the houses. Men and women are arrested and put in vans. There are no windows, no air inside, it is very hot. They are inside for a long time. Then they are driven away. We do not see them again.'

He pushed a hand against his forehead. 'When the children come home from school, their house is empty. The parents are gone.'

I felt sick. 'Denise... I don't wish to—'

'There is more. We are not certain of everything. Rupert says that if they are taking the time with Jews, then they are not searching for us. I am agreeing with this, but then I am not agreeing, if you understand me?'

'Yes, I do.'

He walked to the window again.

'The Gestapo are clever. They try to trick everyone. There were arrests of all male Jews in Antwerp. Many others go into hiding. After some days they release the Belgian Jews. They say there has been a mistake as it is only foreign Jews that they want. Some come out from their hiding and think it is safe. Then they are arrested. If anyone leaves their home, it is searched and anything valuable stolen. We try to warn some friends if we find out a raid is coming. Many times we do not know.'

The father shuffled into the room and knelt at the fireplace, arranging small sticks of wood in the grate. By the time he left,

I sensed the atmosphere had lifted. Denise stayed at the table talking to Rupert who was trying to warm his hands in front of a smouldering fire. Small strips had been sliced from the wood and dried for kindling. Larger logs lay at the bottom. I studied the criss-cross geometry of the kindling in the grate as the damp fought the thin, waving flames – the sole heat for the family unless they lit the stove in their kitchen.

Denise chatted with me and translated for Rupert. We hedged around the war as if no one wanted to be the first to mention it again. A cooking smell filtered into the room. Potatoes again for sure and perhaps turnips and onion – any hot food to burn off the constant, aching cold. My conscience nagged at the thought. This family were managing to shelter and care for me under impossible conditions.

'And now, I must be leaving,' Denise said, rising to his feet. 'This time it will be the goodbye.'

'Denise, I—'

'No more speaking. You write in your note. And we will meet again.'

He grinned. 'Goodbye, my friend, I wish you much luck. Here, we say, *tot ziens*.'

It ended with another handshake, a cheery wave and the back door closing. Rupert headed for the kitchen and a heavy, bleak sensation overwhelmed me. I leafed through the newspaper. The father's voice in the hallway brought me back to the moment. Marcel breezed into the room.

'My brother says you are well.'

'Yes, thank you. Your medicine has helped.'

'Good. I will wake you at five hours, tomorrow morning. We leave for Antwerp at six.'

19

I expected to creep down the stairs the next morning in the same way I had followed Denise at Jos's. The house came alive long before Marcel knocked on my door. A smell of baking bread hit me as I neared the kitchen. The family stood around their iron stove. Rupert was putting on his coat; Marcel broke off from speaking to his parents.

'My brother wishes you good luck.'

Rupert shook my hand then turned to his mother, embraced her and kissed both cheeks. She drew him close, arms around his shoulders, head turning away as her voice faltered. She hurried from the room and I heard her reach the top of the stairs before Rupert had closed the front door.

'Please excuse us,' Marcel said. 'It is sometimes difficult for my mother.'

'I'm sorry. I don't wish to be any trouble.'

'This is not about you,' he said sharply. 'Please sit down. I speak again before we leave.'

His father followed him out and I stood on my own by the kitchen table, unsure what to do next. The family would have sat around it during normal times, when news and a day's work were discussed together over an evening meal, the single occasion when they were side by side. War ripped that apart. How much did the parents know, or choose not to know about what their sons were really doing now?

Marcel returned to feed the stove with twigs from a bucket under the sink. He served coffee and a piece of bread before sitting with me at the table. Coal and dry wood were scarce after the occupation; the family must have fully decamped into the kitchen, living and eating around a meagre heat from their stove. They might have used the back room because of me. I hoped I was mistaken.

Marcel put his cup down as I dipped the last of my bread into the coffee.

'It is time to finish our talk from yesterday.'

I received that serious look again. The man was matter of fact, keeping me lodged between his good manners and a brusque, business-like footing he guarded so carefully.

'*Cartes d'identité, s'il vous plaît,*' he said suddenly.

I shifted about in my chair. He stood over me.

'*Cartes d'identité, s'il vous plaît.*' His voice became impatient. '*Ihre Papiere bitte.*'

I fumbled inside my jacket and handed him the card. He scrutinised the details, then shot me a piercing look before holding out the card.

'What is your reason for this journey?'

I tried to force the card into my trouser pocket.

'No.' He struck the table with his hand. 'No, no. If you are asked for your papers, never show that you understand English. Your face tells everything to me. Keep the serious eyes.' He exaggerated a downcast air and dropped his shoulders. 'You must always be tired and not interested.'

The voice softened. 'I understand this is not easy for you. But the Gestapo, Geheime Feldpolizei or whoever… they can use this trick if they are suspicious.'

He made himself comfortable in the chair opposite and slid a tiny cardboard box across the table.

'This is from my mother, for the razor and soap Rupert gave to you. The box will fit inside your pocket.'

'Thank you. Can I fetch them from the bedroom?'

'They are already inside the box. I have more instructions for you now. The tram station is near but there are checks, so we will ride the bicycles to Boechout and wait for a train to Antwerp.'

I said nothing about my gaffe at Boechout with the ticket collector. Maybe Denise had told him.

'When we leave the train, remember what I say before and walk about a hundred metres behind me.'

He gulped down the last of his drink. 'Later, it is possible that you will travel on a tram in Belgium. Smoking is forbidden. The notices say *Defense de Fumer* in French or *Rauchen Verboten*. This is a new instruction. Trams are often crowded, we stand very close. Belgian people have no choices, they are often near to soldiers. This was not just a problem for us. When the Germans returned to their holes, they removed their coat and tunic. There are many small cigarette burns. I hear also that cigarettes were dropped into their pockets after my friends had nearly smoked them.'

I caught him eying me with another inquisitive look. 'This is unfortunate, yes?'

'Very unfortunate.' I didn't fight off my smile. Our simple exchange had steadied the nerves.

'Did Denise speak with you about the traitor?'

'No.'

'This man is dangerous. You may… what is the word?' He hesitated. 'You may encounter him. He has many names… Jack, Willie, Tom, and he will speak good English with a Canadian or American accent perhaps. He often says he is a British officer or Canadian pilot and you must follow him. Do not go. This man works for the Gestapo.'

My stomach tightened. Things were moving to another level. 'What does this man look like?'

'We do not know everything. He changes his face and clothes, but he has about this height.'

Marcel bridged a hand, level with his eyebrows. I reckoned on five feet eight inches.

'We are searching for him. He has brown hair but sometimes it is grey. There is also a moustache and the spectacles, but not always.' Marcel pinched the top part of the little finger on his right hand. 'This is missing. There is information in our underground newspapers. My friends speak of a photograph. I have not seen it. We must kill him, but he is protected by the Germans. He enters the Resistance and escape routes. Then he disappears when his work is finished.'

The man's height was only approximate and he would likely wear a hat or cap covering most of his head. I focused on the accent, aliases and the little finger on his right hand.

'Time to leave, Ronald, before it is light.'

I shrugged into my raincoat and watched him go into the hall. The elastic bands from Dinah still fitted tightly around my shoes. He returned wearing a grey cap and brown, half-length pea coat.

'This belongs to Rupert.' He handed me a similar cap. 'It will fit you. So now we are both workmen travelling to Antwerp and our bicycles are outside next to the door.'

The cap felt tight. I pushed it higher up my head then made sure everything was secure in my pockets. Right on cue, the father and mother returned. It was a swift goodbye as Marcel was already at the back door. We stepped into darkness and drizzle again. I bent down to tuck the trouser turn-ups into my socks. A run of gritty steps on the gravel and I was cycling after him over the cobbles. We left the village by the south end and I saw no one on foot, only cyclists passing from the opposite direction.

Boechout became visible at first light as a distant, grey cluster of buildings. In the damp smell of early morning I rehearsed Marcel's instructions in my head. Muscles were tight, my skin prickled but my heartbeat kept steady. We dismounted at the edge of the village, pushing our bicycles into a shed behind the nearest house. The garden backed onto fields and was not visible from neighbouring properties or the road.

'Wait here for one minute, Ronald, and then follow me. Outside the railway station, I will give you a ticket.'

He disappeared along the side of the house. Nobody came out to investigate. If the home was occupied they must have known we were coming. I used the time to tidy my windswept appearance and untuck my trousers from the socks.

Drizzle and fallen leaves had greased the cobbles. Workers trudged along in one direction and it took a few minutes to reach the approach road to the station. As I turned the corner, Marcel entered the main building. I waited outside by the fencing and it wasn't long before he returned with my ticket. We walked into the foyer and joined a shapeless queue scrambling for the platform entrance. No soldiers or police. A railwayman, half obscured by the door, hastily checked tickets at the entrance. Was it the same man as before? I had made a huge mistake the last time. *Danku, danker*, or was it *danken* – his drone sounded familiar. He returned my ticket with a mirthless smile, switching his attention to the crowd behind me.

Marcel's grey cap was barely visible amongst the hordes on the platform. He edged closer to me when the train rumbled in. I climbed the steps into the carriage and found a standing space by the opposite door. Marcel stood in the aisle a few paces away. Once our carriage had cleared the platform, passengers around him settled back into their journey with slack-jawed stares. I pushed up against the door and wiped away a square of condensation from the window. Wisps of smoke floated past and the wind made streaky trails with droplets of water on the glass. The train dawdled along between stops. Our carriage was full now. There might not be checks.

We slowed to a crawl, passing bombed-out buildings and rubble. If these were the suburbs of Antwerp then the scars of war from 1940 were still visible. Seconds later we halted at Mortsel station and the men around me left. Thoughts turned to what would happen next – Marcel hadn't said. He didn't move from the aisle until the next stop when a long, island platform with a shelter came into view ahead. It sat in the middle of four tracks. The left one was on our route and served another platform and the main station building. Marcel opened the carriage door opposite me, climbing down the steps as it travelled the last few yards. I waited until the train squealed to a halt before I slipped in amongst the other passengers waiting to leave.

Berchem station was built above street level. The brick building had a square tower at its nearest corner and a slated pyramid top.

Two thin, conical turrets were attached to the pyramid base, creating a fairy-tale look totally out of kilter with the station's formal steep slanted roof and architecture. Black railings lined the back of the platform, and Victorian-styled buildings with shops on the ground floor faced the station from the opposite side of the street. Antwerp's rooftops crowded into the distance and the city appeared undamaged.

Marcel disappeared through an archway. I felt for my identity card and train ticket. It was a return: I must remember that at the barrier, keep Marcel in sight, stay close to a girl in front of me, get through and get out. My body stiffened again. The queue shambled through the doors into a gloomy foyer. Two men were waiting, the nearest dressed in a peaked cap and railway tunic, his right hand taking tickets, the left one handing them back. The other man looked short and squat in his long beige raincoat. He stepped forward, stopping people and asking questions. The queue edged nearer. His gaze strafed the line. A cold stone of fear grew in my stomach. Marcel cleared the exit and his footsteps faded. The girl in front of me passed through. Stares settled on me like ice. I saw my hand hold out a ticket and receive it back.

Someone was close behind. I walked down the stairs trying not to rush, taking careful steps as if my legs knew what they were doing. The cap – I looked for Marcel's cap, not his coat or busy stride. He crossed the street, his reflection gliding past in the shop windows. Wet patches patterned the pavements and cobblestones, and the raised metal railway structure looked crude against the old buildings packed together in a mass of brick red, brown or white frontages. This was not the Antwerp in my school books with its ornate, regal architecture and spires piercing skywards above the port and river Scheldt. A straight road angled away from the station. Marcel turned onto it.

The gap stayed at around a hundred yards. I cursed myself for not checking who was behind me when I had left the station. Most roads and backstreets were empty of vehicles. I walked past women queuing under shop awnings and cyclists criss-crossing the junctions. A bike rattled by with fabric bound tightly around the wheels in place of tyres. Marcel maintained a pattern: stop to look in a shop window or throw a casual glance behind, then cross the street or take a side road if there was activity ahead. He doubled back, often leaving and re-joining streets. I turned up my raincoat collar and kept moving. Gendarmes walked in pairs or cycled. Two German soldiers came out of a shop – it was me who looked away first. No one was following now. We joined a wide boulevard flanked by grand apartments. Two rows of trees ran down the middle. A cream-coloured tram clattered past, the driver in his grey uniform and cap, a conductor squeezing through the standing passengers. Marcel hurried over the tracks embedded in grey cobblestones and knocked at the double doors to a sandstone-coloured building on the corner of a side street. He disappeared inside and a simple truth hit me. I was further away from Spain than when I first landed.

A pile of soggy autumn leaves lay banked up around the step. The left door opened. A woman with gathered dark hair smiled at me.

'*Entrez, Monsieur. Entrez.*'

A drift of onions cooking met me in the tiled hallway. Marcel moved from behind the door to shut out the street. The woman chatted to him in French whilst we walked to a kitchen at the back where an antique cabinet with china and cooking utensils stood against the left wall. Bowls and cutlery were set at a small, brown table. A saucepan simmered on a cream enamel stove, near the sink and wooden draining board under the window.

The woman was introduced to me as Madame Jeanette. She had a thoughtful expression, yet active eyes. Her smooth complexion and smart appearance made it difficult to pinpoint her age. I guessed at mid-forties.

'*Asseyez-vous, s'il vous plait, messieurs.*' We hung our coats over the kitchen chairs and sat at the table. Marcel shut his eyes as if meditating. Jeanette busied herself at the stove, making conversation with him.

'Madame tells me there are extra checks in the streets and stations. Two *razzias* happened near here, yesterday,' he said.

'*Razzias?*'

He opened his eyes. 'They are street raids. Soldiers block off both ends. They line up and walk down. Everyone is pushed into the middle and searched. Papers are checked. The soldiers look for young men hiding from forced labour. Also they find the *smokkelaars* who run black market.'

His words swirled around in my head to the noise from Jeanette's ladle in the saucepan.

'The raids often happen after Resistance work. Yesterday was perhaps a good day?'

Jeanette lifted the saucepan off the cooker. He bent close to my ear.

'Tonight, you will meet more friends. We know you are told to cooperate with the Resistance, but if anyone asks, say nothing to them about the people or the houses where you have stayed.'

'Of course I won't.' For once I didn't receive the Marcel 'look'.

We must have seemed a strange pair, hemmed in between the table, wall and a half-open door into the kitchen. Jeanette sat with us over bowls of steaming potato and onion soup, pushing along with her small talk in French, which Marcel translated. She spoke to me in single English words at first, followed by short French sentences, her accent soft, the poise and delivery measured.

'Madame asks when the Allies will come,' he said.

I edged my chair back against the wall. 'Early next summer might be a good time.'

Marcel sipped his soup and stared out of the window as if withdrawing into our silence. I noticed that a wall obscured any view beyond the yard. Finally he spoke.

'For some houses in cities, the kitchen is in the basement and the family sit in a room above for their meals. Sometimes there is only one room, so a curtain must be pulled across in the middle.' His voice tailed off as if he had run out of ideas to keep the conversation going.

Jeanette began to reminisce through him about the old town and life before invasion. The dark pools in her eyes grew as she walked the streets of Antwerp again, describing its cathedral and sixteenth-century town hall, historic churches and Ruben's house. Her sudden pauses came with a sad and downcast expression on her face. Marcel placed his spoon carefully into the bowl.

'Madame saw the Nazi soldiers marching through the streets. Men and women cried that day.'

Each time I had heard those memories, the words and faces stayed with me like some whispering apparition. The sadness and loss those people carried around hurt me the most. At times my own desperation to get home felt selfish.

'Madame?' I caught her attention. 'Every serviceman tries to escape, so he can fight again. We also long for the day when you are free.'

Marcel translated. She nodded and gave me a quiet smile. I tried to talk of other things.

'You spoke about the wonderful buildings in Antwerp. Were any destroyed during the fighting?'

'The city was not damaged when the Germans captured it,' Marcel said. 'Bombs do this.' His cold stare sent a shiver through me.

'What bombs?'

Jeanette made her excuses, picked up our bowls and went to the sink.

'In Mortsel,' he continued. 'We travelled through there on our train journey. This is the war you do not see.'

'I noticed some wrecked buildings and rubble.'

'The Minerva car factory is used to repair Luftwaffe aircraft. In April this year the Americans arrived during the day. Some bombs miss their target and drop on houses and schools.'

He paused as if waiting for some kind of reaction. 'Hospitals are full of the dying and injured. Many are killed. Two hundred are children. We see photographs in the newspaper. Lines of women in black clothes look down at small, white coffins in a long grave.' His glare cut through me. 'This is not German propaganda. It is the truth.'

My face burned. An acid taste rose in the back of my throat. 'We wouldn't have done that. You know the RAF bomb at night. We are always briefed in detail and bomb on the target indicators. Then later, the reconnaissance photos show—'

'Reconnaissance photos?' Marcel shook his head. 'They show damage, not the dead and injured.'

'I've never bombed Belgium or France. I'm sure the Americans were following their orders. They would see the target and...'

My words evaporated. He threw a glance at Jeanette who was clearing the rest of the table. His expression soured.

'Perhaps the Allies should drop more explosives in Belgium for the Resistance, instead of bombing our towns?'

I bit my lip before answering. He might have lost someone in that raid.

'I am no different to the other airmen, Marcel. I follow orders and do my job. We are trying to help win a war.'

I wanted to say it would save lives in the end and then reel out the remainder of the spiel. We did our bit and they were my honest views, but until our exchange I hadn't recognised the regimented state my mind had fallen into.

'It is difficult sometimes.' His voice sounded weary. He stood and put on his coat and cap. 'We must all do what we can. And now I will leave you. The bicycles wait for me at Boechout.'

I couldn't let him go with things the way they were. I rose from my chair.

'I'm really sorry. If I do get home, I'll tell them what you've said. Right now I want to thank you for all your help and everything you've taught me.'

He waited before shaking my hand with a military precision.

'Goodbye. I wish you luck. Madame says everyone in this building is away until tomorrow. You will leave later today.'

I heard him walk down the hallway. He would check the street through a window, share a final few words with my host and become another memory.

I remained in the kitchen. Later, Jeanette sat with me for coffee, bread and broken conversation. Through our hesitant chat, I learned that her husband and sons were away from home. Jeanette was not her real name; the few unguarded expressions on her face when Marcel had addressed her had convinced me of that. It must have been around three o'clock when she showed me to a bedroom. The building stood on a corner, making her lounge visible from both the avenue and a side street. She said I must stay out of sight and rest until my guide arrived. I avoided asking any questions, it was better not to know.

The door remained half open and her footsteps faded down the passage. A plain pot lampshade hung on three chains from the ceiling. The single wooden bed was next to a window with a decorated plastic sheet covering the glass. Two framed photographs stood on the dresser near a wardrobe. Jeanette was in the first picture, much younger, dressed in twenties-style summer clothes and standing by some garden latticework next to a round-faced man with thinning hair. In the other photograph a tall boy in his mid-teens, wearing an open-necked shirt stood behind a group of adults and children. Maybe Jeanette had hidden the past out of everyday sight until better times.

Holed up inside the same four walls of a safe house it had been easy to become self-absorbed and not look beyond the people sheltering me. Photographs cut through all of that. I had recognised it in the first farmhouse and now again at Jeanette's: a whole family, a snapshot of the past and normality of how it once was, and how it might be when this war ended. I stared at the crowded photos.

How many other lives had these people touched? How many were caught up in this dreadful business? How many would be left at the end?

A French novel lay on the bedside table. I leafed through the first pages then placed it back in the same position. Not a trace of dust, the room had a neatness and preservation, as if waiting for its owner to return. I flopped down on the bed and closed my eyes. Shadowy sleep was out there but I couldn't give in to it. The long drag back after an op had been the same: fight away exhaustion, switch from Group broadcast to intercom, immerse myself in the routine and forget about our gunners' endless search for enemy night fighters.

Clocks chimed across Antwerp, following each other in rhythm before the soulless quiet and waiting returned. Any notion of a safe house being different in the city was a fallacy. Only a sense of being amongst thousands of others offered greater anonymity and solace. Jeanette's marching steps in the passage kick-started my usual fear and shiver. She tapped on the bedroom door.

'*Monsieur...* your *convoyeur*, she arrives soon.'

I followed her back to the kitchen and recovered my raincoat. The guide would be a young girl waiting on the opposite side of the boulevard.

'*Les directives?*' Jeanette's voice dropped to a whisper. 'You understand them?'

'Yes Madame. Marcel has explained about following a guide.'

She left me and entered a room near the front door. I waited in the hallway. It was a few minutes before she reappeared and beckoned me forward.

'*La petite jeune fille,* she waits. *Regardez, Monsieur,* she carries *un sac à main.*' Her hands flapped vaguely in the air for a moment. 'The handbag.'

She passed me a magazine from the hallway table before opening the front door. 'You read in the train.'

I paused on the step to put on my cap. The small girl on the opposite side of the boulevard had shoulder-length blonde hair. Her green coat stood out in the dull afternoon light and she carried a tiny brown handbag. I walked across the cobbles, trailing her at about a hundred paces. She kept to the wide, tree-lined avenues and main roads, occasionally glancing behind before she turned a corner. I thought about Marcel with his cigarette packet and props on the dining table. *Look as if you are going somewhere and don't stare.* He was right about so many things.

Crowds filled the main streets and trams clanked past. Flashes of the girl's green coat weaved in and out of sight ahead. *Look for the tram stops.* I had been told to wait at the nearest one if I lost my guide. *Remember, she does not know you and you do not know her.* How many times had the thought raked through my head?

A dull churning gnawed inside – like dentist day. Crowds were all around, yet I was alone with the dread I might be stopped and asked for a light, or a soldier would try out his pidgin French on me. Forage caps, helmets and machine pistols: the Wehrmacht were everywhere and they were the only ones with cigarettes.

Above the old streets, a flat-topped American-style skyscraper was visible. Most buildings became a blur, except for the medieval structures with their embellished stonework and leaded windows. The girl walked across a cobbled square towards a large grey building with a dome in the middle. Two narrow Gothic-styled towers flanked the entrance on either side. Four levels of large windows and a run of archways at ground level made the frontage look like a church. The entrance was a pulsing mass of civilians, soldiers and baggage. Two grey army trucks stopped and the Wehrmacht spewed out. Black staff cars were arriving and leaving in a chain reaction.

I slipped the rolled-up magazine inside my raincoat. The girl was less than twenty paces away when she sidestepped luggage and walked through the entrance to a wide flight of stone steps with a concrete balustrade on either side. Men and women sat on suitcases in the foyer below and mothers hung on to young children. Luftwaffe, Wehrmacht and Kriegsmarine moved through the crowds or loitered in gangs around their kitbags. I followed the girl down to the concourse. Tannoy announcements, rumbling trolleys and shouts cannoned around the huge space under the dome. Shattered glass in one part of the roof created a jagged patchwork.

'*Attendez ici.*' The girl walked off to buy tickets. I waited by a wall. More servicemen poured down the steps before she returned and stood on tiptoe to get close enough to my ear.

'At Brussels, we journey on the street car,' she said with a heavy French accent.

I struggled to hear above the noise.

'I meet a man. You will follow him… *oui*?'

'Yes.'

She smiled, handed me two tickets then joined the teeming crowd passing under the archways. My brown ticket was for a tram, cost seventeen francs and had punched holes around the edges. I kept a safe distance and joined the queue to a railwayman standing at the barrier. Servicemen passed through an adjacent gate, where a soldier wearing a yellow armband and large crescent-shaped metal gorget around his neck stopped them at random to check their papers.

There must have been ten people between the girl and me. Some civilians showed more than one document to the railwayman. The queue pushed tighter. I couldn't see what the girl had handed over. What to do? It was too late and too close now to get out of the line. The railwayman held me in his solemn gaze. I took out my identity card. He examined it, checked my rail ticket and returned both without a word. I shambled through – surely it wouldn't be like this every time?

A large girder and glass canopy arced above the bay platforms. The girl walked alongside a rake of green carriages. Some had printed notices stuck on the doors and windows. Soldiers clambered aboard, hauling up their kitbags as civilians bowled past, carried along with the herd. A column of steam shot up at the end of the next platform. I boarded the nearest carriage. The girl had positioned herself further down the aisle, ignoring a crowd of noisy soldiers pushing past. I found a seat nearby and the place soon became a clutter of bags and luggage. Marcel had told me separate carriages were reserved for the military. Should I give up my seat for them? What was the form? A woman opposite with a navy handbag smiled at me.

Our carriage jolted forward and the platform slid silently past the window. It took a moment to realise what was wrong. No whistle from the loco or clouds of smoke, this was an electric train. My thoughts stalled at the row of clean shoes opposite. Stares built up around me. Perhaps I was something to look at, other than the enemy? Dressed like this, I wouldn't last long in the cities.

Antwerp passed in a haze through the dirty carriage windows. The Belgians spoke amongst themselves, quietly at first, then louder as soldiers at the other end made more noise. I tried to feign sleep. With my watch hidden and no recollection of a station clock, I lost track of time. Time was abstract anyway: the silence between each noise in a safe house, a passage from one ordeal to another, an interval until the next street corner. Time was sitting in a railway carriage waiting to be noticed, waiting to make a mistake, waiting to be arrested. Time was safely reaching the end of another day.

No one was reading, so the magazine stayed rolled up in my pocket. A blond Wehrmacht corporal tried to start a conversation with the girl. She nodded as he gestured and spoke, she saw his face, yet wouldn't look into it. How had she got involved in this life and death work? Did her parents know? Were they in the Resistance? She was older than Steff, the boy I met in the field, yet moved with the same calm and innocence. I imagined her vanishing into the shadows, like him, then reappearing with no warning in another doorway like some watching spirit. Age didn't matter in this war within a war.

Fields and meadows were swathed in a light mist. We halted at Malines and made other stops. If I glanced up, the woman with the blue handbag always looked away. Passengers had gathered their luggage before I noticed the brick and stone suburbs of Brussels. The train drew into an end platform as soldiers clattered down the aisle. People around me held back until the military left, but the girl had disappeared.

I panicked. Passengers funnelled out and I almost fell in a rush to get down to the platform. The girl waited by the next carriage, our eyes meeting for an instant, enough for her to turn away and take a narrow route alongside the train. No extra checks at the gates. I showed my ticket and walked from the station on to a large square bordered by department stores, shops and hotels. Figures beetled across the vast open space. Soldiers, laden with kit, hung around blocking the pavement. The girl moved off past them as soon as she saw me.

The late afternoon felt damp and cold. Main streets were still busy with people. Women wore neat hats and outfits, the men dressed in suits, overcoats and trilbies or working clothes and caps. It was a weary yet defiant stance to show their best and ignore the occupier. Trams passed me from both directions. They were a yellow ochre colour, the shades differing, depending on their age and level of city grime covering the paintwork. The girl passed numerous tram stops before halting at one where nobody was waiting. I caught up and took a position a few paces away next to an office building. A two-car tram rounded the turn, clanking in our direction. I went to walk forward and froze. On the opposite kerb, a German officer in a greatcoat watched me with the same silent stare as the crowd on the train. He stepped into the road.

20

The tram clattered across in front of me and halted. *If they stop you in the street then they already know who you are.* Marcel had lived inside my head ever since we met. He knew I didn't fit and so did the German officer. Cold gripped my insides like they were packed in ice. The girl jumped on board at the rear entrance. I grabbed the rail, started to climb the step – braced myself for the shout and heavy hand on my shoulder. The tram eased away. My sole thought was to keep away from the girl. No one had boarded behind and the pavement was empty. The officer would be in the second car.

I joined the crowd in the aisle and hung on to a leather ceiling strap. People sat on facing wooden seats, a double on the left and single to the right. Halfway down the car a wood and glass partition stretched window to window across the width, with only the aisle cutting through. A slow metallic screech sounded on the bends. Civilians and military leaned together in one swaying mass. The conductor punched the girl's ticket and worked his way towards me through the damp, soupy air.

Each time we stopped I looked around for the officer. People shoved past with no word or eye contact: the etiquette of a city under occupation? The journey stuttered on through gloomy, late afternoon suburbia before we stepped off the tram, hastening down a side street of narrow, terraced houses. I expected the girl to check I was following. She didn't. Only her footfall and an echo from my own steps sounded in the quiet. If the officer had raised the alarm, I would be in the bag by now. Light was fading. Long gaps appeared between passers-by. A man in a dark suit and carrying a coat over his arm waited alone near a tram stop. The girl spoke to him. He appeared to be giving her directions. She crossed the road. I hesitated. This had to be the changeover. The man gave the briefest of glances my way and walked off slowly down the street. He had a strange gait, dropping his shoulder as he turned into the breeze. His sudden urgent stride went against all my previous instructions. I was certain no one was following me, so was he trying to beat the blackout or a curfew? He slowed near a street corner to speak with a small woman and left before she approached me.

'Hello. What is a Mae West?' she said in a thin, low-pitched voice.

The question didn't take me by surprise. Her appearance did. I studied her in the poor light: a schoolgirl wearing a short woollen coat with large buttons, a pleated skirt and white ankle socks. She had an old-looking face and ear-length dark hair.

'It's a life jacket. You wear them to keep afloat in the water.'

'And what is a champagne glass?'

'A Hampden bomber.'

She stepped closer. 'My name is Lily. Follow me.'

I walked about ten paces behind her. We reached a residential road with adjoining tenement buildings on both sides, a wealthy apartment area with fashioned ironwork on the mock balconies. Lily stopped and waited for me before unlocking a front door.

'Peoples live on the top floor,' she said in a hushed voice. 'They must not hear us.'

I removed my cap and followed her up a flight of stairs to the first level. A tall, thin woman in her fifties with a toothy smile opened the door and invited us in. Curtains were closed and the faintest hint of warmth from somewhere touched my cheeks. Armchairs, a dining suite and matching sideboard with a wireless on top filled the carpeted room.

'This is Mademoiselle,' Lily said. 'Please tell her your name.'

I introduced myself. Mademoiselle shook my hand, welcoming me in smooth English with hardly a trace of an accent. Lily removed her coat. A blue cardigan and white blouse made up the school-like uniform. She gave me a matter-of-fact look as we sat down in the easy chairs.

'Do you have the wounds? I am a nurse. If there are problems we must see.'

'Only cuts.' I touched my face. 'They are OK now.'

'This is good. Please take off your coat,' Lily said. 'A friend will visit soon.'

Mademoiselle had thick, voluminous dark hair set above her shoulders. She observed me from the chair opposite as I draped my coat over the back of the seat.

'Did you have any problems on your journey?'

'No, Mademoiselle. But I only just managed to get a seat on the train.'

After several minutes she excused herself to go downstairs to make a hot drink. During the small talk neither of us had made reference to the war.

'Please speak when you must visit the toilet,' Lily said, explaining it was on a small landing between the first and second floor. 'The rooms below us are for Mademoiselle. We do not know about the peoples…' She pointed to the ceiling.

I wasted no time in making a visit. It was a relief in more ways than one to return and sit in the room again. Lily looked distant and preoccupied. The last chirruping from a blackbird outside stopped. My gaze strayed to the walnut-coloured wireless on the sideboard. It was a home table model with long and medium wave broadcast receiver and an FNR badge at the top.

Lily turned to me. 'Mademoiselle listens at night to the BBC. This is very quiet, as it is forbidden.'

'You mean the same as smoking on the trams.' I repeated the story Marcel told me. She nodded in the right places – I knew it was old news to her. At least there was a chance to say something, an opportunity to talk and stop any silences.

The door suddenly flew open. I recoiled in my seat. A man in his forties with a ruddy complexion and combed-back, red hair blustered in. From his beige belted raincoat and felt hat he could have been the local tax inspector. He peered at Lily through a pair of horn-rimmed spectacles. I hadn't heard him knock or enter the building. Lily spoke in French and he closed the door.

'*Bonsoir*, I am, Georges,' he said quietly.

I stood. We shook hands. The grip was firm and both his little fingers were complete. I gave him my name and rank.

His smile faltered at the edges. He indicated I should empty out my pockets and place everything on the table. Lily passed my raincoat across and Georges stood over me while I searched through my clothes. Magazine, small cardboard box, button compass, identity card, tram ticket and dirty bloodstained handkerchief went on the table.

'Georges asks if this is everything,' Lily said.

'Yes.'

He pointed to the box.

'It's my razor and soap.' I took off the lid.

He picked up the identity card, examining it closely.

'Who gave you this?' Lily asked.

'Some people who helped me.'

'Where?'

'I can't say. I have been told not to speak of it.'

She looked at Georges. They talked. He muttered something and skimmed the card onto the table.

'You have more papers?' Lily said.

I shook my head.

'He has surprise you were not stopped on your journey. Please sit at the table then tell him the name of your navigator.'

I felt flushed and warm. My face had begun to burn as if a hot water bottle was pressed against it. Shivers and a dull throbbing in my legs had started on the train and were forgotten during the tension of the journey.

'My navigator is Sergeant Kenneth Garvey. Do you know about him? Have you heard something?'

Georges rolled my compass between his thumb and forefinger before consigning it to his raincoat. He checked his watch before speaking to Lily again. Mademoiselle ascended the stairs in time to the chink of china. She brought in four cups of coffee on a tray, chatting as she passed them around.

'I am sorry,' Lily said. 'We can tell you nothing about Sergeant Garvey.'

Georges replaced the lid on my cardboard box. 'The discs?'

'Beg your pardon. I don't understand you.'

'You have the identity discs?' Lily said.

'Identity tags. Yes.' They wouldn't find out about the watch, crucifix, pendant and money wallet which were still inside my jacket. Georges ignored the handkerchief, pushing the rest of my things back across the table.

'He speaks to you later about them,' Lily said. 'You will leave very soon.'

I gathered up the things, my throat suddenly sore and dry. The hot coffee had no taste and felt like swallowing broken glass.

'You must change your clothes,' Mademoiselle said, indicating the door opposite. 'There are some in the armoire.'

She showed me into an adjoining room, turned on the light and left. I sat on the bed holding on to my throbbing head. Shivers came in waves. I wiped the sweat off my forehead. The wardrobe door was open: shirts, trousers and two jackets hung on a rail – enough to fill a suitcase. On the shelf above, a pair of braces and some balled socks lay on top of folded underwear. They were all clean clothes and I needed a wash. Lily had already said about leaving soon.

Georges' voice filtered in from the next room. I foraged along the rail. The shirt had overlong sleeves but a striped tie blended in. Trousers and a brown jacket fitted. Two pairs of brown shoes were in the bottom of the wardrobe, one set sporting a mosaic of cracked leather on the uppers. Their soft, close fit around my feet was unforgettable.

Urgent tapping came on the door and Mademoiselle's whispers. 'Are you ready, Monsieur?'

My discarded clothes lay folded on the floor in a neat pile next to the dirty shoes, as if trying to salvage some decorum. I noticed my flushed cheeks and runny nose in the dresser mirror.

'Yes, Mademoiselle, I am ready.'

'Very good,' she said, as I exited the bedroom. 'But you are still too English. Your hair must brush like this.' She swept a hand across her head and went into the bedroom.

Lily stood at the table. 'There must be the photographs and then another journey before curfew.' She picked up my tram ticket. 'You can use this. Georges will be near. The Feldgendarmerie check the trams at night and it is difficult to see them waiting at the stops, so be ready to leave.'

Mademoiselle returned with a hairbrush. My hair felt like a haystack once I had finished the brushing. Georges led me out. We walked through the blackout and heavy drizzle, his masked torch dabbing a small spot of light on the pavement. A wet, clammy film had formed on my forehead and rain dripped off the end of my nose. A sudden bout of coughing hit me.

Georges whispered through the night. 'You have the illness? *La grippe?*'

'It's just the start of a cold.'

Water gurgled down the gutter. Blots of rain spattered on my raincoat. We reached a tram stop. My head and body burned with fever and an ache had soaked its way into my bones. The thick night only focused the rest of my senses on how ill I had suddenly become.

The squeal from a tram sounded, its dark shape looming at the last second. I climbed aboard past the driver poised with his hand on the lever. Blinds were down and barely lit faces gazed through a dusky, yellow hue. The lining inside my nose was on fire. I tried to stem the shivers before sitting down. Georges had taken up position near the front, holding on to a ceiling strap. Only a sudden lurch or my coughing jolted me out of a growing stupor. When he moved past me to the rear exit my body reacted with a series of crab-like movements. I steadied myself, swayed along the empty aisle and stumbled down the step.

The tram clattered away. It had stopped raining. Black buildings loomed on a silent street: no lights or gaps in curtains and no glow from warm fires. I stifled a sneeze into my sleeve. The shakes started again. Georges stepped nearer.

'I help... yes?'

'No. I'll be alright. You're taking enough risks.'

He walked beside me. Pedestrians passed us, their last-minute forms barely registering. We stopped in a residential area. Soft knocks. The front door cracked open.

My time in that house was a muddle of thought and fractured images. A balding man led us into a poorly lit back room, his punchy French triggering one-word replies from Georges. I sat on a stool in front of a backboard of large, chequered squares and blinked into the flash and fizz from a camera. Another man, all head and shoulders in the shadows, took the photographs.

The balding man let us leave by the back way. Another tram journey. Georges stood at the front again, looking ahead into the dark. When he made his move, I followed down the front steps and dragged myself through the streets. At the corner of a crossroads we paused outside a residential building, possibly three floors high. He lit a cigarette before walking a short way down the side street. I had caught up with him when he took a sharp left turn into complete darkness. It might have been an alley, but in my muddled state I struggled to register much except being manoeuvred inside a building. A light came on and a well-built girl in a blue dress faced us. The front door and mat were down the passage behind her. Nothing was said. Her brown hair bounced as she hurried up the stairs. Georges held my arm all the way to the top.

The furniture and décor inside the apartment looked above anything I'd seen before. A young man in a white shirt and striped tie rose from the sofa. His combed hair was exactly how Mademoiselle had wanted mine.

'Hello. I am Henri... Henri Maca.'

He sized me up through thick-rimmed spectacles, as his hand clamped around my palm.

'*Excusez-moi. Bonsoir.*' With a polite nod, Georges was away.

Henri introduced the girl as his sister, Marie. She looked younger than him. The rest of her profile merged into a haze. I sat on the sofa as their voices moved around behind me. Muscles were racked and taut and my skin felt hot. At some point I crawled into a bed in an unlit room, fighting fits of shivers and blazing heat. Fear, uncertainty and an overwhelming guilt at burdening others twisted around inside. I dreamt of falling from some great height and woke with a jolt, sweating. Bedclothes lay crumpled below my knees and swaying patterns on the wallpaper came straight from the delirium of childhood illness. A man's silhouette wavered in the bedroom doorway and the passage light went out.

21

A chill in the bedroom woke me. The clack of typewriter keys sounded inside the apartment. I lay on my back, arms wrapped around a pillow. Curtains near the dresser were open and a fragment of light filtered through the patterned blackout film stuck on the window. My singlet and pants felt cold and clammy with sweat and I struggled into a sitting position before the coughing started again. Henri peered around the bedroom door, tapping it as he walked in.

'*Comment allez-vous? Ça va?* You are well?' He had said it with a worried look.

'Much better,' I spluttered, between the hacks. 'Have you seen my clothes? There's soap and a razor too… and my watch?'

He looked towards the wardrobe in the corner. 'You stay with us now for some days. Please… *mes excuses* for my English.'

'Your English is excellent.' I apologised for not being able to speak French.

The typewriter paused as if listening.

'Henri. Do you know how many days I will stay here?'

The question had slipped out. It was no more than concern for being a burden and risk. Henri didn't know how long. We hedged through a disjointed conversation. It was best I remain in bed. He pointed to my vest.

'*Le caleçon et le tricot de corps.*' He would bring a change of underclothes.

The typewriter started up again.

'It is after two hours in the afternoon,' he said. 'My sister prepares an omelette. Today we have eggs.'

I wasn't sure how to reply.

'My father sometimes brings the meat and flour in a suitcase… and the vegetables. Also eggs if it is possible.' He screwed up his eyes for a second. 'But not in a suitcase. This would be *un problème,* yes?'

'Yes, it might be. Your father is living in Brussels, Henri?'

'Yes, and also, no.'

He walked to the window and fiddled with the curtains.

'My father journeys to Brussels for the affairs of business.' He smiled. 'Then we also see the suitcase.'

'Thank you for helping me, Henri.'

He waved his hand dismissively. 'You wish for the omelette now?'

I spluttered through trying to ask him for just a drink.

He brought me coffee with a bread roll balanced on the large saucer. 'You can put in?' He made an exaggerated dunking action.

'I must get dressed after this.'

'Again I say, please stay there. I will return tonight.'

The smile was back on his face when he laid out a white singlet and undershorts at the foot of my bed. 'For later. My sister sits in the next room.'

I heard him call to Marie and close the apartment door. The typewriter stopped again. My situation felt awkward. It was important to try not to cough or attract attention. A visit from Marie or any well-meant enquiry with me in this state of undress was inappropriate. Did starched British standards fit here? Meeting Henri halfway was best: find my clothes then dress and lie on the bed. I rehearsed those simple movements in my head, tried to swing my legs outside the sheets then gave up.

Something drew me out of sleep. The bedroom door was half open, a light shone in from the passage. My watch and cardboard box were on the bedside table. I didn't recall putting them there. Getting dressed took an eternity. Better to get under the sheets again away from the cold, so I took my watch with me. Strange how none of the clothes I put on at Mademoiselle's apartment had labels.

It was past four-thirty when I finally decided to follow the light and break the ice with Marie.

'*Oh, pardon,*' she said, getting up from the table when I looked in. She wore the same blue dress and like Lily, the white ankle socks pushed back her age.

'You eat… yes? Please, you sit.' She glanced at me as she tidied up scraps of paper.

'I'm sorry if I startled you,' I said.

She smiled uncertainly and left the room by a door I hadn't noticed before. A telephone sat on a polished table in the corner and I recognised the expensive armchairs from the previous evening. Henri had hinted about me not moving on yet. Delays or a change of plan put patriots' lives in danger: best not ask, best not to think about it – best listen to the distant beat of a fork in a bowl.

Marie brought me a glass of water as I struggled through the omelette. An attractive girl with a full face, thin lips and fresh complexion, she manoeuvred about the apartment with an easy air and looked comfortable with strangers being around. My body was racked with flu. Desperate to lie down in bed again, I had to bluff this out and be sure of sitting ready in the lounge when Henri returned.

I shifted in the armchair. Voices outside. Marie entered the room with a woman.

'Madame, *le voisin*,' Marie said.

'Friend?'

'*Oui.*'

Another Madame: she was in her late thirties with dark eyes and hair to match. Her skirt rustled when she moved and her bright face shone as if she could smile for ever. I stood up to greet her.

'Hello.' She shook my hand gently before joining Marie at the typewriter. I sat back in the armchair, watching their lips move in whispers. Madame left ten minutes before Henri breezed in with his briefcase and dropped it on the floor near the telephone.

'*Bonsoir*, Marinette.' He chattered away to her when she came out from the kitchen.

'I see you have better health today, Ron.' He threw his hat and coat on the nearest armchair. 'So, you have met our neighbour. We visit Madame sometimes to listen to the BBC.'

A hammering and tapping sound came from the ground floor. I sat upright.

Henri didn't react. 'A woman, who has the age, lives in the apartment below us.'

'Does she…?'

'If you are asking does she know what happens here, then perhaps? I arrive on a day with one of our guests and she is closing her door.'

He took his briefcase to the table and pulled out a fan of bank notes and papers. 'If she knows, she has not spoken of this. The Gestapo or Geheime Feldpolizei would visit by now, or we have *la surveillance*. I have seen nothing.'

The papers were divided into small piles. Some of them were coupons.

'Henri, may I ask you something?'

He peered over his spectacles. 'Yes.'

'Georges asked me the identity of my navigator.'

'Did you tell him?'

'Yes. I was hoping he might have heard something. Maybe Ken Garvey has passed through?'

Henri licked his finger and began to count the money. 'I remember the *prenom* of some of our guests. I do not identify this man, Ken.'

I decided not to ask about the rest of the boys. The reality of Henri knowing them seemed so remote. He looked up again.

'You can take a bath in our apartment later, perhaps? And then my sister cooks the meal for us.'

I thanked him and thought about how they would heat the water as there was little warmth in the room.

'Good,' said Henri. 'My sister will prepare. Tomorrow we go out and also the cinema. There are more checks on the trams now, and the Feldgendarmerie are very busy, so we must walk some of the journey.'

That would be a daunting test where the prospects of failure were unthinkable.

My bath was a standing strip wash with the water sloshing around my ankles. I shivered and soaped a way through the hasty ritual. Henri had woken me in my room to say all was ready so I never discovered how they heated the water. The name he used to address his sister was another mystery. Later, as we talked and ate a stew together, I settled on Marinette or Marinetta.

For the first half hour I managed to discreetly mash, chew and swallow the softly cooked food down my raw throat. Henri spoke about life under occupation, skilfully keeping to generalities and asking safe questions about the England I knew in peacetime. He would translate for Marie and she asked me through her brother about the meals I ate at home. Our safe talk suited the circumstances: they knew little about me and wanted to keep it that way. Except for the perpetual listening state I endured inside every safe house, my apprehension lifted a little. It was impossible to be afraid all of the time.

'I am sorry, this week there are no French cigarettes,' Henri said.

He passed me a thin pouch, filter paper and matchbox. The loose tobacco contained tiny pin holes and reminded me of clumps of coarse hair lying on the floor in a barber's shop. The papers were thicker than at home. After leaving Marcel's I had craved for a cigarette until I got ill, but all of Henri's smoker's items went straight into my pocket with polite thanks and a promise to roll a ciggy later. My settled thoughts didn't last. He sent a chill through me when he spoke again. I knew what was coming.

22

Henri placed his cup carefully on the saucer. 'There is something you must know. We have information about a man who works for the Gestapo and may be in Brussels.'

He took off his spectacles and held them up in the dull light. 'We know this, and now you must know it.' He polished the lenses with his handkerchief. 'It is unfortunate that a friend has borrowed my photograph of him.'

Henri described the man and havoc he created in the Resistance and escape work. When he mentioned part of a finger was missing, I spilled out everything Marcel had said about the traitor.

Henri put on his spectacles. 'Good. So now we are both ready for him.'

The next day was Monday. Around four o'clock I left the apartment with Henri. We walked together. My legs were like columns of lead and I struggled to breathe. The locals trudged through a foggy afternoon or congregated around threadbare shop windows. Vegetables were priced singly with empty spaces under most tickets. Figures misted in and out at street corners – only passing bicycles and trams punctuated the stillness. A ghostly figure in a suit and trilby waited at the main crossroads. I was sure he stepped in behind us after we passed. Henri appeared not to notice.

Houses with shutters and filigree metal balconies lined the side streets. The cold air filled my lungs – I rattled a cough into my handkerchief. Energy dripped away with each stride; it had been foolhardy not to be straight with Henri about venturing outside. He waited near an old couple at a tram stop. The man we passed earlier arrived and kept a distance from us. I labelled him the Stranger. Henri still ignored him. I tried to breathe deeper without being noticed. Memories of returning to school or work prematurely after illness flooded back. Those first rubbery hours were a warning before malaise and utter fatigue set in again, but there was no choice here. Press on and pass the test.

I climbed onto a crowded tram. Henri had detailed what to do if the Feldgendarmerie boarded. I found a spot half a dozen paces from him next to the partition in the centre of the car. The Stranger stayed further down the aisle, watching a soldier riding outside on the step. After a chain of stop-starts I jumped off at the rear exit, following Henri to an avenue of bare poplar trees. While he waited for a cyclist to pass I rested against a wall. The sheer distance to the opposite side looked unreachable. Soldiers ambled along in twos and threes, couples strolled with their children running nearby, businessmen hung on to briefcases. For a fleeting moment it might have been peacetime with a population who relished every day and looked forward to a future, instead of weary masses struggling through an empty world. Another reminder that reaching home was not solely about my own self-preservation.

Henri stopped near a crowd outside a cinema and we filed into the dark foyer. Glass in the entrance doors was blacked out. People waited to buy tickets or hung about in the auditorium. A flight of stairs curved around a corner and dingy lighting cast shadows on the alabaster ceiling. I shrouded myself near the entrance while Henri joined the ticket queue.

I didn't want a smoke. Cigarettes were the last thing on my mind, but it was something to do, something to occupy my hands and try to act natural. I took out the tobacco pouch and fumbled with the cigarette papers.

'Defense de fumer.' The Stranger's face had almost touched mine. A flash of white teeth and he gripped my arm, steering it subtly back to my raincoat pocket, his hot breath smothering me in a hiss of French words. Henri returned and I jammed the tobacco pouch and papers out of sight. The Stranger took his ticket and glanced around the foyer. I had been warned about small details. What a crass mistake, yet nothing had been mentioned about not smoking in cinemas. It felt so alien against the tobacco haze in the Shaftesbury and Trocadero at home. Now was not the time to apologise. Maybe no one had noticed.

I sat in the stalls at the back between Henri and the Stranger. There was no heating, I was just glad of darkness and rest. The main cinema lighting came on suddenly. Was it a raid? Maybe I'd been spotted in the foyer? No one looked around, nobody moved. A black and white newsreel started up, blaring out a French commentary. German aircraft were pulverising British cities while Nazi tanks smashed through Russia. The film made me think of our bomber stream; I'd still not heard it since I landed. Waves of booing and laughter started. Someone catcalled. The lights must have come on to spot any culprits. It made no difference. What could the Germans do, arrest the whole cinema?

I felt quite buoyant when the lighting dimmed and music began for the main picture – a French love story with crackles. For a while I tried to follow the film, picking out words or gauging the mood from body language and tone of the dialogue. My attention shifted to props and background on the sets – a desk, telephone, curtains and furniture. Each scene triggered some tenuous memory of home. The camera panned across to a straight line of trees at the end of a meadow. I was back under a cornflower blue sky on a Sunday morning with the LDV platoon at the army firing range near Kibworth. Sergeant World War One with his sharp moustache stood behind a few of us lying on the ground in prone firing positions. Two hundred and fifty yards to a set of white square targets marked with a black circle. Beyond the scrubby bank and trees at the end, a goods train clanked along the main line.

The film droned on. I wandered through the first learning drills in my head: British Service Rifle Lee Enfield Mk 3 .303 calibres S.M.L.E. or *Smelly*. Rifle pointing down, finger off trigger, check no round in the chamber, check safety catch on. Make sure no one was between me and the target. Load the rifle, chamber a round. Think about the sixpenny sweepstake for the best shot and a payout later in the Greyhound pub, Great Glen, before an eight-mile bike ride home.

The music peaked. I thought about my aircrew selection at RAF Cardington: the morning medical and slog of educational tests followed by an afternoon interview from a panel of brass hats firing questions and testing my aircraft recognition skills. The throat-clearing group captain asked about my Morse qualifications and experience and the sports I played. A handlebar moustache on the end of the row finally broke his silence after my football and cricket exploits, with 'What, no rugger?'

'Swot up on your maths and go for pilot,' groupy had said. I didn't need maths to know how far it was back to Henri's apartment.

The foyer was a hum of foreign chatter. I stepped out of the cinema into the blackout. The Stranger vanished into groups crossing the street. Henri walked slowly until he reached the avenue of poplar trees. I fought to stay in time with him and my head started to swim. Eyelids grew heavy and my thundering cough hit the night air. A wall leaned out to prop me up, stone steps were invitations to sit and drain the ache from my legs. Henri began to fade. Only his footfall kept me hanging on.

'Alright?' he asked, as we reached a crossroads.

'Yes.'

'A kilometre. We stay together.'

I nodded. My neck felt as though it was the only part of my body still functioning. How much longer? Time was immaterial again: seconds felt like minutes and the minutes were hours. Whether Henri noticed me struggling was no longer important. I looked up at the night sky. Cloud had slipped away and moonlight silvered the street. It wasn't until I heard Henri rattle his key in the front door that I whispered for help in climbing the stairs. I remembered nothing after that except falling into the pit of my bed.

The ache in my legs and shoulders woke me. Marie was speaking in the lounge and I could hear Madame's voice. I hauled myself out of bed. Daylight from the passage was enough to see around the room. My watch lay on the dresser. Past two o'clock: I must have slept for over fourteen hours. The telephone rang. I tidied myself up and waited for Marie to finish the call before tapping on the lounge door. Madame had left and Henri was missing again. He returned sometime after three with a batch of dog-eared English magazines. We all sat together. The room felt warmer and I settled back on the sofa. Everything changed when he went downstairs.

23

A tall, serious man in a charcoal overcoat entered the room with Henri.

'Ron, I am pleased for you to meet Flying Officer Bob Clements. He is an RAF pilot.'

A rush of adrenaline coursed through me – at last, another airman. He looked late twenties with a high forehead and brushed back wavy hair. Henri did the introductions.

'Hullo, sergeant,' Clements said, with an American-sounding twang. 'Been here long?'

'A few days.'

He sat opposite me in the armchair. Marie brought us coffee and Henri asked him if he had eaten.

'Not since noon,' Clements said.

I listened to how he framed his answers to Henri's casual questions. He was Canadian, not American.

Marie went to prepare his food and Henri left us sitting together. We tiptoed around the weather and generalities about the apartment. Clements removed his overcoat, laying it over the chair arm.

'Seen much of Brussels?'

'No. Been inside most of the time,' I said.

I'd given little thought to meeting an escaper I didn't know. In my head it was always one of the boys who would walk in. We waded through clumsy spells of silence, neither of us wanting to stare and yet both trying to form silent judgements from each other's cagey replies.

Gradually, I sensed a cautious relief creep in.

'Seen any of your crew?' he asked.

'No sir. You're the first flyer I've seen.'

A smile showed on his face. He looked surprised. 'What did you do then, walk here?'

'Not quite sir. A train from Antwerp. Then a chap brought me to this apartment.'

He appeared to mull over my answer. 'We're not in uniform, sergeant, and are guests of our friends, so we'll drop the sir if that's OK with you.'

He checked if it was alright to call me by my name.

'This chap?' He emphasised the last word. 'The guy who brought you here, what did he look like?'

'Thin man… spoke a little English.' I opted to say nothing about Lily or Mademoiselle.

'Did he have red hair?'

'Yes. Wore horn-rimmed glasses.'

'It's the same guy I followed here.'

'He asked me the name of my navigator,' I said. 'I'd heard no gen about any of my boys, so thought he might know something.'

'Can't help you.' Clements got to his feet. 'I've met my bomb aimer. Also an American and another bomb aimer who'd been down for months. No navigator though.'

'You've met others?'

'Yeah.' His reply was so level and matter of fact. He ran a finger along his coat on the chair arm. 'Hooked up with my bomb aimer after five days. He was staying at the house I got shifted to. Then I was moved on and we picked him up later in the week. He came here with me. They must have taken him somewhere else after we stopped outside this place.'

'What about the rest of your crew?'

He shook his head weakly, looking in the direction of Henri's voice coming from the next room.

'Reckon the pilot's gone for a Burton. I heard nothing from the gunners after we were hit. Don't know about the rest. Not good. Pretty sure the kite blew up after I got out.'

I never got a chance to respond. Marie came in with a bowl of soup and bread. All Clements got from me was an apologetic nod as he went to sit at the table. What should I tell him about myself?

We weren't supposed to speak about what happened to us, least of all here and to an officer and stranger. He spooned away at his soup whilst Marie tidied the lounge. I discarded a printed leaflet, *Front de l'Independence* and picked up the musty-smelling English magazines Henri brought in earlier. *Used Car* and *Practical Motorist* were dated 1938 and had some pages missing.

Henri had introduced Clements earlier as an RAF flying officer. He wasn't the bomb aimer or flying the aircraft, so must have been the 'second dickey' pilot on his first operation – unless he wasn't being straight with me. I flicked through the magazine, skimming down the classified adverts in *Used Car*: a second-hand Austin 7, a Morris, a Ford and new car radios. The mechanical feature in *Practical Motorist* detailed some 'Get You Home Dodges'. We could have done with some of those. The future remained fragile and fraught with danger and so many questions about each other remained unanswered. Nevertheless, I was no longer alone and there were other escapers. It lifted my spirits.

Madame arrived the next morning for a short visit just as we started breakfast in the lounge. After she left, Marie joined us at the table. I noticed a change and more purpose in the Canadian's words rather than just random talk. Between Henri's translations for Marie, Clements tried to make conversation, breaking down barriers and doubtless masking his own apprehension. He studied each of us, often when he thought no one was watching. I saw something of my own skipper in him. Bill had British reserve with a warm formality. There was rank and respect, but we saw him as one of us. He had spent time socially with his crew, especially in the Horse and Jockey pub at Waddington, much to the displeasure of some fellow officers. Whilst Clements showed no British collar and tie delivery, he would mould his men around him as Bill had done.

'So, none of the guys in Belgium have a moustache?' Clements said, running a finger along his bare top lip.

Henri put down his cup. 'No young men have them after the occupation. It is their way.'

I hadn't noticed. Much of my time outside had been after dark.

'A Resistance guy told me another thing,' Clements said. 'He says a policeman with a number under six thousand can be trusted as they were all regulars before the invasion. Anyone after that was recruited by the Germans.'

'We have also heard these words. But you will follow our instructions and always *la vigilance*... always.'

Marie started to clear the table.

'And now there is business which waits,' Henri said. 'We will speak soon.'

I saw him walk to the next room, emerging seconds later in a heavy brown overcoat and carrying a different briefcase.

'My sister may also leave for a short time. Please do not open our door... to anyone.'

He spoke to Marie again as he left. Clements looked up. I sensed we were both counting Henri's steps on the stairs. The front door thudded shut below. I imagined him threading a route across the city through damp November mist. In the kitchen, Marie hummed a tune I couldn't place.

'Learned one thing on the road,' Clements said in a low voice. 'Don't sew your fly button compass into your shirt cuff.'

He angled his head slightly. 'You didn't, did you?'

'No.'

'Zip fastener on the glove messes with it. I went west instead of southwest.'

We both grinned at his choice of words. I'd ditched my gloves after landing. He didn't probe me any further. My reluctance to talk about what had happened before Brussels was driven by orders. The presence of an officer only reinforced protocol. Part of me wanted to spill out everything since the Lanc got hit, share the scrapes I'd been through and get the lot off my chest. The rest sat back waiting on its haunches. What kind of man would sacrifice his pride and self-discipline to break orders with a virtual stranger? Except in this mess the instinct was to talk, bond and forge an ally with someone whose experiences were similar. If we travelled together there would have to be a reliance and understanding between us. At least he had thrown in some safe snippets of info. They were a starting point.

My head felt clearer. Clements speculated whether Henri's business departure pointed to us leaving later in the day. As much as I wanted to go, if the word came to move on I would struggle. Every muscle in my arms and legs felt soft and weak and the dull ache still nagged at my body. So many questions remained about the journey. How much walking and climbing? How far would we travel in a single stretch? How long between rests? Documents were probably dated to travel on specific days.

We talked generally about aircraft. Clements moved on to the Lanc, its mechanics, flying and handling, but not the ops – everyone avoided the ops. They were always left at debrief. Once that was done you spoke in short about who hadn't returned yet and then, at breakfast next morning who was still missing. After that it was gone. He talked away and fashioned words with his hands. The steady manner and level looks showed no battle-weary stamp on his face, or any of the deep-seated traits the rest of us carried.

'It was your first bombing op, wasn't it?' I came straight out with it.

He gave me a hard stare. 'Yeah. And you?'

'In the twenties. I was ticking them off to thirty and the end of my tour. I should never have started that game.'

Another standoff kicked in as if we were waiting for each other to make the next move.

He rubbed his eyes. 'I was second pilot. Kite seemed pretty clapped out, took forever to climb to nineteen thousand. All OK and four tenths low cloud most of the way. Barrage flak and searchlights over Holland... they weren't close. We were pretty straight and level apart from the usual banking searches.'

Cigarette papers spilled from his hand on to the table.

'Saw a Lanc go down in Belgium. Don't know how long it was after that. We'd just levelled up. Fighter raked us across the stern from underneath... hot metal everywhere, skipper dived to port, cockpit filled with smoke... couldn't see... burning. I opened my window.' He stared into the memory. 'That's what I keep thinking about the most... opening that window.'

He teased out a trail of tobacco into one of the papers.

'Bomb aimer reported thick smoke and fire aft of the bomb bay. Incendiaries were alight, so he jettisoned the whole bomb load. Flames reached the flare chute. Skipper pulled us out of the dive at ten thousand and we turned back. Wireless op and flight engineer disappeared aft to fight the fire. Skipper wanted an update, so I went. Picked up an extinguisher...'

He licked and sealed the cigarette paper then held up his hand. 'Oh, I'm sorry. Is it OK? Marie says she's fine about smokes.'

'It's alright.'

His match scraped across the box. He looked suspiciously down at the bent, wiry cigarette.

'I saw the photo flash was still on board and ablaze. Not much time, tried to push it out. Skipper opened the bomb doors, flames poured in, so he had to close them again. Ammunition started exploding. I went back and told him the fire was out of control. Wireless op said the same over the intercom. Fire extinguishers were empty. Skipper gave the order to abandon aircraft.'

Cigarette smoke pricked at my throat. I started coughing. Someone moved about in the apartment below.

'Sorry.' He went to stub his cigarette in the ashtray.

'No. Please carry on.'

His voice dropped. 'There's nothing more to say.'

I could tell by the look in his eyes, he regretted returning to the memories.

'Tell me what happened to you, Ron.'

I ended at the point my parachute opened. Neither of us had

revealed dates, names, squadron, or take off and target details. My own vague account might have helped distance me from what happened, helped blank out the explosion and flames… make the boys just a position in the aircraft. It could have made me believe for a while that I was detached and telling someone else's story. It didn't, but at least we had broken the ice between us.

The overcast morning lagged. Marie left the apartment without putting on her coat. It took exaggerated OKs and nods from us before she finally slipped out. Clements insisted he went to his room for the next smoke. I took off my shoes, circling the lounge at least a dozen times before resting by the large front window. Through a gap between the frame and curtains I looked down at the deserted street and crossroads for the first time.

Henri returned about an hour after Marie. I must have dozed off later in the armchair as the typewriter keys woke me suddenly. Clements sat opposite reading a magazine. Henri, his tie loosened and shirt top button undone, looked over Marie's shoulder as she typed in the corner. He shuttled between there and a spread of paperwork on the dining table. Around mid-afternoon he became restless, regularly walking to the front window.

'Gentlemen, you leave tonight,' he said suddenly, hastening from the room.

My mind was a storm. Clements peered over his magazine with a startled expression. I rose from the armchair. Marie looked unfazed by the sound of footsteps slowly ascending the stairs. Henri entered with a visitor behind him. I saw the man's dark hair and a cream, round-neck woollen sweater poking above the collar of his brown corduroy jacket.

'Ken.' I had tried not to call out.

It was my navigator.

24

Ken's arms hung limp by his sides. The bandage on his right hand resembled a white, fingerless mitten. He stared at me, eyes wide and expressionless, pain chiselled in his face.

'Ron? It's good to see you.' He went to stretch out his hand then stopped.

'How are you, Ken?' I knew from the instant my words fell out it was a foolish thing to ask.

'A1, thanks. Could do with a sit down, though.'

I did the introductions then helped him to an armchair near the table.

'You don't need to do any of that. I'm OK,' Ken said, easing himself down with his forearms. 'Hands aren't too bad.' He touched the bandage. 'This one keeps me awake at night, sometimes.'

His left hand looked angry and blistered. Another dressing showed on his neck above the sweater.

'You'll be on the move soon,' I said, trying to sound hopeful. He looked at me like I was a complete stranger, as if something lay in wait and I was going to push him there. Marie brought him a hot drink then returned to the kitchen. He picked up the cup awkwardly with his left hand, resting the saucer in his lap.

'My apologies, gentlemen,' Henri said. 'I will return soon.'

He went straight out. The Macas' short absences must have involved their neighbour, Madame. Minutes later, Clements left the room, saying he was going to get some rest. I knew it was for a smoke and the chance to let me catch up with Ken.

'Seen any of the others?' I asked, once we were on our own.

'No. Just two parachutes below me while I was drifting down. Have you?'

'Nobody. Flying Officer Clements met an American and two Raff chaps. Not our lot though.'

'Did he say who they were?'

'No names. He travelled part of the way here with his bomb aimer. The other Raff bloke was one too. No gen on the Yank though. I think he told me more than he should have.'

Ken gave an understanding nod and angled his head at the passage door.

'What's Clements like?' His voice faded.

'Straight enough. He only got here yesterday. I don't know much else.'

He placed his cup down on the saucer. 'Ron, when you get home, you must tell them what happened to me.'

'There's no need to say anything now, Ken.'

'There is… if I don't make it.'

'You will.'

The pain and fear returned to his face. 'I got a GEE fix just before it all happened. Then the bloody shrapnel flew everywhere… red hot.' He swallowed and pointed to the bandage on his neck. 'A piece stuck here.'

'I got away with it,' I said. 'Pretty damn lucky.'

He continued as if he hadn't heard me. 'Copped it when I tried to beat out fires on my table. Maps were alight. Flames must have gone through my gloves. Strange, there was no pain until after I'd landed. Flak kept bursting around me on the way down, tried to miss a hedge and twisted my leg when I hit the ground.'

His words had come with hardly a pause, as if he had to rush through that place and get out the other side.

'Limped around for ten hours. Ten bloody hours… tried farmhouses, couldn't get help.' He wiped his nose on the bandage around his hand. 'Whilst I was walking, I tried to think about what happened. Went through everything to get it all clear in my head.' His voice faltered. 'Couldn't remember parts… only the noise and you standing there waiting for me to put my chute on. I couldn't clip it. Kept trying… and you just stood there, so patient.' He looked away. 'You stood there like you were waiting for a bloody bus.'

He faced me again, a forced smile on his lips. 'Give you the rest later. They've said I might be here for a while until my burns get sorted.'

There was no easy way to tell him I was leaving, no more time to kick around my own doubts about making the next journey, or think about what might have been if the two of us had travelled on from Brussels together. I was only one small cog in a large machine.

'You'd best tell me now, Ken. I'm leaving with Clements tonight. Henri must have been waiting for the right time to clue you in.'

His face dropped to a fixed, worn expression. I tried to reassure him about the Macas and staying in their apartment. He cut in.

'That's grand news, Ron. Did Henri give you a time?'

'No. Nothing yet.'

'Either way, we haven't long,' he said. 'I'll tell you what happened after I landed.'

He spoke in steady, level sentences. I hoped it would bury some of his horrors, for the moment. A hint of sunshine brightened the room and I let him talk without stopping. Almost on cue, he finished as the afternoon light began to dull.

I gave him my account with the same generalities I used before. He took his time to get up and carefully place the cup and saucer on the table.

'Did you catch the train from Antwerp?' he said after a long pause.

'Yes. I got brought to this place after a detour. Still don't know where we're staying. Only been out once and it was dark.'

He looked surprised. 'This is thirty-one, Avenue Val d'Or.'

Clements hadn't mentioned it and I wouldn't ask him. I changed the subject. 'No sirens or air raids here yet.'

We kept to safe topics until Henri arrived. It wasn't long before everyone sat around the table. Ken managed to break bread for the broth soup and took a spoon in his left hand. The time was after three-thirty, less than forty-five minutes until I left. Henri had given me the gen when he returned. Every sound grated in the brittle atmosphere: spoon against bowl, a noisy slurp, the chew and swallow of bread. He began to chat with Ken, working us all into a conversation ranging from German officers and enlisted men hanging on outside crowded trams, to the false façade of central Brussels. I learned how the department stores, patisseries and wine merchants stocked nothing behind their impressive window dressings, except black market items which were snapped up by the visiting German hierarchy or local racketeers. Crowded restaurants and night life on the main avenues were another showcase lie and expensive domain of a privileged few.

'It is the same in Paris,' Henri said. 'If you are there, you will see *la propagande,* for certain.'

I tried to busy myself with the main course of peas, beans and a taste of cabbage. Whatever my thoughts were about moving on, this phase was almost over. I was treading water now.

Marie closed the curtains soon after the meal. Clements sat with me at the table: we were both wearing our coats. Ken had slipped into a fitful doze in an armchair on the opposite side of the room. I thought about the rest of his story and the gamble he had taken after hiding overnight in a wood. He had broken cover the next morning to approach a farm labourer walking down the nearby road. The man hid him in a ditch, came back later with food and returned at night to lead the way to a farmhouse. Two members of a sabotage gang visited and brought him a suit of clothes. The next day he cycled and travelled by tram to the organisation leader's home. After a week there he had to leave in a hurry as one of the saboteurs had been caught by the Germans. The head man passed him to an escape group. I realised that the girl who had brought him to the Macas' apartment was Lily.

Ken knew a lot more than he could reveal. At least there was something for me to report if I did make it home, but care would be required with my account. Ken had said more than he should have and for the right reasons, but that wouldn't cut any ice with the brass hats. How much of his journey so far had been down to good fortune? After what he had been through, he deserved every slice of luck going.

'You are ready, gentlemen?' Henri said.

'Yes. Ready for anything.' I'd rehearsed my answer and practised the tone. This was no simple enquiry or courtesy, each question they asked here carried a greater purpose. Everything rested on my leaving.

'And you, Monsieur Bob?'

Clements smiled.

'That is good. Madame will escort you. You follow her to receive your papers. Do exactly as she says. Then you go with her à la gare.'

'Which station?' Clements asked.

'This is not important.' Henri's eyes were dark and solemn. 'The Feldgendarmerie will check the trams. That *is* important.' He paused. 'You have the journeys left on your tickets?'

Clements took a while to find his. There were three trips on mine.

'Stay near to Madame, but not too close. Always have the certainty that you can see her and be ready to leave, *immediatement*.'

Henri said nothing more. I knew from the cut in his voice that we both bore the same uneasy anxieties. Marie spoke with him in short whispers, her face expressionless until an anxious look crept in behind her falling hair. She left the apartment, her footsteps bouncing down the stairs. I donned my cap and felt inside my pockets: cardboard box with razor and soap, crucifix, pendant, money wallet, handkerchief, watch, matches, cigarette papers and tobacco pouch. Lily had said Georges would speak to me later about the items I showed him in Mademoiselle's apartment. He hadn't.

Henri sat at the table with us, leafing through his paperwork. His eyes moved in small jerky movements and when Clements spoke he replied in that automatic way when the mind is elsewhere.

Marie hurried in with Madame behind her dressed in a long, blue coat.

'Hello, boys.' Madame's voice was casual but her face told me to be ready. She chatted with Henri.

'My magazine,' I said, rushing to the passage door.

Ken stirred in the chair.

'Ron?'

He struggled to stand. 'Good luck. Tell my folks I'm OK.'

'Just you get well and get home, eh? Then we'll have that beer.'

He shook my left hand with his. It might have been a clumsy moment, but the guilt, sadness and regret overruled anything else. My words felt worthless. I could have spoken them in a dozen different ways and they would still have sounded the same. We had been through so much together, but I was leaving and whatever slant was put on that it felt unfair.

The magazine lay on my bed. I rolled it up. Henri poked his head around the bedroom door.

'Leave that here. We have one for you. And I almost forget.' He handed me a small passport-sized photograph. 'Keep this safe.'

My picture was the one taken at the house I had visited with Georges after leaving Mademoiselle's on the first night. It went inside the money wallet. Marie handed me a magazine on the way out and after a firm handshake with her brother I strode after Clements. We felt our way down the stairs with Marie close behind. Someone was talking inside the ground floor apartment. Madame reached the hallway, doubling back along the passage by the stairway. Marie slipped past me and opened the back door. She looked outside, the remnants of late afternoon light framing her silhouette in the doorway. I experienced a strange kind of inertia during the seconds which followed, as if the world had stopped moving and only my racing heartbeat marked the passage of time.

Madame led Clements through the small back garden. I shook myself back into the moment and squeezed past Marie with a soft goodbye and thanks. By the time Madame reached a gap leading onto the side street, I'd caught up with her. Dark cloud clustered beyond the city like an angry range of mountains. Evening would be early. My walking felt fragile and irregular. Madame pressed forward ahead of Clements, while I trailed behind them, coughing from the cold air. Buildings showed no light or life, the late afternoon already shut away behind blackout drapes. Shops were closed and we dodged cyclists and pedestrians heading home. Clements waited for me at the corner.

'Switch sides, Ron. I'll walk next to the road.'

Madame kept moving. In daytime the guides kept longer distances between us, but now it was less than twenty yards. I got a sense we were circling back towards the apartment. In a perverse way, part of me wanted to return there for more recovery time and seeing Ken again. We approached a T junction to an avenue with tram lines and a row of bare finger-like trees behind them.

A tram waited only yards away with a row of figures strung out kerbside. Soldiers checked documents in flickers of dim torchlight. Madame walked through two lines of trees and across another carriageway. I struggled to keep her in sight. No buildings on the opposite side, only a sour smell like stagnant water from beneath a bank running parallel with the avenue. There might have been a park beyond, I couldn't see far enough. Pedestrians passed me before Madame crossed back to the other side of the avenue. If anyone was seriously observing us, our behaviour would stand out a mile. A tram clattered past, doubtless the same one the Germans had checked. At least we wouldn't be riding that route.

The avenue ahead merged into the blackout. Clements' heavy footsteps aligned with my own and once Madame disappeared into the dark and out of earshot, I lost any sense of the distance between us. The pavement ended and we crossed a wide expanse of cobbles. Madame waited in the shadow of a two-storey brick building with lines of windows. I held on to some railings behind her, trying to mask my laboured breathing.

'Stay close, boys,' she whispered. 'No speaking. Say nothing and do exactly with ze instructions.'

'The instructions?' Clements' voice sounded tired.

'Yes,' she whispered sharply. 'Ze peoples will tell you.'

She led us through the open gateway and we stayed close to a building wall. A line of adjoining gable roofs were visible now and stretched away to the left. The space below them looked open apart from support pillars at regular intervals. I guessed at tram sheds and a terminus. There was no sign of life and the unnatural quiet magnified our footfall as we followed Madame into the last shed and almost total darkness. I groped my way slowly along the wall. Clements shuffled along somewhere behind. What looked like a line of tramcars blocked any view to the left. The spurt from a match lit up a narrow wooden door a few yards away. Two eyes stared at me over cupped hands; the shadow of a face hidden under a black trilby. The waft of freshly lit tobacco faded and a cigarette end glowed. Clements was close to my shoulder now. The tip burned red again and the man opened the door.

'Entrez.'

His voice rasped at me, rough and matter of fact as we inched past. A dusky orange light shone inside and the smell of lamp oil and grease choked the air. My coughing started again. In the far corner of the cramped room a light flickered on a small desk surrounded by castings and machine parts. A bald-headed man with rimless spectacles sat bent over a spread of papers. Sheet metal panels leaned against the wall behind him. We waited to be acknowledged. Faint street noise drifted in from the outside. I looked over my shoulder. The figure in the trilby shut the door and faced us. He stubbed out the cigarette on his thumb. It was the Stranger.

He waved us to the desk and the bald-headed man looked up when Madame's shoes crunched on the concrete floor. We were standing over him by the time he spoke to her and took an envelope from the drawer. The Stranger's gravel voice barked out some kind of command. The bald-headed man ignored it and tipped documents, cards and a thin scatter of paper money on the table. His left hand slid to the drawer, hastily covering what resembled the barrel of a revolver. Surely not? The only person I'd seen with a firearm was Denise.

The gunman squinted at the photos on the cards then studied us in turn, the orange light reflecting in his spectacles. Madame chattered in short bursts of nervy French words, then sharper sentences, her hand waving in our direction. She swivelled the cards around to face us.

'*Un carte d'identité* and an *Ausweis*.'

The other two documents looked like passes or permits. There were no photos on those.

'Please remember your new name,' Madame said.

Someone had signed my identity card and *Ausweis*. The photographs on them looked the same as the one Henri had given me. I gathered up the documents and slipped them inside my raincoat pocket.

The gunman raised a hand. The sound of a tram clanked out of nowhere, stopping outside the door. Nobody moved. Voices echoed outside then faded. I waited for a nod to pick up the money. Two taps on the door. The knob twisted. A thin man in overalls folded himself through the narrow gap and spoke to the gunman. Their faces shone in the light for an instant.

'We leave now,' Madame said, forcing some paper money into Clements' hand. 'At the train station, a friend will speak to you.'

The man in overalls hurried back to the door. I was given some Belgian ten-franc notes whilst the gunman was busy stuffing papers into a briefcase. The Stranger had already left.

Clements was ahead of me somewhere between the wall and line of tramcars. In front, Madame's hasty footsteps echoed under the roof. No shouts in German, no screech of tyres or doors banging, no running feet: nothing bar the same stilted quiet. I should have been afraid, yet felt little except numb exhaustion. The man in overalls waited at the entrance, looking beyond the tram lines which arced away into the blackout.

'*Bonne chance,*' he said when we passed.

Madame turned left on to the avenue. Only adrenaline had kept me moving for the last half hour. The night was clear now with no rising moon yet. I caught a final glimpse of the terminus then lowered my head against the wind. We passed the first tram stop. Clements waited at the next one, half a dozen paces from Madame. They were alone and both looked in my direction. Not here surely? Not boarding on the same route and only a handful of stops from the German checks? I rested against the metal base of a lamppost, gulping in the air.

'You are alright?' Madame stood at my side.

'Yes.'

'Please stand where you can see me.' She walked away before I could reply.

A tram clattered out of the night and stopped alongside her. Circular number discs were attached to oblong destination boards on the roof and a small direction light gave the faintest glow near the top. We squashed into the cramped aisle as the car moved off. Window blinds were down and the air around me stunk with a fetid smell of flatulence. Clements steadied himself against the wood and glass partition, his face bland and unfazed. The unknown gnawed away inside me; it had hooked itself in from the second I had jumped from the aircraft. Right now I would be first in line for any ticket check. Each time we slowed down for a stop the seconds cut through me until I saw who was getting on board.

Madame sidled towards the rear exit and Clements moved after her. I squeezed along the aisle between the bodies. People seemed to breathe in and protect their own space with no protest or interest. Relief at stepping down onto the street with nobody following hit me like a flood of morphine.

We kept a tighter line through the grid of dank backstreets. Warehouses and offices butted up close to the pavement and railway wagons rumbled in the distance. At least with our careful pace I could stay near Clements and Madame. She stopped before we reached a main road. The tread of marching feet grew louder. I stayed close to the others in the shadows as a column of soldiers passed the end of the street.

'We go,' Madame said.

A train whistle shrilled. She broke cover, leading us across the road to a cobbled approach in front of a long building with a line of vaulted windows. Some kind of statue was on the roof above a main entrance of stone pillars on plinths, but it was indiscernible in the blackout. Crowds milled around the front as we dodged people streaming away. Madame veered to the left. I hesitated.

'Over there,' Clements said in my ear.

A man next to one of the pillars stood watching us.

25

Madame walked straight past the man. He approached us and I recognised the horn-rimmed spectacles.

'Georges.'

'*Oui. Bonsoir, Messieurs.*' We shook hands with him. 'Please wait here,' he said to me.

I looked across the cobbles for Madame but she had disappeared into the night. When I turned around, Georges and Clements were gone.

Figures passed by in noisy straggles. Trails of French, a spurt of Flemish or German: people I didn't know by sight or name, people with no connection who I would never see again. They didn't know me and I didn't know them. Standing in the dark surrounded by strangers gave me a fragile sense of shelter.

'Follow please.' Georges was back. He pressed a paper ticket into my hand. We moved to a gloomy vestibule inside the train station. A moving crowd navigated in different directions around standing groups. Figures loitered on the fringes or waited while people queued near the ticket windows. No sign of Clements. George led me to a short, stocky man in a cap.

'Here is Sergeant Pope, United States Army Air Force,' Georges said deliberately in my ear as if reciting it from a card. 'You will travel together. Your *convoyeurs* stand by the wall behind us.'

Pope nodded to me as we shook hands. He wore a reefer-style jacket and carried a rolled-up newspaper. Two men stood near a masked station lamp about ten paces away, their outlines spectral in the feeble light. The nearest figure was small and dressed in a suit and trilby hat, the taller man had a thickset frame, overcoat and cap. Georges stood close between us.

'When the *convoyeurs* move, you will follow.'

He appeared to be walking across to speak with them then

vanished behind a group of soldiers. I knew he wasn't coming back when the smaller guide walked slowly away from the wall. The other man tugged at his cap and sauntered after him. Pope moved off with me. Knots of people formed in the narrow space as the crowd trafficked both ways between main entrance and platforms. Our guides reached a barrier where two railway staff checked tickets. I joined Pope in the line.

We passed through to a terminus station with a row of dead-end island platforms, each with its own destination board and metal canopy shelter. The blackout consumed any finer detail. Locos simmered in front of carriages; the air was heavy with a smell of steam, soot and hot oil. Crowds milled around us, all suitcase and shoulders bumping against my body. Uniforms were everywhere again. Our escorts headed along the nearest platform, peering through windows into each carriage. The small man stopped at an open door and climbed in, pursued by a noisy group. I watched the taller guide vanish into the masses pouring down the platform.

Another train journey. The same sick feeling settled deep inside me. Pope climbed aboard first. I squeezed in ahead of another passenger. The small guide shifted slowly down the corridor, glancing in compartments. I noticed his tall friend gazing out through a window near the standing area at the far end of our carriage. His young film-star looks and cap at an upward angle revealing wavy hair made him a 'Gaston' for sure and the shorter man a 'Paul'. I kept close to Pope along the corridor. Compartments looked full and people were still boarding. The crowd set up camp where they were forced to stop. Some sat on upturned suitcases – most stood facing the compartments or twisted around to pull down the window blinds. Paul was a couple of bodies away from us. A woman wedged her bags against my feet and a French-looking chap in a navy-style pea coat peered down the corridor from a standing area at the end. Two young men next to the carriage door nearest him glanced up from their magazines.

I couldn't see any military. Maybe they were sitting in

compartments out of my sight line. Paul kept us in view and appeared to be listening to the low hum of conversation, more than observing activity. His suit jacket was too large and the trousers hung loosely on his small frame. The round face and deadpan expression gave him an uninterested look and I guessed his age at around thirty. Carriage doors banged shut in staccato rhythm; it must have been close to six o'clock. A whistle shrilled and the carriage kicked forward. I pulled out the magazine from my raincoat: *Signal* Issue Number 21 with a photograph of a sly-looking Roosevelt on the cover. Pictures inside showed fighting in Italy, the winter war on the Russian front and U-boats in the Atlantic. Pope unrolled and opened his newspaper, rustling the sheets. He was late twenties, black hair showing below his cap, tongue running nervously over his teeth. I saw him clock the two young men reading their magazines by the carriage door.

The train picked up speed. Someone in the crowd close to me had been drinking and the cold, stuffy air carried an animal smell like wet wool. The Germans would have to turf us off at a station for any checks as they wouldn't be able to move through the packed carriages. When that moment came, Pope and I would be on our own. I felt for my ticket and documents again, even though I knew where they were.

The crush tightened before each stop. Our corridor filled to bursting when travellers attempted to leave their compartments. Once the train halted, the crowd always managed to disentangle itself as if it were a single, collective intelligence. I'd noticed the same behaviour when people left and boarded trams. Stoic dignity in the Belgian traveller bolstered my resolve – a reminder to keep my own issues in perspective. When any scramble started, Paul held his ground, assessing the action and checking the faces. I felt reassurance in that, but never fully exhaled until the first minutes had passed after pulling away from a station.

Thoughts turned to crossing the border into France. I'd avoided considering the problem before. Was that superstition, fear of tempting fate, or the sheer scale of what lay ahead? Or was it just the impossibility of it all? Cutting a path through barbed wire or crawling around mines and sentry towers belonged in films. I skated through other scenarios: jump the train, dodge guards and patrols, change papers, or cross at some remote point – if one existed. I'd wandered around the rim of doubt so many times – best to concentrate on the immediate. Focus on the magazine and try to relax.

More than an hour passed. Days of waiting and listening in safe houses had given me an instinct around a passage of time. The woman next to me with the bags left at Ath, or was it Att? I couldn't tell from the platform announcement. Clements could be on this train somewhere, unless he was travelling another route. I might catch up with him later? A harassed conductor entered the carriage and began checking tickets. Nobody gave him identity cards or papers and he handed my ticket back without looking up. The destination was Tournai. The two young men by the carriage door were still reading when the conductor approached them. That was odd as I had the best of a poor light and struggled to make out any small print. The reader nearest the carriage door had bushy hair and wore a double-breasted, grey-looking suit with large lapels. The other man sported a crumpled fedora hat, open raincoat, V neck jumper and tie. They had both spotted me by the time the conductor left.

The train began its slowdown sequence. Some passengers eased the blinds away from the window, peering through the dark. Paul squeezed past me along the corridor and Pope already had his newspaper folded. I rolled up my magazine before hitting the queue and clambering down the carriage steps with Pope close behind. The station was in total blackout under a high canopy roof. Passengers were no more than a presence or brush against my shoulders as they passed.

'Tournai… Tournai,' a shout rose above the slam and echo of carriage doors.

'Follow.' The whisper fell close to my ear. Paul's short figure moved alongside us. We tacked on after him and my eyes had become accustomed to the dark before we crossed platforms via a subway. Paul pushed on past a black loco with side tanks and no tender. Steam misted across, obscuring the line of carriages. I stayed close, almost treading on Paul's heels. He boarded and entered the first compartment. It was empty and smelled of damp and train dirt. I sat next to Pope who took the window seat. Paul was opposite and secured the window blinds before handing us our tickets. Mine said Rumes. I was puzzling over how he had acquired them when Gaston passed our compartment with the two readers and the French-looking man from the Brussels journey.

The train moved away. Men's voices grumbled further down the carriage and a woman's grating pitch jumped on the pauses. Paul left us and stood in the corridor. No one boarded our carriage at the first stop, so I dredged up my watch, concealing it with a cupped hand. It was well after seven-thirty. The beat from the loco came in rolling drifts, growing and fading against the wind before we stopped again. The trail of noise and dispute further down the carriage cannoned into the corridor then left. Those first silent seconds after the door slammed shut reminded me of the stunning quiet in the Lanc after Bill cut the engines.

Paul made a move towards the door once the train started to slow again. A dull suitcase thud came from the next compartment. I fished out my ticket and followed Pope into the corridor. Paul stood poised to exit. A smell of old clothes erupted behind me. Someone tapped my arm.

26

A thin, wizened man in a faded blue suit rattled French at me. His expression had an uneasy curiosity. My stomach turned. I looked down at a battered suitcase and trousers dotted with spots of oil. Paul answered him above the squeal from carriage wheels stopping. The man pushed by us, opened the door and left. Paul had saved the day. Or had he? No time to think – Pope followed him out of the carriage.

I climbed down as a jet of steam from the loco shot upwards in the cold air. Shadowy figures made for a strip of light escaping from a part-open door in the station building. Pope stuck close to Paul who walked straight past it. I tagged on and stopped between two buildings near the platform end. Pope disappeared into the dark. I held on to the wall and took a step forward. Whispers came from a group clustered together: men's voices, English and American. The shape opposite might have been Pope, or was it?

A woman arrived with three more men. She spoke to them in hushed French then left. I only caught a sense of their profiles once they moved; the rest was swallowed up in darkness. One of the new arrivals was American. An exchange of drawled whispers started. Someone told them to shut up. It went quiet.

The loco whistled, clanking away without its carriages. A man and two more women arrived. They stood alongside me and a gentle tug came on my arm from the taller woman. With a hushed 'follow please' she walked back along the platform.

The station foyer was deserted and no bigger than a large living room. Pope appeared behind me with the two readers I had seen on the Brussels and Rumes trains. We clumped across the floor. The woman looked all winter coat and long brown hair. She turned around when she reached the double doors, her pretty young face waxed for an instant in the yellow light: just a girl of no more than eighteen.

I trailed after her onto a cobbled street with a row of houses on the opposite side. A disorganised tramp of feet echoed behind me. The street looked deserted but my eyes stayed pinned open: shadows and corners still held secrets. Our walking dropped to a tiptoe. We stayed kerbside, took a left turn then sharp right on to the railway line. The track ended after about a hundred yards near a pile of sleepers stacked where the rails had been removed. A chill wind blew in my face. The girl quickened, staying on the empty track bed for around a mile. After a quick check behind her she veered off to the right, keeping to paths or trails through fields. I began to drop off the pace in wheezy, uneven steps. The group stayed in single file and dashed over a narrow road. The girl stopped near a hedge, partway up a beet field. She waited for a break in the swish and rustle of wind.

'Now we walk very close. *La frontiere* is near.' She raised her hand. 'Wis zis, you stop and *s'allongez…* lie down.'

A sudden string of hacks overwhelmed me. Every ragged bite stripped at the lining in my throat. I pushed a hand to my mouth, pulled out the handkerchief and bent forward. The girl raised her hand and we all crouched down. The wind dropped. Silence. Then more silence – the sweetest sound.

When we set off in pairs, I stayed at the back with Pope. The girl carved out long strides ahead, looking around, keeping to worn pathways or zigzagging across open ground. Her field craft reminded me of my first day on the run. She became part of the landscape, vanishing in the dark, only to appear seconds later like a staccato film. Events at the station niggled in my mind. The crowd at the platform end were at odds with everything I'd encountered before, and the absence of railwaymen made no sense. Maybe the ticket collector had marshalled the main travellers through before moving to other duties? Or he knew what would happen next and it was easier to see and hear nothing.

None of us had belonged in that space. Pope was trying to get away like me, the two readers were involved and those American voices surely belonged to escapers. What about Paul, Gaston and the other vague silhouettes? My thoughts foundered again and relief at leaving the village slipped away. I pictured a huge gaggle of us trailing across fields before being cornered in the phosphor glare of searchlights. But the Germans wouldn't wait until then. Easier to arrest us at the station – wasn't it?

The girl's hand went up again. I dropped to the ground next to a shallow ditch. Distant voices passed. We moved off before joining another narrow path. My shoes were heavy with the clag of mud and my body ached like that first day at the Macas'. A wave of despair flooded in: we had covered barely a mile since leaving the railway track. Marcel invaded my thoughts, his voice mutating into my dad's; *'Do as you're told and get on with it.'*

The moon would rise close to three-quarters. If the weather cleared we were an easy spot. The girl stepped down on a stretch of barbed wire so we could climb over nearby. A small line of houses came into view but we headed away from them, crossing a grassy field to a single-level brick farmhouse with outbuildings. The girl trod cautiously across a yard. A lane running past the house was visible through a gap. I waited with the others by a shed. Four taps on the rear door. The girl turned around as if expecting us to be ready at her shoulder. I ran my shoes over a boot scraper next to the wall before she led us into a dark space. Someone shut the door and a shaded light came on. We were standing shoulder to shoulder at the end of a passage. I started coughing again. The reader with no hat inclined his head closer.

'That's a hell of a bark you've got there, squire.'

'Started in Brussels… it's getting better,' I whispered without thinking.

'Best see the MO, if I were you.'

'I will, when I get home.'

He spoke after an uneasy pause. 'I'm Flying Officer Madgett. This is Flying Officer Ward.'

The clip in his accent might have been Home Counties. I

replied with my surname, rank and no handshake. Pope introduced himself. It all felt strangled and socially incomplete, yet my spirits soared. They were both officers – two more RAF.

We followed the girl to a room thick with cigarette smoke where a low ceiling made the space stooped and claustrophobic. Logs burned in the grate and a kettle sat on a metal stove. Four men wearing outdoor jackets or coats crowded around a wooden table with a pasty-faced lad wearing round spectacles. The chairs had been pushed back against a side wall. In the far corner, a sombre-faced woman with an apron tied around her waist rose from an armchair. The men looked at us. One of them was Clements.

'Welcome to France,' he said.

27

The thought of crossing a Nazi-controlled border without checkpoints, towers and sentries seemed incredible, almost impossible. If Clements was in the group at the station, he must have left before us or travelled a different route to the farmhouse. I wouldn't try to make sense of any of it.

The woman wasn't sombre at all. Her homely face and warm voice greeted us like a landlady welcoming in lodgers; a person who deliberately cocked a snook at the enemy with her demeanour. She chatted with the girl who brought us from the station whilst Clements and the three other men emptied their pockets onto the table supervised by the pasty-faced lad in spectacles. Two of the four were Americans and knew each other. They might have been the voices at the station. The other man had his back to me, a riot of unruly, reddish-brown hair mopped on top of his head. He stayed with the others, but in his covert body language there was a sense of separation from them. He spoke only when addressed, replying in terse sentences with a Scottish accent.

Minutes later, a small girl with a pale complexion and her hair in a bob cut arrived with three more men. The French-looking chap from the Brussels train was amongst them. With no space at the back of the room, the new arrivals edged nearer. Clements noticed them. He waved the documents in his hand.

'New papers,' he mouthed.

Two of the latest arrivals acknowledged him. One was a broad, stiff-set American in a black outdoor styled jacket. The other man looked older and spoke with a Northern England accent. The American turned to me.

'Hullo, again.'

I couldn't place him.

'Mills,' he said, quietly. 'We met in Brussels.'

'Yes, we did.' I couldn't think when or where it might have been.

I looked through the smoke at the muted groups standing about. Everyone stayed guarded within their own circle and I would do the same. The pasty-faced lad squinted through his spectacles as he searched through surrendered documents and souvenirs on the table. He reminded me of Bernard from my first Home Guard platoon.

A slim man in his twenties with straight, sandy-coloured hair weaved between the groups to join him. He spoke in French, hardly pausing for breath. My heart raced in a mix of elation and fear. There were more than a dozen people in that room and it flew in the face of everything I had experienced. So many escapers and helpers in one place just didn't fit. The whole scenario was unreal and happening in the midst of the enemy. Germans would be everywhere along the frontier. A lane ran past the front door and other houses were close – Lucie (as I named the host) and the others were taking enormous risks. I tried to detach myself and view the guides and helpers as no different from me doing my bit as a single, microscopic part in the huge war effort. Filing their contribution in a drawer behind some convenient label might have made things easier. It didn't. I still saw them as they were: patriots and families risking their lives for complete strangers.

Listening to the low conversations and ungainly pauses around the room my black humour took over. All we needed now was sherry and glasses to complete some crazy get-together, where the guests were strangers or at best only on nodding terms, and everyone was looking over their shoulders, wary of what they could and couldn't say. It was only then I noticed Paul and Gaston from the train hadn't come to the party.

Wind gusted outside, shaking the shutters. My cough returned with a vengeance in the smoke.

'Could do with the lat,' I said to Pope, between hacks.

'Think its outside.' He pointed past Lucie and the two female guides who were deep in conversation.

The table was covered in documents when I returned. Newspapers, magazines and money were piled on the side along with smoking materials and souvenir clutter.

'*Cartes d'identité, les documentations, l'argent et aussi vos possessions, s'il vous plaît,*' Bernard said.

I joined Pope and Mills. The young, sandy-haired man sorted through cards and papers. Bernard addressed us in French. I handed him the money wallet, identity documents and coins. My rail tickets, tobacco pouch, filter paper and matches came next. I left the cardboard box until last. Bernard took off the lid, holding my razor up to the light.

'No good.'

He returned the box to me with the soap still inside. The razor was added to the jumble on the table.

'*Signal?*'

I passed over the magazine. He fanned through the pages then put it aside. I kept everything else in my pockets, including the French paper money which I had removed from the wallet before leaving the Macas'. There were no watches on the table. I'd been careful and lucky with mine so far, or selfish and foolish, depending on how others viewed things. The sandy-haired man gave me new documents: two cards with my photograph on the inside plus another smaller paper, like a union or membership credential. The French identity card was a buff-ochre colour. I opened it so the halfway crease ran horizontally across the middle. Above a postage stamp and fingerprint, the same flu-ravaged face from Brussels stared back. Alongside were name, profession, date and place of birth, nationality and a round authorisation stamp over the bottom of my photograph. Below the crease I noticed the usual physical description notes, another stamp and boxes for changes. Both cards had been signed and weathered. It was vital I memorise the French papers and practise handling them.

Mills already had his documents. I noticed him watching me as I studied my details.

'These pictures are good in Belgium and France,' he said. 'A guy I stayed with told me. Got mine in a department store.'

'Wonder what job I do?' I pointed to *Profession* on my card. 'Shirt and tie makes me fit for the office... better than being an apprentice machine minder.'

He arched his eyebrows. 'A what?'

I hadn't intended him to hear the last part. It was more of a mumbled thinking out aloud. 'I was in the printing trade before joining the Raff.'

'Is that so?' He gave me a thoughtful nod.

Lucie picked up the kettle from the range. I caught a smell of steaming acorn coffee from the line of different-sized cups. Mills spoke quietly to Pope, the creases deepening on his forehead as they talked. There wasn't much chat to pick up on. Mills lived in San Francisco, less than three miles from the Golden Gate. His kite got separated from the bomber stream after the bomb doors jammed over the target. They were shot up by fighters on the return journey. Pope answered him in slow, short responses which I couldn't hear. It was one of those strange conversations where neither man made eye contact, both staring ahead as if they were looking out to sea.

A mahogany-coloured clock sat on the sideboard further down the room. It was almost ten when I felt a cold draught across my neck. A short, cheery-faced man in a dark blue French policeman's uniform studied us from the back door. Lucie acknowledged him and the quiet fell away as he was absorbed into the room, squeezing past me before speaking to Sandy and Bernard. Perpetually on the move, he chattered in French to the escapers, with sporadic English words fired in like punctuation as every emotion illuminated his face and mannerisms.

'You are RAF?' he said to Clements.

The policeman didn't wait for an answer. He patted his jacket sleeves.

'When I work, I am proud to wear RAF *uniforme*.'

Some of the men looked startled. Any puzzled or blank faces were greeted with the same warm handshake and courtesy before he moved on. His blithe expression instantly vanished once he reached Lucie and the two female guides. They listened to his monologue, heads nodding before he made a sudden, exaggerated military turn and wrapped his knuckles on the table.

'*Et maintenant. Allez, mes amis. Gardez le silence.*'

He put a finger to his lips, then, like some eccentric cavalry officer, made a forward wave to the back door with his free hand. Some of the men smiled. The young girl who escorted our party from the station approached us.

'One group,' she said, pointing to Pope and me. She levelled a look at Madgett and Ward. 'Two group.'

Sandy was buttoning up his navy raincoat. Bernard pushed our Belgian money and clutter into a tighter pile away from the line of abandoned cups on the table. The policeman shifted up a gear, cutting straight past us out of the back door. Sandy left with Clements, the Scottish chap, and the two Americans who were with them when I first arrived. Our group was next. At least ten minutes passed before the five of us exited the farmhouse but I couldn't be certain. I had avoided looking at the clock. The young girl led us through the yard and turned left along the fringe of a field towards the houses we had avoided earlier. I didn't understand it – Clements had welcomed us to France and now we were heading back into Belgium.

28

The wind masked any sound of our movement through the grass. I crawled under barbed wire again. The three-quarter moon peeped between fluffs of chasing cloud, revealing the lightless houses. We trod carefully past some rear garden fencing, making for a gap after the last building. The girl stopped, checked the lane then led us across to a farm track. In the moonlight, ghostly silhouettes of a house and barn were visible further down the pathway.

A dog barked as we approached. The girl hurried on. I was labouring at the back of our group.

'OK?' Pope said.

I gasped a reply. The barking grew louder. A smell of manure thickened. We turned left by the house, the girl striding relentlessly on. The farm was in darkness. I scanned the black windows and door, my heart pounding out a rhythm against our steps – *don't look out, don't look out.* A field slipped into a gradual down-slope and we took the middle route between lines of ploughed furrows, our breath forming clouds in the wintry air. The dog quietened. Men looked about, twisting their heads like anxious sparrows. Perhaps the policeman had inside knowledge of German patrols? I kept moving, hauled on by the girl's impatient waves.

Half a mile later, we hit a narrow village lane. Mist hung around the small church spire and two whitewashed cottages guarded both sides of a bend ahead. The girl signalled us to wait and checked beyond the corner. This time we moved off slowly, our footsteps far too sharp and crisp above the wind. A blurred line of houses showed through the murk, the final home facing at right angles to the others. We trekked through clumpy grass to the back garden. I was last down the path. Barking boomed inside the house, the girl spoke and the noise stopped. Four knocks on the back door – three slow, one quick. Letter V in Morse code – V for Victory? A key rattled.

I groped my way along the narrow passage walls. The girl led us into a large flagstone kitchen, busy with people. Fire glowed from a charcoal hearth, flames blinking in the reflection on the furniture. A meat and herb smell rose from two large pans simmering on the range. The policeman and a small dark-haired woman dressed in black were marshalling escapers to a table, chairs and any spare floor spaces. A blond man in a brown, tweedy jacket stood near me, as if pensively waiting for the nod to step forward. He fumbled out a cigarette and tapped it on a matchbox. A man wearing a double-breasted grey suit leaned against a dresser, arms folded, his forehead ridged with frown lines as he studied the packed room. His hair receded into a parting near the top left corner of his forehead, ageing him at anything from twenty-five to mid-thirties.

Some of the escapers turned to the door behind me. The small girl with her hair in a bob cut steered in Mills and the bloke with a Northern England accent. The French-looking man from the train came in. Everyone from the farmhouse except Lucie may have been there, but their faces blurred amongst a mass of heads and shoulders. Sandy led the girls out of the room with the blond man trailing at the back. He left the door half open and a black Alsatian wriggled through the gap, chased by a boy of about twelve with dark, frizzy hair thatched over the top of his head. He called to the dog before scrambling it out. Escapers were still settling into spaces when the woman (I named her Rachel) reached into a cabinet near me and lined up glasses along the top.

I sat with Pope on the stone floor between the cabinet and a wooden dresser. The policeman appeared with bottles of wine wedged between his fingers. A packet of French cigarettes was passed around. I kept my smoke for another time. Quiet talk rippled amongst the escapers, their words suddenly lost in a clatter as Rachel ladled steaming stew on to patterned plates. The boy shuttled across the room with the first meals and she distributed the rest. Red wine came with it. The smell of tobacco smoke took over. Glasses were more than half full and smiles flickered on tired faces.

'*Monsieur?*' More wine glugged into Pope's glass. The policeman was now a wine waiter, interrupting with a grin or raised eyebrows, angling the bottle to give the merest suggestion that a glass could do with a top up. If the guest spoke any French, a conversation followed with a smile, before the host moved on. I imagined him as the icebreaker at social gatherings, setting a warm, convivial tone, manoeuvring people together to keep the hospitality flowing. But it was Rachel who ran the operation from the moment we had arrived, moving between the visitors and cooking area, collecting empty plates then returning with dishes of apples and cheese without obstructing or crossing the policeman's path.

The food and wine warmed me. I rested my eyes, trying to stay above the low thrum of conversation. Somewhere in the far corners of my head were my parents. I'd shut them out again. That choice always spawned fresh guilt. Thoughts returned to the same thing. I was alive and couldn't tell them, couldn't stop their 'keep calm and carry on' faces, their fragile conversations where neither heard the other's words, or the dread at every knock on the front door.

The policeman raised his glass.

'*Mes amis. Porter un toast à la RAF et à l'armée de l'air Américaines.*'

We toasted the Resistance and an Allied invasion. I saw a room full of painted smiles. The bizarre party I had pictured at Lucie's place had turned into reality.

Loud barking sounded outside. The policeman raised his hand. Everyone stopped speaking. He stepped over the bodies and opened the back door. The man in the grey suit went with him. Some escapers hunched together at the table, the rest of us sat rigid where we were. The policeman returned. A cautious smile broke out on his face.

'*D'accord.*'

It was another stark reminder and an interval before the man in the grey suit reappeared. He stayed by the door, observing the room as wine and cigarettes kick-started conversations again. I decided to name him Pierre. Pope stretched out and said nothing. I picked up on pools of talk as the chat moved around like a gentle tide. The taller of the two Americans sitting together was called Tennessee. He smiled through his freckles, capturing an audience with his Southern drawl and colourful stories. The older, gaunt-faced friend loosened his scarf to join in a debate around the merits and weaknesses of B24s and B17s. His voice came with a serial calm which belied an exhausted look. I hadn't noticed this in the others, it was as if he'd been to war before. The young boy who had dragged the dog out earlier kept close to him, interrupting in French.

The RAF chaps said the Americans were mad to bomb in daylight. The Americans reckoned we were crazy going out at night. It was good-natured verbal fencing and a relief to hear casual talk again, even if Pope and I were anonymous listeners, as were Madgett and Ward, who only spoke to one another in muffled sentences. Nobody noticed us hidden on the floor between pieces of furniture in a packed kitchen. That suited me. With wine loosening the tongues of men who probably knew each other or had met earlier in their journeys, any focus away from us was inevitable.

I did pick up some gen before slipping into a half-doze. Mills and Clements called the bloke with the Northern England accent 'Johnnie'. He'd baled out and landed close to the Dutch-German border after his aircraft hit trees on a hillside in fog. Some airmen had come down in Holland and I wasn't the only one to lose my escape kit when baling out. Tennessee said he landed next to a farm and got shelter there. It was general stuff, although most of us were stretching orders not to talk about what had happened.

American flyers baling out in daylight tried to count the parachutes just as we did. They faced a race against time whilst drifting down. Enemy fighters often circled above and the locals ran to reach the airmen before German patrols moved in on their line of descent, just as Marcel had described to me. Villagers often wanted the silk parachutes, boots, clothes and rations and the Dutch were seen as obsessed with collecting souvenirs. Others tried to help the airman or were pro-Nazi and Black Brigade. An American said the Luftwaffe were machine gunning parachutists during their descent. No one broke into the telling hush with a reply. But what really drove home the most was the narrow escapes and luck we'd all experienced.

Madgett and Ward sat opposite Pope on a sort of carpenter's sawing stool. The wine must have revived me, as we started some small talk around our journey. I told them about bluffing a way past sentries on the canal bridge and how the German officer clocked me in Brussels.

'We had none of that,' Madgett said. 'After the crash we all split up in different directions and legged it before the Jerries got there.'

He looked at Ward. 'Me and him set off southwest. Haven't seen any of our boys since.'

'So what happened before the crash?' Pope said.

'Searchlight beamed us,' Madgett said. 'Got caught in a box barrage of flak.'

His voice grew croaky in the smoke.

'We were peppered down the fuselage. Starboard wing was on fire.'

He drew on his cigarette, looking around at nothing in particular.

'Pilot feathered the starboard inner to reduce the slip stream and tried the extinguisher button. No good. Order came to abandon aircraft. We were too low by then to bale out. Pilot told us to take up crash positions, so I got into the middle near the rest bed. Kite skidded over a field and hit something on the way… made a pretty good landing though.'

Wood cracked and spat in the hearth. The background hum fell away. Some men were oblivious, eyes shut and mouths sagging open. Madgett waited for the murmur to pick up again.

'When I got out, the fire was really burning. We must have

caught a haystack, as it was ablaze. The whole starboard wing outward of the inner engine was a mass of flames. I was glad to get away.'

The French-looking man from the Brussels train was listening.

'So where do you fit in?' Madgett said to him.

'My name is Henri and I am going to London,' the man replied confidently.

'Aren't we all?' Ward said.

There was a ripple of laughter. I hoped it hadn't carried outside.

29

Pierre had eaten his meal alone by the hearth. He stepped over the legs and tapped a wine glass on the cabinet next to me. *'Messieurs.'*

The men roused themselves.

'We must speak with ze quiet. At four hours of morning we walk to Cysoing. Zen our train departs.'

He put the glass down and poked a cigarette into his mouth. 'Our destination is Lille and zen Paris. My friends will give you ze tickets. First we rest.'

The time must have been well after midnight: three hours sleep at most. He lit the cigarette, disappearing for a second amongst the smoke. Pope pushed up hard against the wall and rested his head against the side of the dresser. The others bunked down under their coats on the stone floor, or lay forward at the table, heads pillowed on their arms. Pierre flicked some ash off his lapels as he left the room with the blond man and Sandy. I looked around for the two female guides. They were missing and I had not seen them since they left the room earlier with Sandy. The last thing I remembered before sleep swept in was Rachel watching us from a kitchen chair.

The room was in darkness when I woke. A chill had invaded the house, the kind which settled late on a winter's evening when a coal fire faded. A few red embers glowed in the hearth and the rhythmic sound of men snoring seemed interlinked. The door latch rattled at the far end. Light flooded the room. Tired men stirred.

'*Monsieur... Monsieur?*' Sandy and the blond man tiptoed amongst the sleeping forms, gently shaking them. I blinked into the brightness. On the floor, Madgett roused himself. Ward opened his eyes. He had an easy, yet disciplined demeanour. I sensed a *c'est la guerre* attitude to his predicament, a man who would follow and give orders with no problems. Pope sat up. Clements raised himself from the kitchen chair. I knew where he was going and needed a visit myself. I waited by the door until he returned.

'What time is it?' he said.

'I don't know. It must be after three. That chap said we'd be leaving at four.'

We spoke briefly about the previous evening meal.

'What happened at Brussels station?' I said. 'One minute you were there and the next—'

'Georges took me to a guide where I met Jim and Sergeant Watt. We changed trains at Tournai.'

'Jim who? And which one's Sergeant Watt?'

'Jim, he's still asleep at the table… the Scotsman with red hair. Sergeant Watt, he's the Yank…the fella who was talking in French to that boy last night.'

Clements pointed out the gaunt-faced man sitting with Tennessee at the table. 'Just be careful, Ron, it doesn't pay to know too many names.'

He had made me think. If I did get put in the bag I'd have to be careful with every word. Play dumb and stick to my name, rank and number. The story was ready. I'd travelled alone, seen nothing and heard nothing. How long would that hold up to serious interrogation?

I wound my watch in the lat. Not far off three-twenty. When I returned to the room the last few men were getting a final wakeup call from Sandy. His hand on their shoulders ignited the same half-snore, slurred words and hazy look. Our reactions in those moments made us no different from each other.

'Must be at least a quarter after three?' Pope said to me as I sat down on the floor. 'Are you OK?'

I told him I felt much better. He eyed me with the same foggy expression as at Lucie's the night before when he had spoken with Mills, the American. I still wasn't sure what to make of him. Shutters were down again for now.

The policeman stood at the stove, sharp and pressed in his tunic. Sandy handed out the last cigarettes and the boy passed hot drinks around before he latched on to Sergeant Watt again. Some escapers cradled their cups, gazing into another place and drinking as if it was a job that had to be done. Others hung around in smoky groups or sat checking their documents. Sandy glanced around the room as the young blond man departed by the back door.

Pierre called us to order. We would leave for Cysoing railway station at intervals and in pairs, staying around thirty metres behind our escort.

'Geheime Feldpolizei and Feldgendarmerie watch the stations at Lille and Paris,' he said. 'Also the fraud controllers at Paris… they look for the black market smugglers. Always keep the distance from your guide. The rest you know. Good luck, my friends.'

The blond man returned. Sandy gave out rail tickets for Lille and Rachel handed us each a small package wrapped in newspaper. The policeman ranged amongst us, shaking each man by the hand, giving words of encouragement with an occasional pat on a shoulder. We fell into pairs in a line like parachutists ready to jump from an aircraft. Pope stayed with me. Madgett and Ward were behind us and Watt stuck with Tennessee. I heard Johnnie, the bloke with the Northern England accent, talk to Mills. Scottish Jim and Clements were paired up somewhere – it all became a haze and I hadn't seen Henri, the French-looking chap, since the night before.

Sandy was already wearing his raincoat. The blond man left with Watt, Tennessee and the young boy. We waited for at least two or three minutes. Then, with a nod to the room, Sandy was away. Pope turned to me.

'The name's Harold by the way.'

What a time to finally tell me.

'I'm Ron.'

I felt my way behind Harold along the passage and out into the night. We walked down the back garden and through the grass, with Sandy's slim figure barely visible through a mist of drizzle. He led us around the back of the village. We hastened over a road and cut across fields, tramping through wet, invisible countryside.

'Wonder how long we'll be in Paris?' I said to Harold, trying to break the monotony. My question was left hanging in the rain.

'Let's get there,' he said eventually. 'First, we gotta get around *that.*'

I stopped at the edge of a dark pool of water.

'Go up to our ankles in there, Ron.'

We squelched along the raised bank of a land ditch.

'Could have finished up in Paris, I guess,' he said. 'Started a bomb run in Germany and got shot up by fighters.' He stepped down from the bank. 'Helped fly the kite back.'

'You're a pilot?'

'Nope. Engineer and top turret... B17s. Got about five hours stick time before.'

His short, stocky frame looked ideal for a gunner: B17s were heavily armed compared to Lancs; they had to be for daylight raids.

'So, what happened?'

We walked another hundred yards before he spoke.

'Guess that's another story.'

Sandy's voice rasped through the dark. 'Quiet. No talking.' I hadn't realised how close he was to us. Part of me regretted breaking those orders, but I had gauged no one would hear in the rain-swept wilderness. It had been worth trying to chip away at Harold. Maybe when we could finally speak safely, I'd not have to start all over again with him.

Sandy took a sharp right, near where a railway line crossed the lane. We followed alongside the track and up a wide platform slope. Cysoing was built in the same shape and style as Belgian country stations. Figures crowded under the canopy. A door to the main building opened. In the miserable light from a waiting room, workmen in overalls sat inside on a wooden bench with their lunch boxes.

More men congregated on the platform. Some leaned out peering down the track. Sandy stepped forward as a loco hauled its trail of dark carriages into the station. We boarded, groping through pitch black. Someone struck a match. Three men showed in the flickering light. Two empty seats were opposite them. I took the window spot and Harold flopped down next to me. The carriage fell into blackness again – daylight was still hours away.

It must have been around five o'clock when the train left at a crawl. A regular smell of damp clothes lingered in the air. The three shapes sitting opposite me were dark and still, almost statuesque – more of a presence then anything tangible. A whisper of conversation in the carriage or rasp from a match was all that broke the comatose silence. I imagined the passengers' blank faces around the edge of some gaping hole, staring into the void left in their lives after occupation.

The train halted. No sound of boarding – no banging doors – no reaction in the carriage. Sandy would be nearby somewhere. Time became abstract again and the answer lay frustratingly in my pocket. I hated stops and delays, dreaded the incessant listening, the waiting for sudden movements or a disturbance in the carriage and arrival of a uniform – any uniform.

This was the longest wait yet. A lack of reaction from anyone convinced me the regular travellers knew what was coming. I heard and saw nothing except the red dot from a cigarette or a lighted match. I sat ramrod-straight in the seat, telling myself to be ready for anything, but the bowel-clenching fear still grew in my gut: nowhere to look, nowhere to go, and a giant clock ticking down in my head.

The stop-start went on for hours. It was like sitting in a dentist's chair with the drill grinding slower and slower into my tooth as his foot tired from pressing the pedal. The quiet eventually pushed me into a half-sleep until a sudden noise brought me to. Grey light had filled our carriage. The man opposite wiped the misty window with his coat sleeve. Rain fell in sheets across the fields, Harold read his newspaper and Sandy faced us in a seat further down the carriage. The other men in their rough coats and overalls looked ready for a machine shop or factory. My shoes were sludgy and mud streaks patterned the bottoms of my trousers. Harold's laces were caked with it. I had been warned about being stopped when dirty or untidily dressed. There was no mud on the other men's clothes or boots and our softer-looking civilian outfits looked out of place. Any suspicion or checks could blow everything apart. The carriage wheels clicked into a canter as the loco puffed short distances then coasted before the pattern repeated. Buildings stretched out in the misty distance – surely Lille. We needed to be out quickly, get cleaned up and on a train to Paris.

Beads of condensation ran down the window – small triangles of dirt were lodged in the bottom corners. The precincts of Lille slid past. Men gathered up their kitbags and lunch boxes. I went through my ritual checklist. Sandy held a rail ticket conspicuously between his fingers as he edged to the door. Surely he would get us to a washroom before catching the Paris train? The carriage rumbled over points near the station approach and noise poured in when a door flew open at the far end while the train was still moving down the platform. I waited to join the crowd poised in the aisle.

Shafts of watery sunlight shone through a steel girder roof. A clock at the far end showed four minutes past nine. Sandy moved with the bobbing heads, about twenty paces ahead of us. Another terminus station – five platforms and we were halfway up number three. I stayed close to Harold; it was easy to see over his shoulders. Barriers stretched across all the platforms and queues funnelled through the only open gate. I'd passed through them before, handed in tickets, survived inspections, yet the dread always returned. Pierre's stark warnings about Lille and Paris were clear. Everyone fell under surveillance as soon as they left the train.

Scenarios bounced around in my head: Gestapo and Feldgendarmerie at the barriers ready to demand documents and seize on any uncertainty, observers in the concourse looking for anyone out of place. In the cinema films, men in trademark overcoats and hats or well-heeled women hung about at station exits, poised to follow selected targets. My thoughts had run away with themselves again; I knew too little about too much, it was as straightforward as that. Inside the Lanc, we all understood our jobs and each other, we knew the dangers and wouldn't dwell on them, there was never time. In this world, we relied totally on strangers who sheltered, moved and travelled with us. The hours of waiting, thinking and listening with little idea of what to expect next were wearing me down.

Sandy reached the queue. No sign of the others. The line filed through. Passengers handed their tickets to a railwayman in a black uniform and nobody took out any papers. Another train rumbled in behind me. A crowd waited in a semi-circle on the other side of the barrier. Military gathered separately on the left flank – a noisy set of Wehrmacht and Luftwaffe. I didn't notice the two men in trench coats behind the ticket collector until Harold walked past them.

30

A thud in my chest grew louder. The string of possibilities tightened inside my head. The smaller of the two men stopped a youth. I focused straight ahead across a narrow concourse and reached a large, domed booking-hall with people passing through in both directions. Sandy disappeared into the *Messieurs* and Harold loitered near the entrance. When we walked in, Sandy was standing alone at a washbasin with some of the white splashback tiles missing. He placed a finger on his lips and pointed to a stall with its door closed. Only light skims of mud showed on his trouser turn ups – how had he managed that? I went in the next stall and tried to clean my shoes and trousers. Thoughts stacked up inside my head. Where were the others from the policeman's house? Surely it was too dangerous for any of us to hang around the station or return to the platforms so soon? What about the next train ticket?

Harold waited for me. We moved outside and followed Sandy through the booking hall to a line of busy archways leading on to the street. This was not in the plan. Lille station formed part of a wide concrete square bordered by large buildings and department stores which reminded me of Brussels outside Gare du Nord. Winter sunshine reflected off the wet surface. Near the middle, a green and cream tram curved towards an octagonal shelter with plank-sized advertisement boards around the top. Sandy made for the far side. We could be going to another rail station? I passed two Wehrmacht officers and a gendarme. One thing at a time.

It was a relief to leave the main roads and walk through a network of narrow cobbled backstreets. Houses with wooden shutters and brick or grimy plaster fronts ended any illusion that a city's architecture might be different on the other side of a border. Water pooled over shallow kerbs onto the pavement and women hugged their shawls, watching us from doorways. Sandy stopped outside a terraced-type house. A short man with unkempt hair let us in. We waited in a small vestibule while he shut out the street and spoke in whispers.

'We stay with my friend, Étienne,' Sandy said after an uncomfortable pause. 'The train for Paris departs this afternoon.'

Étienne greeted us and pointed out a door halfway along the passage.

'A young boy waits in there,' Sandy said. 'He waits to go to the school. Étienne will say to him that you are *les Flamands* workers travelling to France. The boy does not understand English, but you will not speak it.'

I heard voices inside the room. Étienne had already entered and it was a while before we were invited in. The space was cluttered with furniture and had no carpet. Sunshine filtered through a pair of worn curtains in thin shafts of light, catching the dancing dust motes. The boy sat by a window, one leg crossed over the other. Short trousers, grey socks and a dark jumper, he looked about ten years old.

Sandy flopped down with us on a couch opposite. *'Bonjour.'*

The boy gave a sheepish smile. *'Bonjour.'*

Étienne went to the window and checked the street. Sandy left the room with him and their voices faded to the back of the house. Harold winked at the boy who was eyeing us over the top of his *Bravo* comic. It felt like being in a doctor's surgery. I waited for the next tramp of feet in the street and a dip in the light as another silhouette passed by the window.

After a long delay, Étienne returned with three cups of wheat coffee or some ersatz mixture. I could see all his fingers were intact. He summoned the boy who rolled up his comic and wished us adieu. Sandy had a strange, oblique expression when he joined us again. Something more than simple detachment lingered on this face. We attacked the newspaper parcels and ate Rachel's bread baguettes, dipping them in the steaming hot drink. I heard the front door close. The outlines of Étienne and the boy slipped past the window. I said nothing – it was time for someone else to ask questions. Where were the other escapers from the farmhouse? They must have been on the train? What was the next move?

Sandy screwed up the newspaper sheets, gathering the balls together.

'We will rest. Our train leaves at fourteen hundred hours.'

'Reckon we might have been clocked at the station,' Harold said.

'Everyone is being clocked,' Sandy replied, emphasising the last word. 'Now please understand about your guides. If they are arrested, many lives in many places are in danger. You must be sure you do not have the attention of the Boche.'

The irritation in his voice caused me to sit up. He got to his feet.

'If there is a problem on the trains and trams, or in the street, do not be looking at your guide. The Boche will see this. Yes?'

Harold stayed silent. Sandy smiled. Not a warm smile, more of a reaction to our lack of response. His eyebrows narrowed in a worried frown.

'Listen carefully. At Amiens, *quelquefois*… sometimes there is the passenger controls. On the train, please see the documents I will hold in my hand. You must show your papers to *le contrôleur* and the man who is with him, it may not be a soldier. It is certain they will watch you.'

He handed us a mustard-coloured ticket each – second-class single to Paris. They must have been acquired earlier or were waiting with Étienne.

Sandy's tone lightened. 'Now, I give the apologies because Étienne has no cigarettes.'

'I've got a couple,' I said. 'They won't get smoked with this blasted cough. I'll leave them for him. I noticed on the way from the station, men were picking tabs up in the street.'

Sandy smiled. 'I think they will not find many here. At night, soldiers are in the city. Before the dawn, some men search with the small *torche* for the last of the cigarette… *le megot*.'

'What? The dog ends?'

'Yes... The ends, but not the dog.' He smiled in a self-satisfied way.

'So what about using torches in the blackout?'

'They are very small and there is also *le mouchoir*.' He took a handkerchief from his pocket. 'This covers much light. Many peoples cannot do this now because there are no batteries to buy.'

Étienne and the boy didn't return. I dozed a little until Sandy roused us.

'*Maintenant, nous allons retourner à la gare.* We return to the station. If I am arrested there or in the street, walk to the station and wait outside for fifteen minutes. My friends will help. If no one comes, you must return there every hour. Hold the newspaper in your hand. Do you remember where the station is?'

He appeared to be convinced by our nodding and took the crumpled, grey felt hat from inside his raincoat, pushing it down tight on his head.

'In the train, you stand near the end of *la voiture*.' The pitch in his voice rose. 'The carriage... car... coach... whatever the word is. Please be standing where you can see me. A friend will meet us at Paris.'

I went to answer but he cut in.

'We must have no delays at the station, so Étienne already buys the newspapers for us. They are outside in the hall. Please, you will both read *Le Paris Soir* and carry it in your left hand when you arrive at Paris.'

The newspapers were on a wooden table in the vestibule. I took a copy and left my two cigarettes in its place. Just after one o'clock, Sandy quietly shut the front door after us. Another shower had soaked the cobbles. Sunlight reflected off the rooftops and the street looked busier. The game was on again.

A horse and cart waited outside a store in the station square. Flashes of home resonated in the bright light. The building was similar to Joseph Johnson's, a large department store in Leicester.

Hotel de Paris next door could have been the Bell Hotel, and the shop awnings of the Grand Pharmacie de Paris belonged on any British city main street. The scene carried nothing of the grey, oppressive feel of Brussels; even the passing tram glinted in the sunshine. A soldier riding on the step brought me back into the moment. Wehrmacht strolled about the square and service uniforms were sewn into the busy crowds moving along pavements. A group of soldiers passed Sandy as he walked up to the station archways. The enemy were still everywhere.

One thirty-eight on the station clock. I didn't require a mirror to know my face was stiffening into that worried, unfocused expression again. The concourse looked busy. I showed my ticket at the barrier. Peculiar, how thoughts kept returning to a steaming cup of tea with sugar. Sandy approached a crowd on the far side where a rake of blue carriages stretched down the last platform. Harold arrived as people bustled past us. On the way from Étienne's, the temptation to glance back and check Harold was still in touch with us had been overwhelming. Sandy waited for the rush to subside. A young man wearing a grey herringbone overcoat hung about behind him with another chap. I rested against a pillar before following them down the platform.

Steam rose at the mouth of the girder archway and draughts of sooty air blew in my face. Wehrmacht were still clambering aboard near the locomotive when we finally found a carriage with some space. All compartments were occupied but the corridor was only two-thirds full. I stood with Harold near a connecting passage into the next carriage where Sandy remained in sight. The young man in the overcoat was three or four passengers away from me down our corridor. I caught his eye for an instant as the train moved out. He didn't acknowledge me.

Railways would never feel the same again. Stations and journeys here were a nasty paradox: a step closer to Blighty, but places of fear and risk. The grand station buildings at home were once part of busy Saturday holiday excitement with a buffet, silver tea urns and white china before we joined the noise and suitcases on the platform. Wartime had turned them into cold, echoing mausoleums where goodbyes vanished in smoke and tears – hopeless places where the shrill of a guard's whistle sent a lurch through the stomach, and a distant waving hand could be the final memory. A chap I worked with at the printers waved his son off. He never saw him again. The boy was lost in the Far East.

Our corridor had smart mahogany fittings. I ran a finger along the wood. Harold pushed up against my shoulder, forcing me into a half-turn against the window. I gave up trying to open my newspaper. Ploughed fields and pastureland raced by in the sunshine. Flak towers had been posted at intervals near the track and security on bridges was tight. Two soldiers guarded at either end near a sentry box painted with concentric white, red and black angled stripes, like a circumflex. The train often slowed to a crawl when crossing. More men patrolled the surrounding area and I felt a surge of optimism. If the Germans were going to these lengths, the French Resistance must be fighting back.

Amiens was the next main stop. I pushed any thought of checks aside – this time I would be ready. The train passed rows of railway sidings stacked with wigwam and star-shaped metal tank barriers. They were sections of rail welded together and a likely explanation for the missing track at Rumes. Square frames constructed in the same way with small wheels at one end were positioned at the bridges, ready to pull across. More lay in piles where the track bed widened. The enemy were making ready against invasion.

The journey dragged. My tongue and mouth developed a dry, leathery feel again which aggravated the coughing. I no longer had the kind of physical exhaustion which started with a dull pain in the feet, worked its way up to the shoulders and finally reached my head. The throbbing ache in my legs and arms kept my whole body strained and taut. Harold hid behind his newspaper. I rustled open my *Paris Soir*. Page two listed what looked like theatre and cinema showings. The man standing opposite me read his copy of *Paris*

Midi. Its front page had a photograph of German troops talking to two women with large baskets balanced on their heads.

We passed a chemical works, smoke trailing from its thin chimneys. Large storage tanks were aligned close to a brick warehouse operating next to bombed-out ruins and rubble.

'*Mesdames et Messieurs, vos billets et cartes d'identité s'il vous plaît.*'

I heard the conductor before I saw him. A dumpy, fifty-something man in a long black coat and peaked cap had entered our carriage through the crowded connecting passage. A younger man wearing a similar uniform accompanied him. Figures around me stirred. I battled with my newspaper, folding it into a crumpled quarter. Passengers were handing over a single card with their ticket. The conductor chatted to some of them – a cordial tone, usually brief, but there were conversations which included the younger man. Identity and ticket check: what the hell would I do if either of them spoke to me? What about Harold? He would be first. I fumbled in my pockets.

'*Monsieur?*' The conductor faced me, hand outstretched.

The documents stuck together in my sweaty palm. *Ticket first – identity card second – no talking, no questions.*

He checked the ticket, flicked open the card and looked at me again.

'*Merci.*'

The suburbs of Amiens were blighted with rubble, shells of buildings and cleared bombsites. Wagons filled the sidings in a large railway marshalling yard. Blackened and burnt-out rolling stock littered the area. Amiens was more of a junction for freight than passenger traffic, its modest station a small island amongst the network of parallel rail tracks, points and storage lines. Our train rumbled into the platform. Station walls and surrounds had been scoured by blast.

Doors banged. Shouts came amongst a thud of sacks landing on concrete. I waited for the announcements. Six words to listen out for: *Controle Allemand – presentez les papiers d'identité.* An eerie stillness settled. In the corner of our corridor, I shut myself off from the world. Paris was a hundred miles away on the atlas inside my head and it would be dark when we reached there. I pinned us to an imaginary map like on the ops board at briefings, with lengths of coloured ribbon between towns and cities on my route from Antwerp.

The clang outside from a wheel tapper's hammer stopped. Still no departure. Two men in grey-green wax coats walked past on the platform. They appeared at the far end of our carriage. A voice near me said the word. It was the same in any language. Gestapo.

31

The two men moved slowly up the corridor, checking faces, peering in compartments, pushing through wedges of people. A bleak silence crept down the carriage. Harold's face had set in deadpan lines, I unfolded my newspaper to the back page: something to do, anything to hide my fear and self-advertisement. The smaller man moved nearer – a pinched face with a granite stare. I looked down at my newspaper, drawing it closer to my chest when the two men squeezed past and disappeared into the next carriage.

The train slipped away after a lengthy delay. Harold blew out a long breath. Sandy was in conversation with someone outside my line of sight. My legs and back screamed for a seat but everyone in the corridor had stayed on their feet. I turned to the window again, watching the town thin out and disappear.

South of Amiens, a loco and carriages lay concertinaed at the trackside. A freight train passed in the opposite direction, armed with anti-aircraft guns on mobile flak cars positioned middle and end. My thoughts moved to Paris, a Paris imagined from newsreels and schoolbooks, where the Eiffel Tower and Champs-Élysées were flooded in sunshine whatever the weather, a Paris with its piano-accordion cafés, waistcoat and apron waiters, wine and expensive restaurants with not a German uniform in sight. Strange pictures after what had happened so far, but I would change none of them until I saw the capital for myself.

Our carriage slowly dulled into half-dark. Interior lights stayed off and nobody pulled down the blinds. Bridges and approaches outside Paris were heavily guarded for miles. Soldiers stood trackside every few hundred yards, silhouetted against a faint orange line on the horizon. The city was shrouded in darkness by the time we reached its suburbs. When the train began to slow, I turned away from the murky rooftops and chimneys. The other passengers were indiscernible now. Sandy managed to manoeuvre into the connecting passage, his profile only apparent by his felt hat. I folded my newspaper. Our carriage passed a stand-up clock on the platform, the luminous hands and figures on its face appearing to hang in mid-air. Almost seven o'clock. Our journey had taken five hours.

Sandy waited near the carriage steps until we climbed down: another station in full blackout. Tannoy announcements bounced around under the high roof as we joined a dark flow of movement heading down the platform. He took his time leading us to a concourse reverberating with noise. Soldiers from the train headed in a direction away from the main crowds. A row of narrow aisles, each with handrails and a small glass booth halfway along, spanned the way out. A bleary, yellow light shone through the glass, ghosting the ticket checkers inside.

I couldn't see much beyond the booths. Sandy stopped at the end of a queue, half-turning our way as he searched his trouser pockets. He'd used the tactic before to check we were still behind him. It reminded me that our man in the herringbone grey overcoat hadn't been seen since Amiens. Harold carried the newspaper in his left hand when we reached the aisles. I copied him. Queue lines were swiftly filing through. At that speed, checks on the other side would have to be random. I prepared my ritual and passed through to a foyer packed with people.

Sandy must have been watching out for us. He cut across in front of me, almost within touching distance before walking slowly to the left side of the foyer where three men waited near the wall. One of them approached Harold first and then moved on to me. Around five feet nine and well built around the middle, he looked to be in his forties, but in the shadows of a blackout it was mostly guesswork. Close up, I reckoned on fair or maybe grey hair, a moustache and what looked like a dark suit, tie and white shirt under an open overcoat.

He held out his gloved hand. 'Welcome to Paris. I am the Chief.'

The accent was French, whipped with a faint American drawl. The Chief smiled revealing a mosaic of white and gold teeth and he greeted me warmly as if he already knew who I was. The whole process was so obvious and public. I looked around for Sandy. He had left.

The Chief asked us to join the two men waiting by the wall. I recognised their silhouettes as Madgett and Ward.

'One of my friends will collect you,' the Chief said. 'Please follow her.'

He described the woman then disappeared into the crowds. We waited next to Madgett and Ward. Sidelong glances passed between us. No one spoke. Were they as nervous as I was? The foyer was still a mass of activity and noise yet that sense of being noticed nagged like a splinter under my skin. Two women came into view at the last moment, approaching us from different directions. The first was tall and upright – possibly blonde with a fitted winter coat and small hat. The other walked much slower. Her short steps fitted the tiny profile and made her appear to dawdle. She looked well under five feet tall, wore black clothes and carried a matching shopping bag. Sandy and Pierre had warned us about the dangers in Paris; surveillance would be tighter. Even amongst the masses and darkness both women looked conspicuous. From the instant they reached us, so would we.

Madgett and Ward followed the blonde. After passing us, the woman in black paused to rummage in her shopping bag. With the briefest glance in our direction, she ambled towards the station exit. Harold moved off first and we kept just enough distance to keep her in sight. She passed under a large canopy before disappearing onto the shadowy Paris streets. It was almost ten minutes past seven.

PART TWO

France

1

Madame Black kept a distance ahead, often fading from sight before a glimpse of her movement kept us on track. We trod the darkness, crossed boulevards, kept to quieter streets. Most shops had shut and pedestrians were no more than shifty footsteps in the blackout. Madame passed under an arched metal *Metropolitain* sign and vanished down a flight of concrete steps between some railings. When we caught up she had already turned away from a kiosk plastered with posters and notices. Footfall came from the street above. We took our tickets from her and hurried into the seedy light of a subway tunnel.

A railwayman clipped my ticket outside a small booth at the bottom of a flight of steps. The platform was half full and Madame stood about twenty paces from us, gently swinging her shopping bag. Soldiers clustered in the centre, ignored by civilians. The low, curved ceiling and station walls were a patchwork of white tiles in different shades of grime. Stale air wafted through in tepid draughts. I checked my ticket – *Seconde Classe Metropolitain*.

Rumbling in the tunnel grew louder and heads turned absently towards the sound. A Metro train of five carriages belched out from the tunnel, the middle one painted red and packed with military, the others a dirty green. We tried to move nearer Madame. Doors hissed and slid open. I was forced inside by the crowd. Standing room only – bodies pressed together in the aisle and some people had even squeezed into the leg space between wooden facing seats. What contrasting worlds: empty streets of fresh air and night-time, set against subterranean tunnels brimming with people cooped up under artificial light and all breathing in the same smell.

Two Wehrmacht *Feldwebels* stood in front of Harold near the door. The gentle whirring changed to a metallic rattle as the train picked up speed in the tunnel. Passengers moved with the swing or stared at their reflections in the dark windows. I held on to a handrail, trawling through events at the railway station. The Chief could have been anyone in a crowd waiting to greet family, friends or acquaintances. When he moved towards us, shook hands and spoke English, it was out of line with what I'd seen before. He had slipped away seamlessly enough, but what of Madame Blonde, tall with an elegant flash of clothes and poise? Madgett and Ward had soon followed her. Even in the abysmal light she was a head turner and more than a glance. With the tiny Madame Black not far away, the two women would have attracted a second look.

I caught a glimpse of Madame near the doors at the end of our carriage. Everyone towered above her. She made her move as the train drew into Republique when she was almost at kissing distance from a row of faces on the platform edge. The carriage spewed us into the waiting masses and Madame set off. It was difficult to keep sight of her, yet I had a sense she knew exactly where we were. Tides of people poured both ways along the subway: Luftwaffe and Wehrmacht personnel, men wearing trilby hats and overcoats, men in business suits, men with black berets, women with smart jackets and dresses leaving wafts of perfume as they passed. There might be safety amongst the numbers?

Republique was a white-tiled maze, with flights of steps leading up or down off its corridors. Trains rumbled in the background – an SS Officer stood under a light studying what looked like a hand-held map of the Metro. Madame seemed to be leading us on a guided tour. I began to think we were going around in circles until she walked under a low archway and we boarded a half-empty train with the military confined to one carriage.

Two stations later, I laboured up the steps of Gambetta to street level. Madame was crossing a deserted road junction. She led us around the block and returned to the same place before changing direction down a narrow street of tall apartment buildings. They were at least five floors high, although shadows and angles could be deceptive in the dark. We followed her into a building with a hallway and winding staircase. She turned the light out and I was last to feel my way up the stairway. Each floor had a small landing where I snatched a rest. Madame was still tapping lightly on a door when it opened. A grey-haired woman wearing a green dress and cream cardigan stood in an oblong of light, wiping her hands on her apron.

We walked into an unheated lounge with a high ceiling and floor-length curtains. The woman called it the salon. She ran a finger along a bureau near the door, glancing at her hand as she motioned us to some chairs. Her upright shoulders were at odds with a posture rounded by age, and her expression narrowed as she looked at us.

'Welcome, *Messieurs.*' The rest of her greeting faded into French.

I waited for a name. Madame Black searched her shopping bag, placing two cigarette packets on the bureau top. A younger woman in her early thirties entered the room. Brown hair curled under her ears, powder rouge cheeks and thin lips gave the face a formal, serious expression. A resemblance to the woman who had greeted us was obvious in her deportment and searching eyes.

'*Messieurs. Voulez-vous vous laver?*' She said something else. I didn't understand any of it.

We were shown to the washing and toilet facilities. Other doors along the short passageway were closed. I guessed they led to a kitchen and bedrooms. Before she left us, the younger woman explained with gestures and random English words there would be coffee soon. Harold grabbed his wash first but it was me who lingered at the sink, drawing a towel up to my wet face. I inhaled the fresh, linen smell, remembering sluicing off the grime at home after a day at the printing machine followed by two hours of night school.

Madame Black had left the apartment when we returned to the lounge. The grey-haired woman brought our drinks in cups with no handle. They looked more like breakfast bowls. She said nothing and left the room. Harold shivered in his jacket. The fireplace was closed off and no heat had reached this room for a long time. A woven scarlet and navy carpet covered most of the floor and we sat in two walnut-coloured armchairs, close to a small, circular side-table. The upholstery felt damp and the arms and fluted legs were moist to the touch. Several paint tins were lined up under the bureau. At least the ersatz coffee was hot.

I was used to the cold after standing for hours on bleak aerodromes and living in draughty Nissen huts. Arctic conditions froze the ablutions solid at Yatesbury Signals School, but things were different sitting here. Since leaving the policeman's house, a chill had slowly worked its way into my bones.

In the next room the younger woman spoke without pausing, all of it with the same nervy inflection. Her voice reminded me of Charlotte's, the only character I could recall from the film in Brussels.

'Something isn't right, Harold.' I shared my worries about the Chief and his two guides.

'Yeah. And how far do you think we'd have got without them?' he said, with a level expression on his face.

'I know that. But we're still trapped up here. It must be at least the fifth floor. What happens if there's a Gestapo raid? We need to check for another way out… just to be sure.'

He rested his cup on the chair arm. 'If we're staying here… then maybe? Only we ain't gonna last long on the streets.'

The conversation next door stopped as if the two women were listening. Things were complicated. I wished Denise was still around with his clear thinking.

Charlotte stopped on her way past the lounge. A key had turned in the lock at the front door. A slim, Italian-looking man in his thirties appeared wearing a brown working smock. He had a clipped cigarette behind one ear and showed no surprise when he saw us. Charlotte took his canvas workbag as he followed her in and greeted us with a *bonsoir*. Flecks of paint dotted his smock and trousers.

'Husband,' she said.

He would be the Painter unless I discovered his name.

A young child's cries came from further down the passage. Charlotte whispered to her husband as he left the room. She led us to a cramped kitchen where the grey-haired woman stood with her back to us at a cooker. Four cane dining chairs were jammed under a table below a set of wall cupboards. In the corner a stove burned faintly near a bucket of wood shavings. A makeshift pipe had been tacked along the wall from the stove to a window covered by blackout material.

This room had a trace of heat. A watery smell of cooking rose from a steaming pan and condensation glistened on the wall. Household clutter filled every available space; the family clearly lived in here. Charlotte asked us to sit and we squeezed past the grey-haired woman. I removed my raincoat, hanging it on the back of the chair just as a shadow filled the doorway. The Painter was standing beside Charlotte with a child in his arms, a boy of around twelve months wearing a woollen bonnet and layers of knitted clothes. He whispered into the child's ear, rocking him gently. Charlotte smiled and kissed them both. The remaining family script lay in their faces: a scene played out every day in the world and a comfort from the misery of occupation and danger.

The knocking sounded after the Painter had handed over the child to Charlotte and exited the kitchen. I looked to the grey-haired woman. Her voice was a whisper, her eyes large and round. Taps came again on the front door – slower, quieter. The Painter called out. Charlotte hugged the child closer to her shoulder and went into the passage. Madame Black arrived at the kitchen doorway with two men. From the startled expression on the grey-haired woman's face, they were not expected.

It was Tennessee and Sergeant Watt.

179

2

'You guys were at the farmhouse,' Tennessee said.

'And at the other place,' Sergeant Watt said, absently.

Madame Black left. The Americans ducked under the wall cupboards to sit opposite us at the table. Behind me, the grey-haired woman barely had enough space to stand at her cooker. Until I had a name, I would address her as Madame and remember her as Joseline.

The muted hellos stopped as Sergeant Watt and Tennessee wriggled out of their coats. Joseline greeted them and Watt answered in French. A hush fell over the kitchen. The relentless, metallic stir continued from the stove behind me, which was a replay of sitting in Madame Jeanette's kitchen in Antwerp. I found myself glancing around to hide my embarrassment. How awkward, ill-mannered and ungrateful to wait for a meal in that way but what else could we do? None of us dared say anything within her earshot, beyond the pleasantries. This damn war – and I still hadn't a clue whether there was another way out from the apartment. At least if Joseline left the kitchen, it wouldn't be long before Tennessee started a conversation.

Our meal was small portions of green beans, potato cubes and stock. The bread slices were grey-brown with a hard crust and moist centre. The same rotten sensation as before flooded through me. This family might have given up their food for us. It wasn't a thought I cared to share with the others yet. After Joseline left us to get on with our meals, we introduced ourselves properly. Tennessee was simply 'Tennessee' and Sergeant Watt remained exactly as that. Watt shook my hand warmly yet I felt the same distance from him as I did with Harold. Both men were aged about thirty and I was just a young English lad.

'The old woman wasn't happy when we got here. Pick up anything?' Tennessee said, with a brief glance to Watt.

'Not much. Some kinda problem. She said something about an uncle a coupla times.'

He changed the subject. Harold joined in their conversations, mostly in reply to questions and always with the same, single-paced delivery. I slipped easily into the background. It was a diversion to listen in on any kind of casual chat in English. Tennessee talked between and during mouthfuls, waving his fork to make a point. He had a myriad of words and phrases I'd not heard before. *Big as hell and half of Texas it was* and *yes sir, enough to make that freight train head straight off down a dirt road.* I never worked out what *a Monday morning quarterback* was. From the way the two men spoke I guessed he was in the same crew as Watt. Despite the American embellishments and drawl, I liked Tennessee. In that interval, he gave me something different to focus on, although behind his bright, young exterior there was another side. I saw it in the few pauses he made, when something serious crept into that face. He was a man with the weight of experiences on his shoulders. I thought about the last time I saw my own gaunt reflection in a mirror and knew I could never be like Tennessee.

'So what happened to you chaps at Lille?' I'd waited a while to ask my question.

Watt dammed his food up on one side of the plate. 'Guide took us somewhere. Paris train wasn't until fourteen hundred.'

He looked up. I said nothing about my visit to Étienne's.

'We were on that train,' Harold said suddenly. 'See anybody else?'

'Coupla guys who crossed the border with us,' Watt said.

Tennessee clattered his fork down. 'Yeah, Mills and that English guy, Johnnie.'

He gestured in Watt's direction. 'Guide took me and the sergeant to some place a few blocks from Gare du Nord station. Mills and Johnnie were there.'

He broke off a piece of bread, dropping it in the stock on his plate. 'Met a man who said he was the Chief. A tall, peroxide blonde was with him. The little woman in black came for us and we followed her to a subway. Got off four blocks from this place and she brought us here. That's pretty much it.'

Some things didn't fit: the enigmatic Chief, his conspicuous guides at the station, Joseline's shocked expression when the Americans arrived and the small portions on our plates from a meal that was meant for two people not four. It had been bolstered up with bread.

'That little woman was waiting for us at the station,' I said. 'The blonde was there as well. Those two RAF chaps who sat near me at the policeman's house followed her out.'

Nobody responded.

'This Chief,' I said. 'Can you describe him?'

Tennessee shrugged and picked up his fork again.

'About forty to forty-five. Light hair and a moustache.'

'Why the interest?' Watt said.

'I think it's the same man who met us at the station. I've told Harold some things about him and there's more.'

The Americans looked at one another.

I took a moment. 'A chap in Belgium warned me about a traitor who gets into the Resistance and escape groups.'

My voice cracked into dry coughs. '… He's Belgian, calls himself the captain or the chief or something. Some other names too… I can't remember them. Follow him and he leads you straight to the Germans.'

Tennessee interrupted. 'So what's this guy look like?'

'He's supposed to be about five-eight, with brown eyes. The hair is brown too, though sometimes it might be grey. He often has a moustache and speaks good English with an American or Canadian accent.'

Watt blinked. He moved about on his chair. 'Is he thin… fat, stocky?'

'I don't know.' I could feel his stare growing. 'Didn't ask. It was early days, my head was full of other things. A description of him is supposed to be in the underground newspapers. The chap who tipped me off reckoned he had a photo but his friend had borrowed it. The Resistance are certain he keeps altering his appearance. They're trying to track him down, but he's well protected by the Germans, does the damage and disappears.'

Watt dropped his gaze. 'What makes you think he's in Paris?'

'Nothing definite, I was just told to watch out for him. The man's very convincing. They reckoned he might be in Brussels. I don't think they knew where he was because he moves around so much.'

I told them about the missing part of his right little finger. 'Did you notice anything about the man you met at that place near the station?'

'It was pretty dark,' Watt said, deliberately. 'We went up a lotta concrete steps and past some big pillars to get in. Sometimes our guy spoke like an American. He had a moustache for sure. Told us he'd lived in Texas.'

He looked at Tennessee. 'Did you see anything?'

'Lot of gold teeth.'

I tried to curb the edge in my voice. 'Did you shake his hand?'

'Yeah. Didn't look at it though,' Tennessee said.

'So he wasn't wearing gloves?'

'Can't remember. But I'm a Texas boy and yes sir this guy had lived there for sure.'

I parked my cutlery on the plate.

'You heard what we were told at the policeman's house about the dangers and surveillance. That station was crowded and there wasn't much light, but the man who met us didn't seem bothered about moving around in full view, speaking English and shaking hands. The little woman in black was barely four and a half feet, and the tall blonde wore posh clothes and probably jewellery. They must have waited at that station more than once and I'll bet the place where you met them has been used before. If the French didn't notice, then surely the Germans have. I've seen enough to worry about all of this.'

Watt rested his elbows on the table, hands together as if in prayer. The kitchen door opened. Joseline waited with a man at her shoulder.

It was the Chief I'd met at the station.

3

The Chief looked different in the sallow light: a thick moustache with fair to blonde hair brushed back high over his forehead. I'd seen Victorian photographs of men like him in long aprons, standing in front of shops.

'Gentlemen, my apologies for the late arrival, please continue with your meals.'

He sidled behind me to stand against the cooker. The others sat stony-faced. I hitched the chair around so I could face him.

'You will have given this information before but I'm afraid I must ask for it again.' He took out a pencil and a small, folded piece of paper. 'Your name, rank and number please.'

Both little fingers were intact. Only then did I unfold my arms, as they had stopped shaking. The next few minutes were a fog. The Americans gave their details with no hesitation. I held back. The Chief scribbled away, the paper resting awkwardly in the palm of his hand. It was dark at the railway station; how had he recognised any of us? Maybe my newspaper was enough? I didn't see Ward or Madgett carrying anything. It must have been a signal from their guides, or did we all appear that obvious in a crowd? I started coughing again.

'We will find something to help your chest,' the Chief said. 'Medicine is difficult to buy, so it may not be tomorrow.'

I thanked him and gave my details. They were only what I would have revealed if I got put in the bag. He slipped the paper and pencil inside his coat.

'Please take off your shoes when you are in this apartment and do not pull the toilet chain. Before I leave, is there anything more you need, gentlemen?'

I ran a finger over my sandpaper face and chin. 'I don't have a razor. It was taken from me.'

Such a mundane request felt out of kilter after the string of events and doubts over the last few hours.

He smiled. 'We will get you a razor.'

I was certain Harold could do with an overcoat. He said nothing. The Chief stopped in the kitchen doorway.

'Sergeant Johnson. Please eat with your knife and fork. Cutting up food and then eating only with the fork is dangerous. It isn't the French way. Thank you.'

He quietly closed the door behind him and we were left looking at one another. More doors shutting, voices and then footfall – every sound echoed and spiralled up from the floors below. A heavy quiet settled again. I'd heard no noise from the family after the Chief arrived at the kitchen door with Joseline.

'Not your traitor guy then?' Watt said to me in a calm and level voice.

'No sergeant. Not my guy.'

He nodded slowly, as if passing judgement. The weak kitchen light shadowed his face, hollowing the cheekbones and dark crescents under his eyes. I couldn't stop thinking about the family we were staying with. Charlotte, her husband and son would be shivering in another room, and what of Joseline? Was a part of our meal meant for them? Best not mention any of this, I'd said enough already. My thoughts moved to Bob Clements. Chances were he caught the same train as us at Lille. He seemed a distant face now. This was how things would be. Apart from Ken, my navigator, the only person I'd formed any sort of bond with was Denise. The others were allies and nothing more. There were too many shackles and complications for men to forge closer ties in this kind of adversity.

Joseline came into the kitchen, took away our plates and placed an ashtray, matchbox and cigarette packet on the table. Sergeant Watt spoke to her in French again. Their conversation stuttered as she busied herself at the sink. Harold struck a match and Tennessee bent forward for a light. Smoke fogged around them as Charlotte returned, avoiding eye contact with everyone except her mother who passed her three cups and a child's bottle on a tray. Both women left after Joseline had served us coffee.

'So what did she say to you?' Tennessee said, as soon as the kitchen door clicked shut.

Watt put down his unlit cigarette.

'They've had no fuel to heat the apartment blocks for almost three years. There's electric and gas in the evening, just enough for cooking. Most places have put a stove in somewhere, but getting wood is pretty impossible. The woman apologised because she has to go out early every day to join queues for food. There's some kinda black market though.'

Tennessee drew on his cigarette. 'She say anything else?'

'Not after the younger woman came in. I'm sure she's the daughter.'

'So what happens next?'

'It's getting late. I guess we'll find out soon enough.'

The Painter's voice came from somewhere deep in the apartment. I took a tentative sip of my drink. Joseline and Madame Black squeezed into the room. They looked like a deputation.

'*Photo d'identité,*' Joseline said, looking to Sergeant Watt and Tennessee.

Madame Black gave a nervous smile. 'Follow please. The photographs. Then we return.' Her English came with a pronounced French accent, the first time I'd heard her voice outside of whispers. She glanced at Joseline and then Tennessee.

'Boys. The smoking… it is not correct.'

She demonstrated how we must hold a cigarette between our thumb and index finger.

'Guess we'd better go,' Watt said, unravelling his legs from under the table. 'Let's move. We'll see you guys later.'

He forced himself into a stooped position to miss the cupboards above his head. Tennessee struggled past behind me and joined him in the passage with Madame Black. They left without another word or glance behind. The glow in the stove had almost died but my shivering was not from the cold. It came with a worry I might not see the two Americans again.

4

Harold spoke after a long hush. 'Ain't it kinda late to be getting their pictures taken?'

A wave of fatigue washed through me. My eyelids felt heavy. 'Can't be curfew yet?'

'Won't be any stores open,' he said. 'They must be going to someone's place.' He was looking suspiciously around the kitchen. 'Don't know the time. Have you seen a clock anywhere, Ron?'

'No. But we've only been in here and the next room.'

'Still think it's strange,' he said. 'I've stayed in a lot of these places and there's always a clock. Nobody wears watches.'

'A chap I stayed with in Brussels wore a wristwatch. The man who introduced us at Brussels station had one too.'

No response came. I seized the moment. 'Nothing's changed. The Chief isn't the man I was warned about and these brave, kind people are most likely exactly that, but there are bigger things which still don't feel right. So do we find another way out of here, just in case?'

'We'll do it tomorrow. But we still don't know the goddam time, do we?'

I produced the watch from my raincoat hanging on the back of the chair.

'It's just after ten.'

He stared at it. 'How the hell did you manage to hang on to that?'

'Hid it in my coat. Knew it was risky, but it was something from home, the last thing to hold on to, I guess. Kept telling myself, as long as I kept it I might just make it back.'

His surprised look disappeared. 'You're a dark horse. They took mine the next day, lost a lot of military kit when I landed. Darned nearly broke my back when the chute opened, then folks were running to the landing place. Hit the deck pretty hard and rolled over. Girls started bundling up the silk before I could unhook my chute. Mae West and helmet got grabbed by another guy. A boy pointed to timber nearby. I near on ran with him to a hedge then stumbled and fell. He pulled off my flying boots and threw them in there. Then this other guy picked them up and walked away.'

His gaze moved slowly around the kitchen.

'Next day, the guy I stayed with took the rest of my military, except the shoes. I was still wearing those. Three old timers got me some pants and a coat. I left the overalls behind with the guy. He kept my leather jacket and burned the other clothes.'

Harold had opened up and caught me by surprise. I pictured him baling out in daylight. Then the darkness and flashes caved in around me again, pressing against my forehead like cold, sharp fingers. Flak bursts, a sickly smell of cordite as I swung about in the icy night air, then the terror – the rigid, paralysing terror of hot shrapnel setting fire to my parachute.

'You OK?' He pushed the cigarette packet across the table. 'Smoke?'

'No thanks, it starts me coughing again.'

I mentioned how I'd still been walking around in my uniform the day after landing and how the shoes I was given had barely fitted. He listened with the same unreadable mask on his face and when I'd finished, he rose to open the kitchen door.

'I'll smoke this out there,' he said.

Joseline returned to the kitchen just before ten-thirty with the tray and cups Charlotte had carried out earlier. We soon understood it was time to retire for the night. Harold left with Joseline first. Watt and Tennessee hadn't returned when she came back for me. A racket of thoughts raced through my head as we entered the lounge. I'd brought my raincoat for extra warmth in anticipation – would it be a camp bed or the chair?

The section of wall at the end of the chimney breast had been pulled open. A small bed with a blanket and top sheet filled the space inside. A white towel hung on the hook screwed into an interior wooden framework supporting the plasterboard. I was still staring at it when Joseline left the lounge door ajar and switched out the light. A glow from the passage was enough for me to climb into bed and pull the raincoat around my shoulders.

Exhaustion rolled me up like a rug, yet my mind circled around the edge of sleep. Somewhere in the void I heard a tangle of voices from the passage. Watt and Tennessee must have returned. Noise stopped once the passage light went out. A hiss from the toilet cistern faded and the night drew in around me.

I woke pressed up tight against the wall. Someone was gently raking the stove in the kitchen. I turned over and manoeuvred to the end of the bed. Light sneaked through the open lounge door, making shadows on the furniture. The cold was interminable with my every breath visible. It was well after nine o'clock. I bent down to find my shoes then remembered what the Chief had said about not wearing them. My trousers looked like I'd slept in them: I had. I walked slowly towards the lounge door, slipping on my jacket. A razor lay on the bureau top and a stale cooking smell from the previous evening lingered in the empty passage. Harold appeared at the end of the corridor with a towel.

'Have you seen Tennessee and Sergeant Watt?' I whispered.

'They've gone.'

'Gone? I thought I heard them come back last night?'

He joined me at the lounge door. 'They left before it got light. It could have been that Chief and the little woman with them.'

He spoke as if it was some throwaway remark.

'So what's with that?' he said, gazing at the open false wall in the lounge.

'You can't see much from here but there's a hidden space behind it and a bed. Where did you sleep?'

'A room down the passage. It's two rooms now, if you get what I mean. This place is full of twists and turns. I bunked down inside a gap near the floor. It was like climbing in the bottom of a dresser.'

The child started grizzling. Charlotte's voice came from the kitchen.

'I best get rid of this,' Harold said, glancing at his towel. He wandered back towards his room.

Charlotte appeared, framed in the kitchen doorway, rocking the child in her arms. The day looked dreary through lace curtains behind her.

'*Bonjour,*' she said, showing me to the table.

The stove was unlit. I guessed Joseline might have left early to join the food queues. Harold came in buttoning his reefer jacket and sat down opposite me under the cupboards.

We didn't get any breakfast, only bowls of the acorn coffee, or was it chicory? Charlotte's footsteps faded down the passage and the child's murmuring stopped. Harold blew into his cupped hands. He remained unflappable with that sit back, say little and do nothing indifference. In the gloomy morning light I searched for something behind his gaze but it never settled on anything for long. Was that just simple detachment or an action preventing him from thinking too far into the future? The last dregs in my cup disappeared, but the bitter taste stayed around the roof of my mouth.

I made straight for the window. Beyond the lace curtains, the backs of apartments tapered away in a long row: six storeys, a single sloping roof and unfinished grey plaster walls with stove pipes jutting out at obscure angles from the windows. We were on the fifth floor of this block. Down in the courtyard I saw no sign of a fire escape or metal staircase.

The front door slammed. Joseline bustled into the kitchen with her shopping bag.

'No talking. *Quelqu'un…* someone visits.' She urged us out along the passage with a stream of French words clipping our ears. Charlotte began to close all the doors.

'My apologies for this,' Joseline said. She shut us in a bedroom. Harold stood with his ear pressed against the door. I pitched my voice at a whisper.

'There's only one way out of this apartment.'

The two reflections in the dresser mirror didn't move. The first one sat perched at the end of an iron bedstead, shoulders hunched and hands in his trouser pockets. The other was some way behind him in a wicker chair next to the bedhead. Both strained to hear the deep voice coming from the kitchen, and both knew that neither understood any of its monotone words. Only the sound mattered. While the voice stayed, the reflections in the mirror would have to remain still and silent in the bedroom, fighting the shivers, listening to their own breathing. They wanted the voice to stop – they wanted the front door to open and close – they wanted to get out of that room.

Harold stared at the crucifix above the bed and shifted in his chair. We had both discovered how to fidget without making a noise. He tapped his wrist. Chatter droned in the kitchen. I took out my watch and held the face up to him. More than half an hour had passed. Maybe the fog between us might finally start to lift. He had distanced himself from so many things, yet underneath there was another man, a brave one from the little I had learned from him after leaving the policeman's house. For a while, Tennessee had broken through that deadpan expression and quiet. Harold had started to speak more although I learned nothing about Harold the man. I might never get to know him. That might be too much to expect, as it was with the rest of the escapers. I'd hardly been forthcoming myself. Before we left the bedroom, maybe some of the barriers between us might vanish into the smell of damp linen and mothballs.

Another twenty minutes passed before Charlotte let us out and we followed her to the kitchen. When she left, Joseline pulled up a chair next to me.

'*Messieurs*… please. This *après midi* you walk.'

'Are we leaving?' I asked.

'*Non.*'

She tried to explain. All three of us stumbled over our words. The conversation circled for another attempt at landing. We would be accompanied separately today for exercise. I couldn't understand the rest of it. One thing I had discovered was whatever my worries were around the Chief, his associates or the apartment, I'd begun to warm to this family.

Joseline excused herself. I heard the front door close again. The world inside a safe house would always revolve around every noise and small sounds of life. Worries crowded in again. The walk was a sign our departure must be close. Getting into Spain meant crossing the Pyrenees. Harold was ready, yet I'd struggled to climb the stairs the previous evening. The enormity of a mountain journey dwarfed any other dangers.

Harold stayed inside the apartment. The Painter checked up and down the winding staircase before easing the door shut. The landing fell into near blackness. I groped my way down the stairs, finger-tipping the rough plaster. Our tread on the stone steps echoed around the walls. Comings and goings were easy to clock.

The double entrance doors were open and dusty daylight streamed into the hallway. Two women stood talking in the street and spoke to the Painter as we passed. The afternoon sky was a still, winter grey and apartments lined the street on both sides much as I had imagined them from their dark shells the night before. The grimy white façades came from a classical Paris seen on film, some with false balustrade balconies supported by plaster corbels and fronted in black sea-scroll metalwork. Attic dormer windows were prominent at regular intervals along the stretches of sloping roofs.

I crossed the same junction at the end of the street as the previous evening. Roads converged on it like spokes to the centre of a wheel. The Painter kept to wide avenues and boulevards and made no detours or double-backs; maybe we had less chance of being stopped on the main routes or trapped by a roadblock. A couple of trucks and cars were parked, other vehicles had the road to themselves, except for a horse and cart, bicycles and a strange covered contraption half the size of a rickshaw which carried a single passenger towed by a cyclist.

Shops were open, some with sparse window displays and queues outside. Pavements bustled, cafés looked busy and soldiers were impervious to the crowds. People milled around a newspaper kiosk. Nazi posters and official notices in bold, black lettering were sandwiched on boards and walls between coloured bills advertising Paris entertainment. Along the main streets, this city had adapted to occupation.

We walked along a boulevard lined with bare trees. The fresh air smelt good and I took longer strides until coughing fits returned. The Painter steamed on until we broke out onto a bridge spanning the River Seine. My black and white pictures of Paris became reality in full colour. Despite everything it was a special moment. The Painter stopped short of the middle span. We leaned on the white stone balustrade, looking across the water. I hadn't a clue what he was saying to me and didn't notice a figure approaching, or see the hand which gripped my arm.

The whisper came close to my ear.

'Stay where you are and please do exactly as I say.'

The Lewis crew, ground crew and driver RAF 44 (Rhodesia) Squadron in June 1943 at Dunholme Lodge before the crew transferred to RAAF 467 Squadron, Bottesford after Lewis was promoted to Squadron Leader. The nose art is a beer glass tipping bombs with the accompanying text 'Good Health Then'. Pictured L to R: Stead, Mallin, Bayliss, the driver, Scott, Garvey, ground crew, Lewis, ground crew, Morley and 3 ground crew. (Author)

L to R: Mallin (hidden), Garvey, Lewis, Scott, Bayliss, Morley and exiting aircraft, Stead. (Author)

Morley before his transfer to RAAF Bottesford. (Author)

'Steff's house in Oevel. (Author)

Blacksmith's house in Oevel, now a café.
(Author)

Above: 'Maurice's house in Voortkapel.
(Author)

Right: 'Denise' after joining the British
Army in 1944. (Author)

II

Staf, Denis & Ron 1986.
(Author)

Sasse Bridge – the bluff past the guards. (Author)

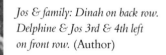

Jos & family: Dinah on back row. Delphine & Jos 3rd & 4th left on front row. (Author)

Jos's house in Achter Olen.
(Author)

'Lily' in England after her escape.
(H Hanotte)

Mlle Helene's apartment in Brussels.
(V Schutters)

*Tram terminus in Brussels where new
identity documents were given.* (Author)

Maca's apartment in Brussels.
(V Schutters)

Rumes Rail Station. (H Hanotte)

'Lucie's' farmhouse at Sartaigne nr Rumes. (Author)

Henriette Hanotte k/a 'Monique' ('small girl with her hair in a bob cut') and Amanda Stassart k/a 'Dianne' ('the girl no more than 18') who escorted Morley across the border in to France. Pictured in Brussels with the author in 2011. (Author)

'Lucie' extreme left standing next to her sister Nellie who was not seen by Morley the night he was at the farmhouse. (H Hanotte)

'Bernard' (H Hanotte)

'The Policeman' & 'Rachel'. (H Hanotte)

'The Policeman's' house in Bachy. (Author)

Café Larre outside Bayonne where the evaders hid and the Germans arrived. (C Padgham 2009)

Mandochineko borda where the evaders waited with 'François' for the Basque guides. (C Padgham 2009)

VI

R Morley   *R Clements*   *K Garvey*   *H Pope*

G Madgett   *G Ward*   *G Watt*   *T Johnson*

J Harkins   *D Mills*   *E Johnson*   *H Neuman*

J Kennedy   *C Passy*

Photos on false identity cards: R Morley (Author) *All other images* (Comete Archive)

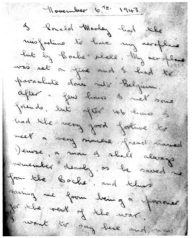
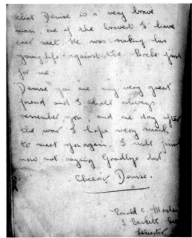

Morley's note to 'Denise' Pages 1 and 2.
(D Vanoystaeyen)

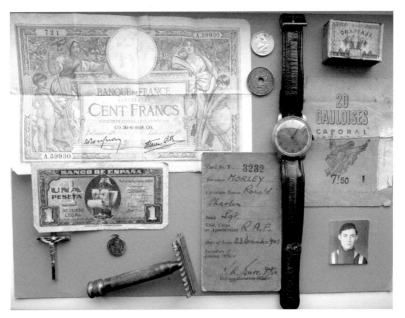

Morley's Items
L to R: French 100 Francs, Belgian and French coins, RAF Watch, Belgian matchbox,
Gauloises cigarette packet, Spanish Peseta, Gibraltar temporary ID, misc. photograph for
ID, Belgian crucifix, Belgian pendant and razor from the British embassy in Madrid.
(Author)

5

The man pushed closer behind me. 'I will ask you some questions.'

My stomach caved in. The voice was cold, matter of fact and distant, as if rising from the waters below.

'What is PT?'

I tried to turn but the figure was too close.

'PT – what is this?'

It sounded like the Chief. I couldn't be certain. The black glove moved down my arm and released its grip.

I gulped in cold air. 'It's physical training. Did it at school, did it in the Forces. Shorts and singlet... exercises swinging your arms. We—'

'Stop. We have company.'

The voice became fluent in French, an arm outstretched moving with the river flow, a finger tracing and pointing as if highlighting some distant landmark. Footfall sounded on the bridge before I heard the men's chatter. Steady steps at first, one set heavier than the other. Boots and German words, sharp against the droning voice at my shoulder. The men's conversation passed by. A few paces from me, the Painter stared down at the grey river washing under the bridge. After a long pause the voice spoke again.

'Now tell me about the jankers, please.'

'I've never done it. You get confined to camp, put on a charge for a breach of discipline. You have to do punishment jobs. Anything worse and you get put in the glasshouse.'

A flock of birds skimmed low over the river.

'What is a wingco?'

I stared down at the water. 'A wingco? He's a wing commander.'

'Thank you. We must be certain who you are... there have been arrests. Now please return with your guide to the apartment. Good afternoon.'

I turned around, but the voice was striding away, grey overcoat flapping in a sudden breeze off the river.

The Painter avoided my gaze. He knew exactly what he was doing in bringing me to this place and that solitary thought blew straight through like an east wind. I felt adrift again with the same rubbery sensation in my legs as standing all night on Home Guard duty then having to leave straight away for work. The Painter handed me a green Metro ticket. He had neared the end of the bridge before I finally took off after him.

A strange car with a line of cylindrical tanks on its roof rattled past in a pall of sulphur smoke. Harold would get the same interrogation, for certain. It was not the right moment to think about that or mull over anything except keeping the Painter in sight on our weary drag back to the apartment. He looked in no rush and disappeared down a flight of steps where people were ascending onto the street. Against all the rules, I began to hurry.

Crowds streamed past me in the Metro subway from the opposite direction. The Painter had vanished around a long bend when I blundered into an oncoming figure.

'Oh, sorry.'

A startled face stared at me from below a Wehrmacht forage cap. I tottered past the soldier, tried to catch my balance, expecting a command to halt and the shrill of a whistle. The shapeless masses pouring both ways became a godsend. I walked on through a blur of people and noise, instincts steering me to the blind side near a subway wall. People ahead were indistinguishable except for their footsteps keeping time with my own. The Painter waited, studying the faces as they passed under a light. Did he see what had happened? Should I try to make him understand when it was safe to talk? He moved away in the direction of a ticket checker. Events on the bridge flashed through my head. I would say nothing.

We changed trains numerous times. Some stations were closed and their platforms stacked with crates and boxes. The Painter's face remained solemn. When crowds thinned, he ignored vacant seats, held on to a rail and made no move to leave at Gambetta. We slipped out at the next station, a look cast in my direction being enough of a signal for me to move. He must have seen what had happened in the Metro.

Evening pushed away the afternoon. Sundry autumn leaves dotted the pavements and I crowded deeper into my raincoat as we reached Rue du Cher. The street was deserted, apartment buildings blank and cold against the last of a wintry day. The Painter disappeared into number seven. I hurried inside and took a moment to rest on the first landing as he climbed the winding stairs. *You were careless and very lucky.* Dad's voice came through the dark in a tone he always kept for matters dealt with after the evening meal. He was right. It made no difference that the crowds had saved me or the soldier didn't recognise English – I should have paid for it. The last few hours had changed things and I was uncertain now what to expect in the apartment. At least if Harold had received the same grilling, I might have an ally. When I reached the final flight of steps, the Painter waited at the top urging me on with exaggerated waves. Light from the open door and the gargle of a gramophone inside made his actions appear almost music hall. I gave in to the nervous smile on the edge of my lips.

He went inside. The music stopped. Charlotte led me into the kitchen lit by a glow from the stove. Harold was absent. She placed a kettle on the range. The matchbox and a fresh packet of cigarettes lay near the ashtray on the table. I didn't want a smoke but couldn't sit still. Working my way through a cigarette and not inhaling was an option. She switched on the light, slid out a board from under the sink and fitted it into the window space before closing the curtains.

'Excuse me, Madame.'

She turned around from the range. I held up the brown packet of Gauloises.

'May I?'

'*Oui. Certainement.*'

Charlotte appeared normal, whatever that was. After Chamberlain's broadcast, *normal* became an abstract word. If conversations at home mentioned 'we used to' or 'before the war,' they didn't go much further. I was steeling myself to face the Painter again when he shouted to Charlotte from down the passage.

For a while, I stood alone against the stove with a lit cigarette. A tepid heat had reached the metal by the time Harold brought in the cold from outside and slumped onto the seat opposite. I pushed the cigarettes to the middle of the table.

'So what happened to you?'

He gave me a wary look. 'You go first.'

My walk to the Seine and events at the bridge came out slowly and carefully, with no mention of the journey back. He lit a cigarette, taking in two long draws.

'I walked with the old woman to a park about six blocks away. Nice place with trees and paths... a lake too.'

Smoke rose in wispy trails between us.

'When there's nobody around, this guy comes out from nowhere and starts walking behind me.' He placed his hands almost together. 'Real close, like this, see. Tells me I gotta look straight ahead and keep going. Starts asking questions.'

'What, the same sort of things as me?'

'Yeah. Flyboy stuff like ETO, CQ and what's a blanket drill? Then I'm waiting for his next shot and he's gone. Didn't see where he went.'

'Where was Madame?'

'Walking on ahead.'

I noticed him glance at the stove, massaging his sleeves as if trying to squeeze out the chill. He pushed the cigarette back into his mouth.

'That big shot who grilled you is the guy from the park and the same one who came here. Couldn't see his face but the voice is right. Yep, I'm certain that he met Tennessee and his buddy before we saw them last night.'

He gave me a disapproving look. 'And he ain't that captain you were talking about either.'

'But he might have been. I had to say something, too many things were wrong. Surely you can see that. And Sergeant Watt told us he'd heard Madame saying there was a problem.'

I tried to hold his stare. 'The chap on the bridge said there had been arrests. Did he tell you that? No, I'll bet he didn't. We're all still in danger up here, but as you've said before, we should just let them get on with it.'

My words had tailed off into sarcasm.

'But you don't, buddy. You don't let them get on with it.' A twisted smile played about his mouth. He leaned nearer to me. 'You ask too many goddam questions and you think too many things. What kind of escape drill did you guys get? When you're in with the Resistance, you do as they say.'

'They told us the same. Except, somebody said to go it alone if you were stuck more than a week in one place. I didn't take much notice. Wasn't going to finish up like this, was I?'

I tried to continue but he waved his arms across each other. 'No. You hear me out. Sitting there all bug eyed, I'm gonna give you a last piece of advice. Stop beating yourself up with stuff you can do nothing about, or you'll mess this whole thing up.'

He set his fingers together in a steeple. 'Neither of us speaks the lingo. Goddam it, we can't even ask for a train ticket.'

'I don't know what happened to you, Harold, but I went through some near misses getting here. After I landed, there was one thing in my head. Go to a farmhouse and get help.' I took a drag and blew the smoke straight out. 'I had this picture of travelling through the countryside at night with blokes in berets carrying sub machine guns. It's nothing like that. And there's this constant thing banging inside my head.'

I placed my cigarette on the ashtray. 'We never know anything about what's happening or what's coming next, until the last minute. I understand the reasons why but it still eats away inside me.'

I went silent for a while, stiff and bristling. Harold sat back in his chair, fingers laced behind his head.

'Well, I reckon it's time to ask the last question,' he said. 'When can I get a darned thicker coat?'

Joseline walked in with a scowl on her face. 'Boys... stop this now.'

She banged a pack of cards down between us and left. The rasp of a hard broom came from the apartment below. Sound carried through this building: two men arguing in English, it was unthinkable. I looked away first. Part of me wanted to brazen it out with Harold – the rest knew the right thing to do. Instinct and stupidity often went hand in hand. Despite my worries around our situation, conflict between us would never happen again. Harold was a realist and he was right this time. However vulnerable we were by staying here, we had no choice. Our chances of reaching Gibraltar without organised help were almost non-existent.

Harold peered over the fan of cards in front of his face. We had settled on playing Rummy. Hardly a word had been spoken. It was the only cards both of us knew and an easy route to avoid conversation. Strange, how the gap between us could be shored up for a while by playing a simple game. Against the bubble and steam from saucepans on the range, I kept a vague score in my head, placing and picking up cards with little thought. They were different to home: the Ace with a numeric figure one, Kings showing the letter *R*, Queens *D* and Jacks a *V*. Card games were supposed to be an opening for easy conversation, a neutral ground for small talk, jokes and male camaraderie. At home they filled our family parties and get-togethers. I stared at the table, thinking about my relatives and what they were going through.

Thoughts slid back to training at RAF Sutton Bridge. Radio parts lay scattered on the table when the order had arrived for me to report urgently to the Signals Room. A tall officer held up a note.

'Your mother has been in contact. I'm afraid your father is

seriously ill and taken a turn for the worst. I'll arrange a pass for you to go home immediately on compassionate leave.'

I chain-smoked the hours away, powerless to reach home quicker as the train rattled through the countryside. Dread rose inside me with every step away from the railway station. Through the tram window, afternoon life went on, indifferent and detached. The single thought in my head was turning the final street corner and seeing my home with all the curtains shut.

They were open. Doctor McKay was shutting the front door. He waited for me on the path.

'You made it, then.' He lowered his voice. 'I'm sorry. It's advanced pneumonia. I'll call in tomorrow morning, but he might not last the night.'

As soon as my key turned in the lock, I could hear the death-rattle breathing from upstairs.

I existed on the edge for days, yet there had been something tangible in a physical presence upstairs lying between life and death. All my parents would have now was a CO's letter to go with the telegram reporting me missing after operations. Did Mum's tears fall on the bedroom lino as mine had when I swept the floor around Dad's sick bed? If they did, she would have made sure no one saw them. Dad was a survivor too. Wounded and gassed twice in Belgium, he came through again. It would take more than the Germans and events in a Paris apartment to stop me doing the same.

The evening meal was potatoes with stewed beans. The Painter sat with us to eat. He was all smiles, quirky expressions and French. Joseline and Charlotte left the apartment and took the child with them. The Painter had stayed behind to keep an eye on us, of that I was sure. After what happened earlier I could hardly blame him. More unsettling was where the rest of the family went. When they returned after an hour, Harold excused himself and I soon retired for the night, relieved to retreat into the secret annexe and my own space.

I left the lounge door open enough to let in light from the passage. For the first time in weeks my aching muscles and bones felt down to nothing more than physical effort. Tomorrow was another day. That expression carried old-fashioned British stoicism, but somehow it didn't fit anymore. So many things would have to change during the next twenty-four hours. I lay in bed listening to the family slowly shutting down for the night. Joseline's clunky shoes were the last to pass the lounge. The passage light went out, a key rattled in the front door and her footsteps faded down the stairs.

6

The tread of marching feet worked its way into my sleep. I woke with a start, heart racing. Soldiers were outside, large numbers and closing in. I rushed out of bed, flinging open the door. At the end of the passage Harold stood silhouetted in the early light. Charlotte came out from the kitchen. She must have seen the look on my face.

'*Les soldats. D'accord…* it is alright. *Toujours* they march and they go.'

She pointed in the rough direction of Rue Belgrand. It was at the end of Rue du Cher – I knew that from my walk with the Painter. We got a reassuring nod and she returned to the kitchen. The marching songs came in eerie drifts over the tramp of jackboots. There was discipline in those voices, steel in the steps, but no soul in their singing. The icy passage floor struck up through my socks, Harold stepped back into his room and I returned to the refuge of my hidden space. The morning heartbeat started in the building. Noises rose from the street and I began to sift through the last twenty-four hours and my own dark imaginings.

It was well into afternoon when I decided to visit the kitchen and brave the room's cold embrace. Joseline was raking the stove. She had been in and out of the apartment all day.

'*Il y a une coupure de courant,*' she said, without turning around. '*Il n'y a pas d'*électricité.'

We had no electricity. The area often suffered power cuts during the day. Harold arrived and glasses of water came with our bread rolls. We played some tentative hands of cards until the light faded and both of us retreated to the darkness in our own rooms. About an hour later the passage light came on of its own accord and a thick aroma of cooking soon reached my room.

Later that evening Joseline took us down to the ground floor hallway and a door near the stairs. Harold held on to the pack of cards and she led the way into an apartment. A tall pair of steps leaned against the wall next to paint tins, a wooden box of brushes and decorating equipment. We were invited into a well-furnished room, lit from a central shade above the dining table. An elderly man, muffled in coat and gloves, sat in the corner with a blanket around his legs. A plate with the remains of a meal lay near his feet. He kept looking at the fireplace and a dome-shaped metal heater about the size of a lantern which resembled the paraffin lamp we used at home to stop our toilet pan freezing in the winter. This room carried the same cold, damp feel as upstairs.

The man struggled to his feet. '*Mon mari,* my husband,' Joseline said.

We shook hands with him. The puzzle of her frequent absences was solved. She pointed to the dining table after Harold held up the cards. With the language barrier, I half expected our game to become another conundrum. Harold sat opposite me with the deck between us – he always did. A lace cloth covered the table in a diamond shape, leaving shiny mahogany triangles at the corners. Joseline went to help her husband who waved me away when I tried to assist. The family set-up was clear now. Charlotte, the Painter and child lived in the fifth-floor apartment and Joseline joined them at intervals during the day while her husband remained downstairs, likely staying in bed for long periods to keep warm. It was a grim thought that most of the French in Paris shivered in their homes.

The elderly man sank into a chair. Hands deep in my trouser pockets, I felt guilty at wishing a pair of gloves were in there. The evening meal earlier had been awkward. The Painter had squashed up next to Charlotte and the child. Joseline left us in the cramped kitchen after she served green beans and potatoes. Everyone showed exaggerated interest in their food and I winced at the clatter of cutlery. Family smiles came with hushed exchanges, although it was the diversion of a child which had lifted the strange atmosphere.

Harold fanned out the cards, shuffling, straightening and stacking them. The low light cast everything in a dull, weary look. I noticed a framed sepia photo on the nearby dresser. A young couple dressed in their best Sunday clothes stood in raised chin studio poses. Joseline returned with the blanket and a large book which she thudded down next to the cards.

'*Voila.*' Her finger tapped the front of a French-English Dictionary. She wrapped the blanket around her husband's legs amidst fussing French exchanges and the man's wheezing. She taught us Belotte, a French partner whist, with thirty-two cards, plus the dictionary.

'We play. *C'est bon*… it is good for my husband.' I dealt us five cards each, with the top one in the pack left face up. Each instruction ended with a whispered *voila* or finger directed at the object lesson. Everyone took turns at dealing. I teamed up with Harold and stumbled through the rounds. The man broke into husky laughter with fits of coughing when he played a winning hand. After more games I gestured we could swap pairings.

'*Non.*' Joseline said firmly. 'You boys play the cards together… always.'

The old man began to tire. During the final game, Joseline's gaze strayed to the framed photo. Behind the shadows the light cast on her face, the age lines fell away.

Later, I lay awake tiptoeing through events from the last few hours: the apprehensive start, a closer entente cordiale with Joseline and signs of a thaw between Harold and me. Was thaw the right word? The distance in our relationship remained unfathomable. At least the Painter and his wife had grabbed some privacy while we were away, and the old man visibly picked up. How many other escapers had stayed here and played 'The cards'?

I wiped condensation off the bathroom mirror. A misty portrait in a singlet rubbed its chin. Steam rose from hot water in the sink. Restless after another early morning marchpast, I'd requested it for a strip wash and shave whilst Paris struggled to boil a kettle in the coldest winter for years. There was something malevolent in the soldiers' steps as they marched together, despite what Charlotte said. When they were alone or in small groups in the street, I had mastered walking past them without looking down at my shoes. I survived next to the military on station platforms, trains and trams and had escaped from my collision in the Metro subway. But from the foot and cycle patrols right through to marching columns, the troops were different once regimented together.

I bent over the sink, blowing bubbles, rippling the water over my cheeks. It stung my face. Too many cold shaves and hacks at the stubble. I curved the razor around my chin and the mirror fogged again. Sanctuary existed in this room: quiet privacy, a place for uncluttered thoughts where I could close my eyes and return home to the corporation white tiles, frosted glass and toothpaste tube – the hanging face flannels, white bath and proud taps with their 'hot' and 'cold' labelled tops. It was the sole place in my house I could think about now without pain.

How long would I stay in this apartment? For as long as it took.

Ripples of afternoon sunlight streamed through the kitchen window, reflecting off our empty plates. Tepid warmth stroked the side of my face and dappled shadows danced on the floor.

'Do you want to play cards in the lounge?' I'd been thinking about asking for a while.

Harold stretched out, arms above his head, fingers almost touching the cupboard above. He shot me another of those get to the point expressions.

'I know the room's freezing cold,' I said, 'but we're cluttering up the place in here. It feels like we've parked ourselves in somebody else's life. The family must want to eat and have time together. Besides, we might be stuck here for a while.'

He squinted into the light. 'What makes you think that?'

'Nothing, it's just—'

'Just nothing?' He shook his head.

I could have started another spat but didn't pursue it, not after the previous day. I went to change the subject and the words froze behind my lips. Noises sounded on the stairway, a rapping came at the front door. We were up on our feet. Charlotte hurried in, waving us to sit. She grabbed a set of keys from a drawer and called out as she shut us in. The knocking came again. A key jiggled in the front door. Her words sounded straight and level, the men's replies always quizzical. I could smell the same fear as on the inside of my facemask in the Lanc. Harold showed a nervous flash of teeth but he kept silent. We both felt it – the terror of being trapped, our backs now pressed up against the kitchen door as if standing on a narrow ledge. I swallowed hard. Gestapo and Geheime Feldpolizei would be inside and down the passage by now. Charlotte continued her guarded speech. The front door shut quietly. I breathed out and we stepped away. Joseline looked into the kitchen. 'OK?' More French words trailed out before she left.

'That's twice it's happened,' Harold said.

The two women talked as they moved between the other rooms and the child chuntered along with them. It sounded like three singular French conversations.

'We know there's some sort of internal decorating business going on,' I said. 'That must be why the people are coming up here.'

Harold nodded but didn't reply.

'Most of the kit is in the ground floor place with the old chap,' I said. 'There's some paint tins here under that bureau in the lounge, but they were used ages ago. I guess you saw them the night we arrived.'

'Yep,' he said, picking up the cigarettes from the table. 'They can't get hold of much paint, that's for sure. Want a smoke?'

There were two left. It was the last packet.

'Probably no wallpaper either,' I said. 'They'll use distemper or whitewash. We have this awful battleship grey colour in Leicester. Most people don't bother with it.'

He shoved a cigarette into his mouth, waving the packet weakly at me before tossing it on the table.

'You can have the last one, Harold. I'm not ready for them yet.'

'OK. Thanks. Now listen up.' He stopped to strike the match. 'I don't like this any more than you. But I've been thinking. We can hear folks coming and going in this block all day and the old woman is up and down them stairs like a jackrabbit. Yeah, the family don't always know when folks are going to come calling and it's pretty quiet at night, but maybe we won't get noticed in a place like this, and that's why we're here?'

'Fingers crossed you're right, because if somebody does blow the whistle we're done for. For what it's worth, I think the old lady is fully au fait with what she's doing. They all are.'

His face brightened. The conversation moved to shortages of everything in France and Belgium and what supplies were like at home. I listened intently. Rationing in America was nowhere near as severe as Blighty.

He pulled up his coat collar. 'Let's go and play cards.'

The lounge door stayed open. It felt more tactful than disappearing from the kitchen and shutting ourselves in. I opened the false wall to show him my bed and hidden space in more detail. We sat by the small table in the same chairs as on the first evening. He hunched his shoulders, rocking slowly.

'Maybe we'll get more smokes soon?'

The last one was still in the packet on the kitchen table. 'Yes,' I answered, routinely. The family never touched our cigarettes and we always left them in the kitchen overnight.

'Haven't seen any of them have a ciggy,' I said. 'Caught a whiff of tobacco when we walked in on the first night and the painter chap had half of one tucked behind his ear. I suppose they can't get hold of them… or afford them. Ours must come from the black market and we haven't offered a single one. They can have most of my share.'

He nodded thoughtfully. 'No, Ron. We'll both do it. Next

question is, what are we gonna do about the cold in this place? Things ain't getting any better.'

He waved a hand in the general direction of the kitchen. 'There's no fuel, so the stove ain't fired up till late afternoon. Then nothing much comes from that sawdust.'

'Warmer in bed than being out here,' I replied. 'Seems like we'll stay on two meals a day so there's no point in getting up until after two o'clock. We're better off keeping out of the way unless they give us a shout. I've got the watch, so I could tap on your door.'

'No need. I'll be listening out for you.'

We had made progress and reached the boundaries of cordiality for one day. Too early though to share with him how the cold lived inside me and still kick-started my coughing whenever I lay down.

We were still in the lounge when Madame Black arrived with more cigarettes. I got a packet of ten. She gave me a small half a crown-sized tub from her black shopping bag. With part-sentences and mimes, I was told to rub the ointment on my chest at night. Joseline brought in four navy berets with different stages of fade and showed us how to wear them on a slant, angled down from the right side of the forehead. None fitted so Madame Black measured us up before she left.

Harold split and shuffled the deck. 'Cut,' he said as if talking to himself. 'Your deal.'

His face carried that empty expression again. The armchair swallowed him up as he sat back. We stopped playing cards when the light became impossible. Neither of us made a move to put up the blackout cover. He took out a cigarette then returned it to the packet without comment: our matches were still in the kitchen.

'Funny, ain't it?' he said.

'What?'

'The soldiers. They march past... we don't hear them come back.'

'There's probably a barracks nearby.'

I rose to my feet and tiptoed around the room. 'Saw plenty of military a couple of days ago when the painter chap took me out... most of them on my way back to here. Some blue Luftwaffe uniforms too. Did you see many?'

'No. Most were young kids and guys over thirty-five... old soldiers too,' he said. 'The rest looked like officers or Krauts on leave.'

I told him about the Antwerp train full of soldiers with their kit.

He stifled a yawn. 'Lots in Brussels. The folks I stayed with reckoned most of them were doing office jobs or policing.'

Charlotte came in to cover up the window and draw the curtains. I sat down once she switched on the light and left us. Even with no shoes on, wandering around in one place for too long attracted attention from the apartment below.

'Sorry, Ron, I'm plumb tuckered out. Gotta hit the sack for a while.' He picked up his cigarettes and left.

I dealt out a game of Clock Patience. Life clattered on in the apartment while I turned the cards. How sensitive I'd become over the weeks in recognising signals from a host's demeanour or the behaviour of other escapers. The airmen were guarded and initially suspicious, but their circumspect, esoteric attitudes, their voices and the facial expressions revealed more of themselves than they realised – more than I would have picked up before all this happened. Harold still remained something of a mystery and battle ahead. If we did stay together it was crucial to improve on the current status quo between us.

I left the cards and tiptoed to the bureau. French newspapers and magazines lay piled on top. I flicked idly through them. Propaganda showed Parisians living alongside Nazis and carrying on with the good old days before occupation when theatre, music hall and cinema thrived. Press pictures featured tourist areas bustling with daytime activity. A uniform or swastika was always lurking somewhere in the photographs.

Later we crammed into the kitchen with the family for another evening meal of green beans and potatoes. Joseline had cooked something out of nothing again. After serving us, she ladled the last of the contents from the saucepan into a terrine. I offered to help when she made a move to carry it out, but was waved away again. Navigating the unlit staircase was precarious, but a worse thought than her struggling down to her husband crept up on me. When we ate without the family, was there a darker reason?

After the meal, we offered our cigarettes. Joseline was still missing and when the time came to withdraw and give the family some privacy, both packets were left on the kitchen table. I'd lost track of the days since Brussels. What day was yesterday? I had travelled to Paris on a Wednesday. Before asking, I would check the newspapers in the lounge. The false wall was still open when I entered. My bed had been made and someone had cleared the bureau top.

Time forged a long chain of daytime links until blank sleep overtook me late in the evenings. The marching Germans were an alarm call before the pattern of a new day mirrored the previous one. The Painter left at dawn before Joseline's blustery morning arrival and her string of absences. Charlotte's worn path continued between the bedroom and kitchen. I lived in the present only when I ate, got close to the stove or played cards. The remainder of my day existed in a near future: the wait for the next meal, hot drink or visit from the Chief with news that we were leaving. At night the present crumbled and there was nothing to hold on to except memories of home, or facing up to my worries of capture and trying to deconstruct them. The Chief told me on the bridge there had been arrests. Something must have gone wrong and we were stuck here. My natural reaction and desperation to leave for the next stage of the journey battled with a reality I was still not fit enough to tackle the Pyrenees.

Beyond the constant listening out for the stairs and front

door, my time alone spawned an odd lethargy. I drifted into a flat, colourless world where I eked out the routines, took twice as long to do everything, tiptoed down the passage to the bathroom and lingered with my ablutions. The contents from my pockets were laid out on the bed again, checked, counted and recounted: a silent, steady ritual repeated over recent weeks. It was in total contrast to my kit and equipment checks amongst the noise and chaos in the squadron's crew room before an op. Best I could do there was to find a corner away from the parachute packs and harnesses mixed up on the tables amongst navigation bags, flasks of tea and flying gear.

Callers to the apartment arrived at various hours. Every set of fresh knocking during the morning threw me straight out of bed. Only the family and Madame Black entered the apartment until one afternoon, when a swarthy-looking man in a rain-soaked overcoat carried a sack into the kitchen and emptied cuts of meat onto newspaper in the middle of the floor. He bore a resemblance to the Painter and left with hardly a glance at Harold or me sitting at the table. When the Painter arrived home early and Joseline told us to find our shoes, I sensed things were about to change.

7

'Your journey… *beaucoup de kilometres,* many kilometres,' Joseline said, rubbing salt into the meat. '*Et bientôt,* soon for you, perhaps many mountains, yes? *Maintenant,* before you leave, you must walk… *l'exercice.*'

She made exaggerated steps on the spot, puffing out her cheeks. It looked comical, although there was nothing funny about her words. The Painter gave me a probing look. He knew what I was thinking.

Paris was heading home in the dark when he led us slowly through Gambetta. I paused behind Harold, drawing in the sheer depth and texture of a street again. This district was middle class, perfect before the war for small businessmen and office workers to live. Squinting through a rainy night in the blackout to make that kind of judgement on buildings and the people inside them was as unreliable as it was unfair. I mulled it over while trudging back to the apartment. How easy it had been to pigeon-hole a complete family who had sheltered us and put their lives on the line. Was that the British way of labelling folks? Back home, the snotty-nosed slum kids at my old school were urchins, people who had bought their house had money and the man who owned the printing works where I was apprenticed was a Jew. The Nazi ethos was terrifying, but the British way of looking at some things had caught up with me. This war transformed everything. The world would change when it was over, although some people might still sit in the same narrow judgement as they had always done.

Charlotte opened the apartment door before the Painter could put his key into the lock. A smell of meat cooking hit me. Joseline met us in the passage, animated, brusque and waiting to hustle us into the kitchen. More cigarettes were on the table beside two black berets. Madame Black must have visited again.

'For your journey,' Joseline said.

Harold tried his on. It fitted. A steady ache throbbed in my legs in time to my heartbeat. My knees buckled when I tried to ease down into the chair. If it got noticed, no comment was made. I made sure my beret was OK. Reality was arriving too soon.

We feasted on a casserole and potatoes. The meat carried a beef flavour with a sweet taste and no string or fat. It surrendered as my fork pressed against it. I made tiny squares, shunting in small pieces of potato to make each morsel last. Joseline stayed with us, cutting up more meat into bloody-coloured steaks.

She turned around. '*C'est bon*. It is good yes?'

I agreed.

'Ah. *Le cheval*,' she said. 'The horse is good, always.'

My stomach was undecided what to do next. Harold stopped mid-chew. I lay in bed later, working through the day's events. For the first time since arriving I couldn't bring myself to think about food.

The lounge door was part-open again the next morning. Was that a subtle hint for me to start getting up earlier, or ensure I didn't fall over in the dark? My chest felt easier; the last of the ointment had done its job, even if it did stink out the room. A chorus of wailing air-raid sirens instantly spread across the city. I dived out of bed and stepped into my shoes. Harold rushed in. We met Charlotte in the passage and were marshalled back inside.

'Do we stay here?'

'*Oui.*'

She shut us in, rushing away as a barrage of anti-aircraft fire opened up. Another door banged – it wasn't the front one. We took cover behind the open false wall which might shield us from the blast if the window and blackout board were blown in. The steady drone of bombers above increased and the pounding of guns grew louder. Joseline and the Painter would be out somewhere in the city.

Harold closed his eyes. 'B17s.'

No whistle of bombs came, only explosions and the child screaming in another room before a distant crump of more hits. It was a while until the all-clear sirens sounded. A raid by our own side; the whole episode seemed outlandish. My thoughts were still on Joseline and the Painter when Charlotte opened the lounge door and stood comforting her child.

The raid must have started around ten forty-five as it was after eleven when we were invited into the kitchen. Joseline returned at midday and the Painter called in before leaving again. They both looked unperturbed. That evening, we ate more horsemeat. How different it tasted when you were seriously hungry.

The Painter took us out later for another walk to a small, backstreet cinema. Auditorium lights came up when the first newsreel started. The audience spoke amongst themselves with no sign of the derision shown in Brussels. I dozed through the main picture and by the time we returned to the apartment, I recalled little of it except men in suits and women with cigarette holders and long necklaces. The next day, the Painter took us to a football match in a half-empty stadium with swathes of open terracing and crush barriers. We were dumb mutes for the afternoon. Even with a military presence it was easy to blend in amongst the crowd and say nothing.

Joseline didn't take us down for cards so often. Our evening walks continued before or after a nightly meal. If there was any daylight left the Painter walked well ahead, always leaving a gap. He varied his routes around the grid of apartment blocks, houses and shops, speaking to us in short bursts of French when we were together. I never understood a word and the sole building I recalled with any clarity was an old sandstone-fronted structure with three arches, a bell tower and large clock face. None of it worried me – my fitness was improving.

Four nights after the bombing raid we were late getting back to the apartment. I had begun to feel edgy about our sudden detours through different back streets. The Germans could have blocked off a section at night in less than a minute and rounded up everyone caught between the barbed wire and barricades. The Painter sauntered through the apartment with Harold behind him. I was last inside. The kitchen door was open and Madame Black waited beside Joseline. Documents lay spread out on the table.

'You leave tomorrow night, boys,' Madame Black said.

I had waited for days to hear those words, yet they still took me by surprise. She pointed to a stamped official letter and what looked like a travel permit.

'*La chemise, des pantalons et la cravat,*' she said, gesturing at my tie. Her voice was soft but firm. I must change my shirt and trousers before the journey and remove the necktie as they were not suitable in Southern France. Joseline spoke to her. Both of them studied me. A sudden hot flush warmed my face. The conversation rattled on and neither woman looked happy. Madame Black gave me a worn white shirt and pair of trousers from her shopping bag. I could keep the jacket, but she looked uneasy about my raincoat.

'This ain't right.' Harold held out a printed letter with a photograph waxed into the top left corner.

'*Qu'est-ce que c'est?*' Joseline asked.

His eyes narrowed in desperation. 'This is Johnson. Madame, this picture is Tennessee Johnson.'

8

Madame Black left in a hurry, pursued to the front door by Joseline. Harold fumbled out a Gauloises. The match snapped in a fizz of flame and went out. He tried again, steadied his hand and took a long pull before exhaling the smoke as if he'd drawn in his predicament and was trying to blow it away. I saw him as the kind of man whose anxieties might harden into resolution by the morning, but with no matching photograph he would not survive serious checks. That created huge risk for all of us. I had enough experience in the printing trade to know the work involved in replacing photographs and documents. Harold's chances of departing the next day were slim and it would be difficult to predict my feelings if he was forced to stay behind.

My new papers were still on the table, a tactless reminder of our predicament. I shoved them inside my jacket. The family left us to eat our meals together, which we did in virtual silence. Harold went to bed early, taking his documents with him. I was about to turn in for the night when the Painter brought his newspaper into the kitchen. He hadn't done that before. The front page was dated 30 November. We had been in the apartment for at least a fortnight.

I woke early next morning thinking about Mary. She was always in my thoughts, but I couldn't let her into this world – not here and not now. It was bad enough imagining her wandering through the same void as my parents. All she could do was wait and listen to Lord Haw-Haw's propaganda radio broadcasts from Germany each night to see if my name was amongst the casualties and captured from bombing raids over Germany. At least there was still hope for her: no news was good news. She must have been told that dozens of times by well-meaning folk. I could feel the hurt. Her sister was widowed seven months earlier and had only been married for days before her husband sailed for the Middle

East. He was an army non-combatant with a safe desk job away from the fighting. The telegram still arrived. A freak stray shell had scored a direct hit.

A multitude of worries about home bulldozed their way into my head. The next day was a Thursday. Would Mary still be going to Mum's for tea? Would Dad walk her part-way home later through the blackout? Would he take the dog with him? Even simple domestic thoughts brought me no solace. Back here, the daily apartment routine rolled into action and returned me straight into the moment. Would this family's life ever return to how it used to be? A dark and uncertain future faced us all.

I was sitting on the bed when Charlotte tapped on the door and entered. We exchanged a greeting. The family usually avoided entering the lounge until after I surfaced and decamped to the kitchen. She removed the blackout cover from the window. Daylight flooded in and I was left alone again with my thoughts. Not my place to ask her for the latest news about Harold's documents. That had to come from him because serious questions to the family or helpers were off limits since my spats in the early days here. I placed my watch on the bed. The time was moving towards midday.

The kitchen stove remained unlit. Patches of blue sky showed between pale streamers of cloud above the apartment roofs. Harold dealt the cards in lines between our empty cups, turning them over and bending the edges with his thumb so they made a crisp, slapping noise.

'The daughter's in your room, I can hear her talking to the kid,' he said. 'She's getting your bed ready for the next guy, eh?'

'Madame told us to be ready by four o'clock. She should have been back by now.'

'And we've been waiting since a quarter after three. Sit down, Ron. Wherever she is, the old woman ain't gonna get back any quicker.'

He threw me the cigarette packet. Neither of us had mentioned his documents. Joseline had left the apartment around midday so must have been confident the problem would get sorted. That was what I kept telling myself.

I listened out for the front door. Wearing a beret felt strange. Me, a typical Frenchman from books and films – only the bicycle and onions were missing. Harold drew deeper inside his jacket. The beret highlighted his dark features and non-European face. I thought about the German officer who marked me in Brussels, plus the rest of my scrapes. This entire journey had been like tracing my finger along a tight thread which held everything together, never knowing when it might break.

Joseline roared in on a flood of French and dropped her shopping bag. She tutted, adjusted the angle of our berets and stepped back to inspect the work. I willed her to break some good news.

'*Nous allons,*' she said, quietly. 'We leave.'

Two sandwich-size paper bags were placed on the table. '*Du pain pour votre voyage.* The bread.'

Her words struck with a worrying inevitability. No mention of Harold's papers. I squashed the bag into my raincoat pocket. Harold gathered up the cards, running his fingers around the edges to neaten the stack. They were someone else's game now.

'*Maintenant,* we go,' Joseline said. 'I say adieu to you now, boys. Soon, we see my friend and you will follow her.'

It appeared I would keep my raincoat. Like the other articles, it was a part of me. I waited my turn to shake her hand. The Painter had left early in the morning and Charlotte was somewhere behind the lounge door which stayed shut. Such a strange goodbye after staying with the family for so long. We crept down the stairs to the hallway – a while since we had played cards with the old man. I missed those games and would miss the Painter too. From the moment he walked into the lounge on the first evening, his gestures, garrulous French and smiles helped smooth a way through. The rapport between us called for no English words.

Joseline forged ahead to the far end of Rue du Cher and around the block before joining a main avenue. The wind billowed around her coat and we all stayed a distance apart, with Harold keeping to the back. Paris streets were busy again. Less than an hour of daylight remained. Madame Black walked out from near a café, close to a junction. She paused by the window, looking in her shopping bag. Joseline had turned into a side street before Madame saw us and sauntered to the middle of the avenue where a railed entrance led down to the Metro.

The train was dirty and half empty. Madame sat where she could see us. We changed twice, our final carriage with its blinds down covering the windows. When the train clattered away we were the only ones left on the platform. Madame waited at the bottom of a long flight of stairs down to the street. It was fully dark and a stiff wind blew in my face. The Metro continued above us onto a steel girder bridge. We crossed the street and descended concrete steps to a walkway. Ahead were the black waters of the Seine and, against our backs, a high wall up to the road. The shadow nearest me moved. A red fleck of light glowed then dimmed. The outlines of a man and a small woman approached. The man spoke, his face shaded under a hat and raised overcoat collar.

'Good evening, gentlemen. I would like you to meet my friend.'

It was the Chief. He shepherded Harold straight to one side. I couldn't hear what they said. The woman wore glasses and a knee-length coat and she greeted us while the Chief handed out smokes.

'I am sorry your stay in Paris has been so long,' the Chief said to us, holding out his cigarette for the woman to light from it. 'Your train leaves at twenty-two hundred and the station is near. You should arrive at Bordeaux after nine hours if there are no delays. I wish you a goodnight, gentlemen, and good luck.'

He disappeared into the dark. I looked around for Madame Black. She had left. Harold waited alongside me making shuffling noises with his feet. What thoughts had crashed around in his head since leaving the apartment? What did the Chief say to him? What happened about his documents? A Metro train sparked as it crossed the girder bridge over the river. The woman's cigarette tip glowed.

'We walk. We eat. Then it is the train.'

She waited for a couple to pass by. 'No English. If I speak to you, you will say *oui*.'

We walked back with her towards the steps.

9

The woman led us away from the river and through a network of dark backstreets. We entered a small corner restaurant just as the rain started. Two gendarmes were leaving. I was close enough to catch the draught as they shut the door behind me. We sat away from the other three diners. An elderly couple chatted in the corner. The business type near them sipped his drink and studied a newspaper.

Wafts of boiled cabbage drifted over as the waiter fussed in and out the kitchen. He was a fizzy little man with thinning hair and short steps. The woman passed me a menu. Behind her thick glasses and smiles, she was a young thirty-something with long, bouncy brown hair. I named her Susanne. The waiter arrived, twiddling a stumpy pencil. Whatever Susanne said to me, her face and hands appeared to hypnotise him as she spoke.

'*Oui*,' I said. He scribbled on his pad and the charade repeated with Harold until the waiter swivelled around and beetled off to the kitchen. I caught Harold's eye – anything to elicit a signal about his papers. He looked away.

My soup was vegetable. The main course of white meat with greens and potatoes arrived piping hot. Heat was all that mattered: days in a freezing apartment had revolved around the next warm drink and meal. The waiter loitered around our table until someone from the kitchen called. As we neared the end of our meal, Susanne passed us our rail tickets under cover of the menu. They were paper: SNCF to Bordeaux. My travel particulars had been handwritten and showed the same false name as my identity documents. As soon as our plates were empty, Susanne took out food coupons from her handbag. The clasp clicked shut. This brought the waiter scurrying to our table and she counted out the coupons in front of him. He still insisted on accompanying us to the door.

We walked on to the dripping street, our footfall echoing through great rafts of quiet. It was different territory from my first journey to the apartment with Madame Black, but an enemy could still be around the next corner. The rain stopped. My feet pounded the cobbles up to the railway station – we were on view again, even in the dark. I kept a distance from Susanne and walked under a small girder bridge which entered the upper frontage of the station. The night was playing tricks again: the night saw everything, heard everything: my heartbeat, my breathing, my own distinct footfall. It knew every thought and messed with my head.

A parked truck nearby looked unoccupied. I saw no other vehicles. A steady stream of silhouettes shadowed in and out through the station entrance. It was eerie how the door guillotined conversations when it closed behind the figures entering. Susanne led us along the frontage. Large, wooden signs were on the wall or jutted out at right angles above our heads. Servicemen and civilians milled about the foyer and concourse which had the same cavernous feel as Antwerp, Brussels and Gare du Nord. The minute hand on the station clock shivered into place. Eleven minutes past nine, late for children to be running around their parents and suitcases. Susanne bought magazines at the newsstand where a Kriegsmarine waited nearby in his naval overcoat. She walked straight by him to pass us a *Signal* magazine each and we struck out for the ticket barrier, her route threading through civilians to avoid the military standing groups. There were more commissioned ranks than before. Officers chatted together as orderlies waited nearby with luggage. The checker returned my second-class ticket and I passed through behind Harold. Under the roof, platforms stretched away into blackness – less than fifty minutes to departure and passengers were already boarding the train.

The first carriages were in total darkness. Someone inside pulled up a blind. They rapped on the window. We manoeuvred through the crowds and luggage and it was a relief to climb aboard further along nearer the locomotive. Susanne found a compartment with spaces. She pulled the door, which folded across instead of sliding. Harold went in first and we occupied the first three seats. I was next to the door and Susanne sat between us. Luggage thumped on to the wire rack above our heads. The two places opposite me stayed vacant. A Messerschmitt with camouflage marking filled the front cover of my *Signal* magazine. Except for feigning sleep, reading was still the only refuge from eye contact or a risk of someone trying to pull me into conversation. I leafed through the pages. Amongst a gallery of crashed Allied planes, German soldiers bossed the scenes or smiled for the camera. A sudden commotion developed down the corridor. Two German officers bucketed their way into our compartment and sat down opposite. It was as if I'd stepped off a precipice.

The men were tall and from the rank insignia on their greatcoats, probably lieutenants. My chest and stomach tightened and the rest of the faces became hazy, featureless ovals. This night would be a hanging hell and the train was still in the station. I hid behind the pages and glimpsed Susanne, her head down reading a film magazine. A couple near the officers spoke in strained whispers, others kept quiet. Jackboots stretched out in the letterbox view below my magazine: jackboots rubbing together, jackboots crossing, uncrossing – jackboots squeaking and sliding out of sight. The officers spoke in German. One of them cleared his throat. I had an urge to keep licking my lips. Harold had his eyes closed, head resting back on his seat. Somehow I had to get through the night and fight my fear until the train reached Bordeaux. If the officers spoke to me or became suspicious, it would be over.

People cluttered the corridor. A whistle blasted down the platform and someone in the window seat checked the blind was secure. I slipped the magazine inside my raincoat, shut my eyes and kept perfectly still. Paris was almost behind me now, yet memories loomed with scant chronology. The previous fortnight had frayed at the edges, a string of events merging into a collage instead of a calendar. I'd seen the River Seine but nothing of picture-book

Paris. My random recollections always homed in on the flat hours at the apartment and worries of how long Joseline and her family could carry on before they were caught. How many of our helpers would stay free?

I longed for a solid block of sleep, yet dreaded dozing off then speaking out in English. The carriage rattled over points. I came to and looked straight into the nearest officer's frank, blue eyes. The lights went out. A night bulb came on, tinting the compartment in a dim, bluish glow. The officer might be waiting to alert the ticket checker. If I slipped out at the first sign of any disturbance in the corridor, it might be enough to save Susanne.

This journey came with the same stop-start as our travel to Paris. Sabotage and Allied bombing on the railways were doing their job. In the hollow hours of early morning my mind and body opened themselves to sleep, while other senses resisted. I tried to focus on home but the thoughts were full of holes. A rustle of paper distracted me; Harold had started on his bread. The main carriage light came on and a railway official entered the compartment.

'Vos billets, s'il vous plaît.'

Susanne took out her ticket. I copied her and it was over without incident. The Germans rose and left. By the time they returned, the blue light shone again.

The beat of the journey worked its way into my all-night thoughts. I fell into snatches of tormented sleep and it was a heavy thud above my head which woke me. The compartment light changed to yellow. Passengers lifted down their suitcases and the two officers moved into the corridor. *Bordeaux... Bordeaux* – the shouts outside were clear enough. A queue slouched past the door. We were the last three occupants in our compartment, surely the right time now to leave and blend in amongst the crowd.

Carriage doors slammed. Susanne remained in her seat. I felt a squirm and twist inside me again, like trying to run away in a dream and being unable to move. She finally got to her feet, checked the corridor then pulled the compartment door shut.

'Vos papiers. Vite. Le train part.' She was facing us now, hands outstretched, her back rigid. The crease lines deepened on her forehead. 'Give me your papers. Quickly, the train is leaving soon.'

I handed over my documents in a bunch. Harold did the same. Leaving a carriage late would attract attention. The window blinds were still closed. How far up the platform were we?

Susanne sat down where the Germans had been. Our surrendered documents lay fanned out on the next seat and four official cards appeared from her handbag. Like some casino croupier she picked up cards and papers from the seat, merging them with the others cupped in her left hand. Whatever she passed to me I put straight in my raincoat pocket before following her out of the compartment. The corridor was still empty. She halted at the end and touched her hair, gathering herself like an actress ready to go on stage. The Chief had not prepared me for any of this.

A whistle shrilled outside. Our carriage door swung open. A wave of bustling noise hit me. I climbed down the steps and moved after her with Harold at my back. It wasn't light yet. A high wall stretched up on my right to a curved glass and girder canopy. The damp air clung to my face. Susanne moved to a shielded lamp above steps leading down to a subway. We emerged behind her in the middle of an island platform as the train we had travelled on was pulling out. The first signs of a purple dawn showed through the large windows lining the far station wall. She approached a man dressed in a half-length coat. He was standing alone.

'Bonjour. I am Max. I 'av your rail tickets.' He passed them to us with a handshake.

'I need the can,' Harold said.

'Ze can? What iz ze can? I can… you can?'

Harold took a step nearer and explained. Max led us back via the subway to the platform where we had first arrived. Most of the military had left. Sufficient light emanated from a solitary bulb in the men's ablutions for me to check my rail ticket. Dax: I'd not heard of it. A large scar cut across the bridge of Max's prominent nose, and his red lips and smile were at odds with the probing, confrontational eyes. He looked the Resistance type who wouldn't shy away from action.

When we returned to the middle platform, Susanne was missing.

'Cigarette?' Max held out a packet. The escape lecture said they were as good as a meal so I kept mine for later. A freight train rumbled north through the station and workmen began to gather on our platform, most of them wearing berets. Max waited for the wagons to clatter past.

'Always, many peoples on ze train. When it arrives, follow me. On ze train I will leave you, but I am zare, I can see you. At Dax... er, *je t'attendrai sur le quai.*'

I must have given him a blank look. He rubbed his chin.

'I wait on the quai. You look... I find.'

'Do you mean the platform?'

He nodded. 'Ah *oui.*'

A clock hung at the far end of the station. In the early dawn light I couldn't make out the time. A smaller train steamed in. We boarded a suburban carriage and stood shoulder to shoulder along an open aisle next to wooden seats. Max squeezed down to the far end and merged amongst passengers once the train had pulled out. Bordeaux suburbs turned into misty, grey fields and bare trees. Most conversations stopped after the workmen opened their lunch-boxes. Between stops, the countryside slipped by in flat lines. I rested against the carriage window, chewing on the bread Joseline had given me. We had managed to reach Bordeaux without Gestapo control going through the train, or worse still, stopping it and ordering us off for checks. This was Southern France now and frontier country which made it more likely they were on board already or the Feldgendarmerie had men waiting at stations along the line. The odds were shortening. Max was out of sight at the end of the carriage and I knew why. Was Dax a final destination before the border, or was it to wait for another train? Whichever alley my thoughts ran down, Germans always blocked the way. I sneaked a quick glance at my documents: a new identity card, another permit or pass and what looked like the *Ausweis* I had given to Susanne. Harold moved further down the aisle without making eye contact. Was that a signalled answer about his papers?

10

Passengers gazed out at the countryside. The land rose in steady inclines before falling back to scrubby flat fields and trees where the cycle repeated. I expected rock faces and plunging valleys, not pastel-green hills misted in the distance behind a winter haze. The train chattered through swathes of woodland. Country stations were Alpine-style buildings with an upper level and cross-wood lattice on the walls. A small group of passengers slipped out at Labouheyre, heading away to the town. We drew in under a gable roof canopy at Morcenx station on the edge of a forest where a line of worn faces waited on the platform. Still no ticket checks. Max said he would find us at Dax, or we must look for him. It was all so vague. Should we hang back at arrival and risk drawing attention, or make for the exit under cover of a crowd? A whistle blew. The journey since Bordeaux had slowly wound itself tighter around me. I was desperate to leave the train and get away. In an endless replay I saw myself descending the carriage steps and leaving the station with Max.

At least half an hour must have passed. Houses slid by the window: cream plaster walls, wooden shutters and terracotta-tiled roofs. Our carriage stopped opposite a Dax station sign. A canopy covered the platforms and the far side was completely open. I could see through to soldiers guarding the railway sidings.

Harold walked well ahead of me down the platform as the crowd uncoiled itself in front of him. Max was waiting and moved off when he saw us. No sign of checks at the departure gate. I handed in my ticket, following Harold through the wide station approach to a street crowded with soldiers. A column marched past in full kit. Troops loaded spades and shovels into an army truck – they were no more than boys. Max approached a young man pulling out bicycles from under a rickety shelter. His dark wavy hair, leather jacket, slacks and mustard-coloured sweater could have placed him straight on a film set. Two men waiting nearby took the bicycles from him. I recognised Flying Officer Ward. The other chap grimaced, pinching the bridge of his nose. His brown, breeze-blown hair showed lighter flecks and the face was pale and drawn. I hadn't seen him before.

Max pushed a couple of black bikes over to us. 'You can ride the bicycle?'

'Yes,' I answered in unison with Harold.

My frame was heavy; the saddle felt hard and worn. Ward acknowledged us. He spoke with the other chap and they walked across with their machines.

'Name's Kennedy... Squadron Leader Kennedy,' the other man said quietly in a Canadian accent. Max stood up after examining my chain. He looked from Harold to me and then at the man in the leather jacket, sitting astride his bicycle, hand against the shelter wall. 'You ride with him to Bayonne.'

'I go with you,' he said to Ward and Kennedy.

Max scanned the hills with a pained expression, as if we should have been up there hours ago. People were starting to notice us when they passed – soldiers, a man with a handcart, a woman in a ragged coat. We'd been standing around for too long. Max spoke in a low, dry voice with bites of French and broken English. The man in the leather jacket would lead. I was to follow a hundred metres behind, with Harold an equivalent length in the rear. Max would head the next group a further distance back from us. If there was danger the guide would wave his beret and we were to get off the road.

What about roadblocks and spot checks? Germans and gendarmes would be just as vigilant in border country. What of Harold's documents?

Kennedy closed his eyes. 'How far is Bayonne?'

Max mounted his bicycle. '*Cinquante kilometres*... fifty.'

I bent down to tuck my trouser bottoms into my socks when Kennedy jammed a beret on his head.

'*Allez,*' Max said.

Ward climbed on to his bicycle. 'We've got to reach Bayonne before nightfall,' he whispered to me.

Fifty kilometres was over thirty miles. The more I thought about it, the longer it seemed. The army truck started up, firing out a mushroom of black smoke. I rode off down the street. The man in the leather jacket headed away from the station past more soldiers, young troops with triangular badges on the shoulders of their tunics. I saw no more petrol-driven vehicles, only bicycles and a stationary cart, the horse shaking its head against the bridle. My saddle felt like a wooden block. I swerved around potholes, the front brake lever flapping loosely as my feet hit the road to slow down. We turned into a side street, the free wheel tick of another bicycle close behind. I named the man in the leather jacket 'François'. His machine was more smooth-running than mine and he pedalled faster causing the gap between us to grow.

The town sprawled out with the same look as other places after Bordeaux. Gaps stretched between buildings and there was none of the covetous fencing dividing properties like at home. Parts of this place belonged on an artist's canvas where one sleepy day painted over another and life meandered through on a brushstroke like a slow-moving river, instead of the restless noise and running sore of occupation. The thought triggered a realisation which kicked inside me. My swelling anxiety had started to ease, but how had we avoided document checks?

I tried to keep up. Leg muscles were softening and François slowed down, glancing behind with that *get a move on* body language. We cycled up rising ground towards woodland. Dax was gone. Hills and valleys stretched ahead in the distance.

The frame and balance of my bicycle was top-heavy on the inclines, shaking right through to the saddle. I struggled to keep pace on steep hills, back lanes and the winding tracks which passed under heavy, twining tree branches. The sole respite was freewheeling into dips before taking turns with Harold to lead on the flatter sections, even though we were supposed to stay apart. Neither of us spoke.

I pictured my Sun Club Racer bike in fine detail with its *Lauterwasser* handlebars and French Simplex Derailleur gears. Sunday trips with the Cyclist Road Club when Matlock was a sunny two-and-a-half hours ride away from Leicester were good times. Any thoughts away from the snarling pain in my feet and legs now became a godsend. François moved out of sight over a hill. I finished with the cycling club just before the war because it meant missing Mum's Sunday dinners. That told a story and I was paying for it now.

On the open flat stretches, fields and pastureland ran up to ditches on both sides of the road. Autumn still crouched behind winter in the sheltered places, where the cold air smelt of earthy damp and decaying vegetation. My mouth felt caked and dry as brick dust, the snatched guzzles of water in the ablutions at Bordeaux, long past. A young woman cyclist joined François up ahead and they kept to the deserted back lanes and tracks. Minutes ground out the hours – pedal and chain, chain and pedal – freewheel down the hills. The blurred pattern of gravel passing under my front wheel had a queasy, hypnotic effect.

François and the woman stopped. He beckoned me forward. I dismounted, battered and bruised in difficult places. Harold arrived moments later. No one waited for Max and the others; we wheeled our bikes between clusters of thickets. The woman looked young, athletic and alert and her slick machine carried a pannier on both sides of the rear wheel. I laid my bicycle next to Harold's on the damp, sedge-like grass. This was a sheltered spot surrounded by bushes well away from the track. The woman knelt on the ground and spread out newspaper, battening the sheets down with bottles of wine, baguettes and cheese from the panniers. Max arrived with Ward. Kennedy staggered in behind them, dropping to his knees in the corner. His face had a sickly, grey pallor. I found my watch. It had stopped somewhere after ten and we had been cycling for hours.

The woman busied herself preparing food. A yeasty scent of baguette bread reached me. When Max joined Kennedy, François took up position where he could see the track. Ward sat between Harold and me and we stared at the picnic, a world away from blue skies, cucumber sandwiches, home-made cakes and lemonade. *Thank you* felt such an inadequate response to the woman as she placed bread and cheese into my hand. I was so exhausted and grateful I couldn't remember hearing my words, so said them again. Only after the wine bottle got passed around did I manage to eat.

Kennedy stayed propped up against the hedge. François returned to sit with Max as the woman gathered up newspaper and remnants from the picnic. A frozen stiffness had set in my calves and left hamstring. I started to massage the muscles and looked across to Ward.

'Where's Flying Officer Madgett, sir?'

'He left Paris before me. We were together... then Kennedy arrived and took his place. He could be in Gib by now.'

The woman secured the panniers on her bicycle.

'*Mes amis.*' Max tapped his wrist and waved us to our feet. 'We must leave.'

'What do you make of Kennedy, sir?' I bent down to adjust the socks tucked in my trousers. Ward did the same. We straightened up in unison.

'This is where we do a song and dance,' he said.

We laughed. He moved nearer as I picked up my bicycle.

'I don't think he's well. Says he's alright, but he was tail-end Charlie all the way from Dax. Told me in Paris his father is Vice-President of the Canadian Pacific Railroad. You heard him say he's a squadron leader. Well, he nearly put us in the bag on the train to Bordeaux. Someone left the bloody compartment door open and he shouts out in the most appalling French, *fermez la porte.* Two German officers were sitting near us.'

'What happened?'

'It wasn't very nice I can tell you. I told him quietly to shut up.'

'Two of them were sitting opposite me on the way down here,' I said. 'I daren't move. Very tricky just sitting there and stewing. I could have murdered a pint though.'

'Like right now, sergeant.'

Ward appeared quite personable. We had hobbled on to the track before Kennedy struggled to his feet with Max fussing around him. I set off behind François with new heart. The line rode off in the same order, except for the woman who cycled some way behind us. Lanes and tracks stayed quiet but things changed after we hit a wider road. An aircraft droned above the low cloud – it sounded like a Junkers 52 transport. The road stretched to the top of another incline, or ran to infinity on flat ground in the kind of straight line which foreshortened distance and would have held a shimmering heat haze in summer.

Long spells passed with nothing except bicycle rattle or wind sweeping across the fields. Hamlets sat back off the road behind hedges and wooden slat gates. Valleys were replaced by the slog of more level terrain, then gradual, tilted climbs as if the landscape was playing games with us. I dismounted on really steep tracks and hills. Walking eased the pain in my legs and I could make up time by freewheeling on the down sections.

François slowed in the distance. Harold gained ground on me and the three dots on the rise behind him were climbing nearer. My eyes felt rough and gritty, exhaustion swallowing me in a confusion of thoughts. Surely Bayonne was close? The voices I heard came only from inside my head: a story from school of Christian and Hopeful on their journey to the gates of the Celestial City, how they kept going, how they never gave in. I was half slumped over my handlebars when Harold caught up. The glances between us were enough.

Occasional petrol traffic passed; there were no cars. Exhaustion soaked through me in huge, great waves and my vision grew hazy. The road became a blurred, restless nightmare. I slipped into a stupor until the whine from a heavy truck jolted me back as it thundered by, canvas billowing. I stared at the tailgate to focus my faltering attention.

Gloomy afternoon skies had moved in; less than an hour's daylight left. The line of distant buildings ahead had to be Bayonne. François turned off the road, leading us through a village with houses similar to Dax. He was indestructible, his focus unrelenting, the drive always onwards, head constantly looking and listening. My single thought now was pushing the pedals with enough momentum to force the chain around. If I stopped, I wouldn't start again.

The lane passed through a large spinney. François waited at the edge, bicycle slewed in a half-turn, his legs astride the saddle, feet on tiptoe to the floor. At last, a rest. The others caught up, except Kennedy who trailed in with Max then collapsed as he tried to dismount. Ward helped him to stand. The woman had left and Kennedy was now a serious worry.

Both guides urged us forward into the same broken formation.

'Bayonne,' François said.

His words lifted me. In fading light, I followed him through the narrow backstreets darkened by four and five-storey buildings. Soldiers were about. Figures appeared from the shadows with no warning. François became a blur, sliding around bends and corners. I pedalled after him, rattling across a stone bridge spanning a wide, grey river. No road blocks or manned checkpoints – no guards or gendarmes. Without a backward glance, François reached the far side and veered off into more side streets. I cycled on to a smaller bridge traversing what I guessed was a canal or narrow river, just in time to see him freewheel down the slope towards a road along the waterfront. The tall, slender buildings wedged together reminded me of Amsterdam.

A stiff breeze off the river blew around my legs. The same stinging cold hit my face as on that first morning with the motor cyclist at the canal. I'd travelled a long way since then. One of my first COs might have twiddled his moustache and referred to it all as jolly good character building. Nothing about self-preservation and fleeing for your life resembled that. Harold caught up and passed me. The road had become a rough path which followed the river under a railway bridge. Buildings nestled on top of a steep slope to the right and fields butted up to the opposite bank. Wind swept through grasses and over the water in a whisper. Harold turned off the path ahead.

Lanes and tracks steepened as if nature was preparing for the mountains. I heard nothing outside the wind except a muffled beat inside my head and the clank from a bicycle somewhere in front. My mood began to bend and twist with the miles. Max had set our destination as Bayonne and the town was behind us now. A final surge of darkness closed in. The track tilted up to a black space. How difficult had the last hills really been? How much was down to total exhaustion? The bicycle fought against me. My full weight pushed on the pedals by standing up from the saddle and pulling hard on the handlebars. The back wheel spun and the ground lurched up to meet me.

I was dusting myself down when Ward arrived.

'Are you still in one piece?'

'I think so.'

He dismounted. 'We'll stick together. Kennedy's riding with Max. He says we're nearly there.'

A slice of moon appeared between the clouds. We lugged our bicycles to the crest of the rise where François waited with Harold.

'I make sure it is safe,' François said. 'Stay here.'

As he cycled down the slope, Max arrived with Kennedy and helped him walk across to us. I peered through the blackness. A fleck of light winked in the distance.

Max looked nervously back down the hill.

'If I say go, you go.' He pointed to the field opposite. I doubted we would, once our legs realised what they were supposed to do.

François whistled and cycled out from the dark. 'Follow me.'

The group collected itself together, freewheeling behind him down the slope to a solitary house near the road. He marshalled us to the back. A door opened and a middle-aged man and woman stepped into the thin bar of light.

'Ici,' François said, pushing his bicycle towards a small outhouse. His energy after such a long journey was unreal. The middle-aged man helped wheel our machines out of sight. Max hurried us into the kitchen and we followed the woman through a large room set with tables and chairs like a typical French café. She led us up a stairway and waited at the top while we slowly battled each step.

'You are zair,' Max said, pointing out the last door in a short passageway. The woman led us straight to it. Slim in a dusky red blouse and beige skirt, her eyes shone with a liquid sheen below her bouffant style black hair.

'I am 'ere wiz *mon ami*,' Max said, disappearing into the next room. The woman opened our door, motioned us inside and then slipped noiselessly away down the passage.

Twin beds butted up close together as if positioned to halve the chances of their occupants falling out on to the floor. Two wooden chairs were up against the wall. Kennedy collapsed on the nearest bed, Ward sat on the other, trying to prise off his shoes. I dropped onto the chair next to Harold.

'If we're stopping the night, I'm sleeping on the floor,' I said. 'Finish up with a back like an *S* if I sit here.'

Ward looked up. 'Can I smell cooking?'

Kennedy lay on his back, staring at the ceiling. The spicy smell reached me. I was too tired to speak. Someone paced about in the next room, probably Max. He was killing time and waiting for the boss. François had said little, but he was running the show. The two of them were in conversation when they entered our room. François explained a meal would be brought and we were to keep quiet with no moving about, because the café was below. He lowered his voice.

'We leave tomorrow morning at zero five hundred.'

'I say goodbye now,' Max said. *'Bon courage mes amis.'*

Both men left us. The woman soon brought our meals on trays: wine, a bean soup, flat bread and pork. I warmed my insides with some spicy hot grog – a cross between watered rum and brandy. We sat with full glasses. Cigarettes got passed around.

I knew from the look on everyone's faces they had heard the same noise. The drum of a heavy exhaust – nearer – louder. Ward went to the window and peered through a chink in the thick curtains. An engine stopped outside. Doors banged shut. He swung around.

'Germans.'

11

Men's voices sounded outside. I got to my feet in that missed heartbeat moment when time stops: Ward, mouth open by the window, Harold, an unlit cigarette frozen between his fingers. The Germans must have seen our light. I waited for the stomp of boots on the stairs. Someone moved outside in the passage. The door cracked open. Fingers appeared around the edge. The middle-aged man from the house looked in – lank, dark hair, sweat on his forehead. He stepped inside, easing the door shut.

'Boche,' he mouthed, pointing a finger at the floor. Mumbled French followed.

'They're downstairs in the front part for a drink,' Ward whispered. 'No noise or moving about, I think that's what he said. Ciggies out lads and turn off the light.'

'*Tais-toi,*' the man whispered as he left.

Ward tiptoed slowly back to the bed. He paused as if his stooped body was forced to think about every movement. Kennedy lay down again. It was ludicrous – this place was in the middle of nowhere and the enemy were only feet away. Chatter grew louder downstairs. I carefully took the plates and glasses into a corner and killed the light. It was all quiet next door but in our room there was no move to sleep.

I sat under the window, hands covering my face, the tracks and roads still moving under the bicycle front wheel. My body cried out for rest, even a doze was impossible. Every time a door opened downstairs the laughter and racket coming from below rattled through my head. Dad used to rap on the bedroom floor when I switched on the radio after a late night out.

'Turn it off.'

'But Dad, it's the Duke.'

'Bugger the Duke. Turn it off and come to bed.'

I'd smiled about it then, but not tonight. At least Duke Ellington led me to a safe place now for a moment or two. I needed to railroad more of those thoughts in – anything and everything.

Eventually the laughter and chat moved outside. I heard the engine fire and a spin of tyres as the vehicle turned and sped away. Only the wind remained, buffeting around the building.

'What time is it, Ron?' Harold whispered.

'I dunno. Must be well after midnight.'

He fidgeted in his chair. Kennedy's breathing sounded like bellows. Movement in the café below became a more friendly noise – the clink of glassware and quiet words in a tone of someone clearing up before calling it a night. The middle-aged man came to collect our plates and glasses. He appeared older than I'd first thought. I removed my raincoat and lay down on the floor. For the first time since staying at the Macas', I didn't feel so cold.

Wind hooting around the eaves woke me. Rain spattered against the window. My mouth had furred after the hot grog. Every muscle ached and pain jolted through my legs when I tried to stand. Harold stirred in his chair. A tap came on our door and François entered. He turned on the light, wet glistening on his leather jacket.

'*C'est quatre heures du matin*. Zero four hundred, gentlemens. We leave at five.'

The others had surfaced by the time the woman brought us coffee and bread. Ward and Harold looked set for the day. Kennedy sat propped up in bed. I couldn't think beyond finishing my drink; we hadn't seen the real foothills and mountains yet. It might have helped prepare the mind and body, instead of perceiving a distance and panorama built only in my imagination. Bayonne was nearer the border and we were further south, I knew little more than that.

After breakfast, Ward started to make his bed. Kennedy worked with me to tuck in his sheets and smooth them out. The stretching might iron out my own aches and pains. A tired, tense silence replaced any small talk. François hastened in, brushing the wet off his shoulders.

'You are ready to leave?'

This was not a question, but an order packaged in pleasantry again.

'We ride the bicycles. Then we walk,' he said. The smile wobbled at the edges, as his gaze crept back to Kennedy.

Everyone donned their berets while the dark-haired woman waited in the corridor. She made no attempt to enter the room and François didn't invite her in. I was first out after him. She smiled at me, her sable eyes searching beyond mine as she spoke. I saw the same expression at home with Sid's mother. My friend had a motorbike for his twenty-first birthday present then rode out on it and was killed. Stan, my next-door neighbour, died in early 1939 after a road accident when he collided on his bicycle with a lorry. He was only fourteen when his parents had to put on their brave masks. After the war started, the same expressions began to filter into the streets, trams and pubs. The sadness at loss and separation was everywhere.

François descended the stairs two at a time. We followed him down and through the café, some of us as stiff-legged as the furniture. I reset my watch by the kitchen clock when he gathered us at the back door.

'We will ride. Please to remember… no speaking. There are Boche patrols and gendarmes. I am the only guide now, so we bicycle like yesterday, but closer.'

With a firm nod and twist of the door knob he stepped out into a windy blast. The house light shone briefly across the yard, reflecting the wet on our bicycles propped against the outhouse wall.

'Come,' he said, turning up his coat collar.

I wiped the saddle with my handkerchief and waited against the wall, eking out some final seconds of shelter. François walked along the line to Kennedy. Whatever they said was lost in the wind. We pedalled off in pairs then turned on to a steep, downhill track. I went last, wheel to wheel behind Harold, my feet scuffing the ground to steer and brake. Cold fingers of rain ran down my neck, wiry undergrowth scratched at my ankles. Between blustery gusts, a noise of running water grew louder. I veered onto a track running alongside the river. We had reached the bottom of the valley and it was still too dark to see the opposite bank.

My wheels sank in a porridge of mud and slush. A different challenge now: pedals down slowly, keep away from the water's edge, miss large stones, grass clumps and bushes. Mud stuck everywhere; my shoes became heavy like clogs. Strength ebbed from my legs – a slide back into thick glue was inevitable on the narrow pathway. We dismounted and pushed our bikes for short distances until firmer ground. The downpour hammered down in angled sheets, the gale always in our faces. I managed to keep sight of the figure in front until it turned off the track into woodland. The first signs of a rain-laden dawn appeared above fields beyond the river.

The air reeked of leaf-mould. Snatches of grey showed through the canopy. Rain spattered on the trees, every sound sharp and magnified. François pressed on through a hilly forest riddled with fast-flowing streams. I slogged up and down the narrow back lanes catching only snatches of the others unless we assembled for an order to cross a junction or an open road.

The wind finally softened, turning rain into heavy drizzle. I caught up with Harold when he dismounted. We pushed our bicycles along the edge of a field to a line of trees and bushes. François and the others stayed partly hidden in a damp mist until we reached them. Kennedy was on his knees near the bushes, vomiting. Ward went over to him. I thought about the chap at Dunholme Lodge who was sick by the same tree near the aerodrome entrance every time he returned to ops after leave. Didn't see him for a while and then I moved to Bottesford. He might have been transferred to another squadron or just went for a Burton with the rest.

Harold checked his chain again. We had been together in Paris for weeks – square pegs in round holes, as Dad would say. Neither of us belonged there and I felt just as guilty thinking that way as when we had crossed the border into France. We might never have fitted into those round holes, but I didn't see us as square pegs; just different shapes from each other – literally.

Kennedy rose to his feet. I knew little about him, only his physical state. Ward was a pleasant man, the kind of sociable chap to join in a conversation or pal up with you at a training course to get through the days. But here, he was a serving officer and that line could not be crossed. I tried to imagine both men in civvies and meeting them once the war was done. My thoughts couldn't stretch that far. Whatever distance existed between any of us now, we had to stick together. If things went wrong in the mountains we would depend on each other.

I started to scrape the clods of mud off my shoes with twigs and leaves. François took a small bottle from his jacket, passing it to me first. We were all shivering. My clothes hung wet and heavy and I felt no sensation below the knees. The brandy scorched down my throat, its warm glow spreading across my chest. François studied our tired figures in a manner I'd become used to.

'Gentlemens.' He paused to lean his bicycle against a bush. 'This way.'

A small gap between the trees was large enough for us to crowd together. The countryside merged into greens and browns amongst the bad weather. In the distance, a misty line of mulberry-coloured hills and mountains poked above the rest of the landscape. He pointed to the horizon.

'Spain.'

We set off for freedom. At last there was something to latch on to. I held my hand out in front of my face for a few seconds as we cycled along. It completely covered the Pyrenees. The foothills were a patchwork of trees, fields and pastureland, with sparser terrain on the higher climbs. More hills became visible. François raised his arm and we gathered at the edge of another clump of trees. He looked around as if searching for something, then pedalled over to the bushes.

'We hide the bicycles here,' he said, pushing his machine behind the greenery.

Kennedy crumpled sideways. He grabbed at the handlebars and managed to land on his knees. We laid our bicycles behind the bushes, covering them with branches. François gave Kennedy another shot of brandy then inspected the camouflage. All I wanted was water.

'We walk together,' he said.

'How far before we stop?' I asked.

'One hour. We must arrive before the night. Then we wait.'

He led us in single file. Rain turned to hail; water sluiced down the grassy slope. We were just a faceless, soaking mass, bent against the wind. I gave up trying to see anything except the man ahead and my own steps on the slippery ground. The route passed through remote, open stretches, the party often halting if someone lost their footing. In exposed places the silent hills saw our every move. We trekked up rising ground for more than an hour, slipping on patches of slimy grass and mud. Kennedy fell again. François stayed with him after that, heading towards a large wooden shed on the apex of a hill. The last half mile passed with the hazy view of a farm in a valley to the east.

The shed was a small barn. Two wooden doors leaned at weary angles against the inside walls. I ploughed through a carpet of sheep manure on the earth floor and collapsed with the others against the back wall near some large oblong flagstones. The place stank of wet, dirty clothes and animals. We were all shaking and Ward gave up trying to unbutton his coat. I'd no memory of how much time passed.

François waited at the open barn front, staring into mists of drizzle. The hillside sloped down out of sight – a hundred yards away could have been the edge of the world.

The wind blew around my feet, snags of sheep fleece waved on the wall next to my head. How far from total collapse were we? This was no ordinary fatigue: a grey, mortuary cold had settled into the marrow of my bones. It was vital to take off our sodden clothes. Harold rose, wrestling to remove his reefer jacket. He held it up as if ready to put it on a hanger.

'Heavy as hell. See if I can dry it.' His words tumbled out in shakes. 'We can light a fire. There are pieces of dried wood and brush in the corner.'

François turned around, shaking his head.

'I am sorry. No fire.' His face narrowed into a grimace. 'It is dangerous. No peoples must see we are here. The rain is very bad, so we are safe.' He shrugged his shoulders. 'For now.'

He approached Kennedy and helped him to stand. 'Please gentlemens… the clothes.'

The rest of us removed our outdoor coats, laying them on the flagstones close to where we sat. My shoes squelched with water. I took them off and wrung out my socks. François produced a bottle of wine from a pile of dried ferns in the opposite corner and looked down a row of cold, exhausted faces.

He held up the bottle. 'For later.'

Kennedy stared into thin air. I unbuttoned my jacket. The rain had soaked through all of my clothes.

'Please do not go outside,' François said. *'Pour uriner,'* he pointed a finger at the corner of the barn. 'You will leave when the guides arrive. Do everything they say. There are still many Boche. Also… in the hills *et les montagnes, c'est très dangereux*, it is easy to slip and fall.'

'How far? How far is the border?' Harold asked.

'At night, six hours or seven. *Mais…* for some peoples it is a longer walk. In Espagne, also you have the danger… and the Spanish prisons are bad.'

He stopped. I could hear water running off the roof.

'If you are arrested, tell the Spanish Police you are aviators and have escaped from the prisoner camp in Germany. You journey through France, steal the clothes and food.' His voice quickened. 'Every man must try to escape from the prison camp. This is normal.

Yes?' A shrug of the shoulders seemed to animate his expression. 'If you have not been in a camp and the Boche has never captured you, the Spanish can escort you back to them.'

He removed his coat to shake off the water.

Six hours to the border and that was just the start of it. Stories of escaping from a POW camp would never hold up to serious Spanish questioning. I forced my feet back into the saturated socks and shoes. Harold fumbled with a soggy cigarette.

'You guys got any Benzedrine left?'

Nobody had. We stood up every half hour, turned our coats over on the flagstones and walked to the barn door and back. Only Kennedy remained on the floor. François spoke with him at intervals then sat with us to pass the wine around. His eyes told a different story to the look on his face.

The singlet pricked at my midriff. My skin itched. It felt raw and angry. I'd been scratching around my waist without realising. I moved to better light near the entrance and pulled up my shirt. A rash with red spots and blotches clustered around my middle.

François called me back. 'Gentlemens. Your money and identity papers on the floor please. *Merci beaucoup.*'

We rummaged about inside our clothes and searched the coats on the flagstones. A small pile of notes, coins and documents grew next to each man. I kept my French banknotes. As with the other items I'd hung on to; if any of them were taken away, I wouldn't make it home. Perhaps that superstition was a throwback to the boys carrying lucky charms on ops. I never took any, but putting trust in simple faith now was no longer enough.

François gathered the hoard together, separated the money and shoved everything into his jacket.

'*Maintenant… les manteaux, s'il vous plaît.* Please wear your coats.'

The rain stopped later. Light was fading under a blue-black sky and it was almost nightfall when we finished the last swallows of wine. François rose to his feet in an instant. Harold raised a hand for quiet. Footsteps swished through the grass outside.

PART THREE
Spain
1

Two men in thick coats, leather trousers and balaclavas appeared by the shed entrance. Each carried a bulky goatskin bag slung across his body and a large stick. The taller figure had a pack on his back and exchanged words with François. I named him Stéphane. He explained in sharp sentences, which François translated, how we must walk in a close column and watch for his signals. We followed him to the entrance where François gave us all a vigorous handshake.

'Good luck, my friends.' He patted Kennedy on the shoulder as we walked away.

'*Messieurs.*' The smaller man handed out four long sticks from against the outside wall. Stéphane went on ahead, while we waited behind the other man's raised hand. How absurd we looked against them, dressed so inadequately to face the mountains. Just after six o'clock the group moved out. I stayed three or four paces behind Stéphane. Harold came next, forward of Kennedy and Ward. The smaller man kept to the rear, feeling out the track on both sides with his stick. Wet clothes welded to my body, trousers chafed against my legs and the state of my underwear was foul. I itched and scratched a path through the long grass and away from the barn. Every week at the aerodrome I parcelled up some of my laundry and posted it home to Mum. Every week it came back washed and ironed. I had mailed the last package on the day we were shot down. I prayed it had arrived before the telegram.

The night was thick. Tracks narrowed into short, undulating runs where Stéphane rustled on through ferns and the mushroom smell of undergrowth. A half-moon shone between breaks of cloud, casting shadows against the hills. The wind had eased, letting in a sly, tactile cold against my wet body. I rammed the stick into clumpy grass as the climbs grew steeper and downward slopes became more difficult.

Our guides displayed a cautious animal craft of their own, the furtive body language which sat with hunter and hunted – the psyche of men who knew every inch of their terrain. We walked along the foot of a valley, Stéphane hiking in and out of view and glancing anxiously at the sky as if trying to predict the next show of moonlight. It wasn't a glow, but easily distinguished our movement along the landscape. His hand went up and the line halted.

Clumps of trees bunched into the rising hill ahead. Stéphane tied a white handkerchief to the top of his stick. 'Les mouchoirs,' he said, indicating we should do the same. A raised hand or waved stick in the air meant stop and stand still. A downward sign meant lie on the floor. At least three of us had followed that drill when we crossed into France. The smaller man arrived and the procession started up after a swig of wine from his goatskin bag. Hours passed. The guides called to each other at intervals in a nasal, bleating sound. We crossed a stream, where a thinly built man stepped out from behind a line of saplings. He took up a rear position when the group moved past in single file. The smaller man departed at the next hill. A thick blackness enveloped us suddenly on the path. Stéphane appeared only as a handkerchief on his stick as we dropped below the skyline and onto a narrow sheep track grooved into the hillside. The moon shone clearly for several seconds. Hair rose on the back of my neck and arms; I was less than a foot from the edge of a ravine. Something struck me hard in the back and Kennedy crumpled at my feet. Harold grabbed an arm. I took hold of the other and we raised Kennedy into a sitting position, his legs still splayed over the edge. Ward and the other guide almost tumbled over us.

Kennedy's breaths came in snatches. 'Been getting these darned headaches.'

248

The guide crouched beside him and made a birdlike whistle. Stéphane took a while to retrace his route along the track. He bent down, tilted the bag and splashed some wine into Kennedy's mouth. We all took a drink, a simple process of angling our head back and waiting. The sweet taste thawed my numbed lips, but the trickle did little for my thirst. A huge cavern of hunger growled in my stomach, there was nothing in that empty space now except the cold. Stéphane inspected the line. I helped Kennedy up and Harold returned the stick to him. He stood behind, hands around Kennedy's waist. The track was too narrow to take more than one man, so the party trailed up the rise in a single column. The whole drama had been played out with less than half a dozen words.

We halted in a dip below the valley ridge. Stéphane held up what could have been five fingers. Kennedy sank to his knees. Ward squatted down beside him and the guides huddled together in their big coats and balaclavas. Stéphane drank from a small bottle after the other man had declined it. I set my shoulders, trying to stop the shaking.

'How long till the border?' Harold said.

Stéphane raised a single finger.

Kennedy groaned when he tried to stand. I hobbled across to him.

'Are you OK?'

What a ridiculous question, but this was not a moment for tact. He stared at the ground and the guides came to pick him up. Stéphane had indicated an hour to the border – a lot could happen in an hour. I thought about the dinnertime factory whistle before the war, a spill of people dashing through the grime for home and a hot meal. I cycled from Bells Printers in the city centre to our council house near the eastern edge of Leicester and back again every weekday. Margaret Pick caught a tram to the Shaftesbury cinema then boarded the Outer Circle bus to Ireton Road which was close to the fields. She would have passed Bill Ross walking more than two miles through the city to rows of terraced houses in

Brunswick Street off Humberstone Road. Even the old timers, Sid and Cyril, managed to make it home on their boneshaker bicycles – all there and back to work in an hour and a quarter. Strange how those thoughts invaded my head at that moment. Time would pass if I stayed on my feet and remembered the easy things.

François reckoned on six hours to the border and we had walked for nearly five. I made my legs start moving again. The next valley ridge became the foot of another massive hill. The guides pushed and cajoled us along. I shifted the strain from my calves by leaning on the stick. Stones dislodged by the others bounced down the path, hitting me. Rocks and clumps of grass protruded from the path causing trips and falls. The strain of hiking uphill began to tell. We were slowing down.

I knew our order by the rhythm of the men's steps. The group climbed over the rise and into a dense wood. No more stops or rest, only a glimpse of the white handkerchief ahead. Dad marched in a column of exhausted soldiers during the Great War and managed to doze at the same time. Impossible now and one more reminder of how much I longed for the soft, dark warm of sleep. Amongst the trees, we held on to each other's sticks in a long, climbing daisy chain, despite overhanging branches poking me in the face. How could Stéphane or his friend see where they were going? We sloshed through fast-running streams, the freezing water sluicing around my shins. I focused on something visible to aim for: a shape ahead or gap through the tree canopy – one small chunk of distance and time. When there was nothing I picked a number, counted my steps and started again as soon as I reached it. The mentality would work. I learned in an ops crew to think and speak only of things possible on the day: bacon and eggs, a letter home, the target briefing or beer and banter. No future existed beyond a crew's silence at the dispersal pad and the smell of leather, dope and oil inside the aircraft. There was nothing after a setting sun and take off until I stepped down onto the runway and sniffed the still morning air of another dawn.

The ground dropped sharply. We used our poles to slither down through scrub and grass. Stéphane changed direction to walk alongside a brook. Bare trees and saplings lined the water on both sides, giving us some scant cover. He moved to the back of our line while the other guide scouted ahead, making frequent hand signals for us to slow or stop. We halted opposite a gap in vegetation on the far side of the brook. Stéphane encouraged us towards the bank. The moon cast a phosphorescent sheen on the frothing water. Beyond the brook a long clearing ran about three hundred yards up to the foot of a steep hill. He pointed to the top.

'*Espagne.*'

My heart thumped faster. Ward nudged me. A quarter of a mile to the top of a hill – Spain was seven hundred strides away – a walk from home to the end of Mallory Place and back. No towers and guards, no criss-cross stakes or barbed wire.

'Can't hear him. What's he saying?' I whispered.

Kennedy pushed closer to me, panting. 'We walk to the hill. Then we run.'

I splashed into the water and bent a branch back to get through. Broken cloud slipped across the sky, thin and unpredictable. Stéphane moved on our flank. The other man led, urging us into pairs. I stayed alongside Ward. The wind dropped. Shadows were suddenly still and the hill became more black and brooding. We stopped. I heard the noise. Stéphane raced to the front, snapping gravelly French commands over his shoulder. The other guide ran in a different direction – there was no caution now. I was grabbed and shouldered back to the trees. A thunder of hooves grew louder. The sound was everywhere around us – thumping gaits and snorting, the churn of dirt, a clink of harness and beat of the earth as the crescendo passed.

I lay still in the wet. Noise from the horses faded. Ward was lying in front of me next to the other guide; the rest were getting to their feet nearby. I could see them all – shadows on the edge of a moonlit stage, with Stéphane waving frantically now.

Ward started off towards the hill. I whispered after him.

'What's he doing?'

'He says run... run for it.'

That single thought was the only thing I could hold in my mind. I crashed through the undergrowth, heard the gasp and heave of running men, then a crack of rifle fire. My legs tottered. I fell amongst the grass, clawing myself back up and throwing my body forward in a thrash of limbs. A figure crossed ahead of me – the hill grew steeper. I was climbing not running. The final yards were legs raking the ground and fingers tearing at soil. I collapsed on my stomach, gasping for air.

Someone retched nearby. I gulped in big breaths, trying to slow my thumping heart and stop the coughs. A presence knelt down next to me. White eyes peered through the balaclava. Stéphane helped me to stand and move away from the slope. Black shapes either side of us made for a figure waving near the bushes. Another shudder passed through my body: I'd remembered the gunfire. Everyone crowded together away from the hilltop. The guides stayed in a huddle.

'*Patrouille Alpine Allemande,*' Stéphane whispered in a husky voice.

'That was close,' Ward murmured. 'German Alpine patrol.'

Harold was still on his knees. He looked up.

'Where the hell's Kennedy?'

2

The guides fell silent.

'Anyone spot him on the hill?' Harold said.

'There was shooting, back there,' I whispered.

'Sounded like distant firing to me.' Ward paused for breath. 'I didn't spot him. Can't see much now, the moon's gone behind cloud again.'

My stick was missing. It must have dropped when I got pushed back to the trees. We searched around for Kennedy. Ward spoke to the guides. French spiralled up from the huddle. Raised arms and fingers pointed into the darkness.

'Haven't a clue with half of it,' Ward muttered. 'They say it's too dangerous to go back as the Germans are based only a couple of hundred yards away on the French side. There was something about Spanish patrols around here because of trouble in the mountains after the civil war. I've told them we won't move without Kennedy.'

Harold stood up straight, cautiously flexing his legs. 'Guess we'd better go find him then.'

Ward laid his stick on the ground. 'I'll come with you.'

'No, I'll go,' I said.

'Two of us will do, Ron,' Harold said.

I crept after him. Footsteps brushed through the grass behind us. Stéphane drew alongside and placed a hand on Harold's shoulder.

'Non... non.' He waved me forward with Ward. 'Allez.'

I wanted to go back and find Kennedy, wanted to take this solitary chance of making a difference without relying on guides and helpers. We had fought this war in teams where survival depended on each other, so why not now? Harold's thinking made sense, but it was Stéphane who had stepped in and made the final decision. They were both right. Why risk all three men?

I slithered down the hill with Ward. Nothing else stirred except the wind and rustle of grass. Time protracted and sharpened its claws; the German patrol could be spreading out along the hillside. What madness to risk everything, yet it was the right thing to do and nothing else mattered. Ward crouched close to me. He whispered in my ear.

'You look left and I'll take the right.' I felt his hand, hard on my shoulder. 'Let's go.'

Partway down, he changed direction. We had both noticed movement at the same time. Kennedy's indeterminate shape was trying to stand. We grabbed his arms and heaved him up the hill.

'He'd passed out,' Ward said, when we reached the top. Harold grappled with Kennedy's right arm, trying to make him stand on his own. Stéphane strode back to us.

'Très bientôt, nous arriverons à une ferme.'

'A farm, very soon,' Ward said to us.

Both guides were moving out. Ward picked up his stick.

'If I don't sit down soon, I'll bloody well fall down.'

I gripped Kennedy's arm. 'Come on, they're leaving.'

We tracked the others down a steep slope. Two yellow spots winked near the bottom of a valley. Kennedy faltered. I kept hold of him, oblivious of everything except the lights. The last time I'd seen any at night was below the Alps in summer when Swiss anti-aircraft batteries fired up token warning shots at us. The mountains and a carpet of glowing dots in the valleys had been bright and clear.

The farmhouse nestled on the hillside and its lights burned more orange than yellow as we drew nearer. I could almost smell lamp oil, feel the heat from a log fire and taste hot soup. A woman and a bald-headed man watched from the open doorway. The two guides assembled us in front of them and the conversation became a jumble of voices and covert gestures. The bald-headed man gave single word replies aimed in our direction. We were a ragged mess. Kennedy's trousers had torn at the knees and mud was caked on my clothes. I noticed an outbuilding tacked on to the farmhouse and the guides marshalled us to it.

'What the hell? If you—'. Harold's words were trampled under a churlish *'allez... allez,'* as the guides manoeuvred us inside. The wooden door shut in his face, pitching us into blackness. Something fled from around my ankles in a flutter of feathers and squawks. The stink of poultry manure and mould was overpowering. Someone gagged. Harold struck a match and panned it around the shed. Plaster walls, chickens cowering in corners and an earth floor of dung and feathers made me heave. The match flame flickered and died.

'We must get some air in here chaps, or we choke,' Ward said. The smell filled my empty stomach – maybe a smoke might dull the nausea. He forced the door open and a cold draught blew in. I fumbled inside my jacket. The matches were damp. It was beyond belief how Harold had managed to strike his after the soakings we had suffered. My cigarettes felt wet and no strength remained for me to do anything. The dumb miles we had covered after leaving Dax raked through my head. I relished that kind of solitude before the war. Bike rides and birdsong walks in the countryside on hushed Sundays when a city rested were a world away from the clatter of printing machines and traffic. They were dusty memories now.

I slid down the wall onto the floor. Voices from outside jolted me back into the moment. It was Stéphane and the other guide. Were they bringing food? The talking stopped. Their footsteps passed the shed and left us with nothing but silence.

'They'll bring food from the house... sure thing,' Harold said. The red tip on his cigarette glowed. Nobody answered.

I thought back to the volley he had fired at me in Paris when I was asking too many questions and *not letting them get on with it.* The bread roll and coffee at the café was eighteen hours ago and we would get no food tonight, whether we let them *get on with it* or not. The slow retreat in his voice told me he already knew that. I threw down my limp cigarette and the cold took over.

3

A man waited in the shed doorway, all bright face and black jacket. I blinked at the grey morning. He looked like the chap from the farmhouse. The others stirred. Ward got to his feet, hands pressed into the small of his back. Harold stretched across the floor to nudge Kennedy. The man ignored us as he entered the shed, firing off words in a rasping dialect. A cloud of flies flew up in the air when he waved his arms to shoo out the chickens. My whole body creaked and pain knifed through the right leg when I tried to stand. I steadied myself, bracing for the torture of the next movement.

The room darkened. A stout man sporting a beret and thick, weathered clothes had appeared in the doorway. He flicked his fingers and pointed outside.

The rest of us helped Kennedy to his feet. He straightened up. 'I'll be alright once I'm walking.'

Harold slipped his arm around Kennedy's waist. 'OK buddy, hang on to my shoulder. We'll start like this and see how it goes… yeah?'

Ward gave me a wry smile as we hobbled outside. Chickens pecked about in the yard – the cold air cut sharp inside my nostrils. Steep hills of scrub, bushes and clumps of trees rose on three sides. Harold and Kennedy stared up at the rising ground. The farmhouse was lodged on a wide shelf, before the slope tapered down to the bottom of a valley. The stout man passed me a stick, shorter than my last one. He could have been Pablo from the film *For Whom the Bell Tolls:* Pablo with a goatskin bag slung across his shoulder, Pablo buoyant with a full breakfast inside him.

'When will we get food? How long?' We had all thought of saying it. Harold was the one who asked.

Pablo gave us a vacant grin. He surveyed the untidy line for a moment, angled his beret and headed towards the hill, as if throwing down a challenge. We passed the farmhouse where four small faces pressed against a downstairs window. I kept walking, each step jolting my body as we climbed the valley. Another range of hills and foggy grey mountains came into view under a pewter-coloured sky. I stopped at the same time as the others, gazing at the panorama. Pablo pressed on and the worries engulfed me again. We were empty shells and four blank faces looking at the impossible. Ward moved off and the rest struggled after him.

Vultures circled high above. Finch-like birds with grey feathers and white breasts skimmed past us over the ferns and scrub. The soil was a yellow ochre colour and a herby smell rose if we walked through vegetation. Kennedy managed short distances unaided, but our pace slowed. Rest times became longer and Pablo constantly scanned the horizon as he rallied us up and down the rugged tracks. We stopped under a ledge close to some sheep crowding in a sheltered spot on the rim of a valley. Ward joined me. Harold shared a cigarette with Kennedy who sat crumpled on the ground like a pile of rags. I stayed on my feet, watching the distant peaks fight off a wandering mist. No one had passed us since leaving the farm.

'Any idea where we are, sir?' I asked Ward.

'Can't be too far off the target now. I'll be glad to get out of sight. We could all do with a good pit stop and refuel.'

The skin under my arms felt chafed and angry and the sore itch had spread all around my waist.

'These people are not like Max and the others,' I said.

'It's a different fight for some of them, sergeant. Last night was hardly the Ritz, I know, but we have to get on with it and keep moving. You heard what the guides said about the Germans and Spanish patrols. These men are taking big risks for us.'

'I realise that, sir. But it doesn't feel the same as before.'

'What do you mean?'

'I get the feeling if we can't keep up with them, we've had it. The climbing and weather are getting worse and they're in enough danger already, without us slowing things down. We have to stay together, keep our eyes open and really look after one another.'

'I'd expect us to be doing that, already.' He focused on Pablo, standing separate from the group. 'You can't argue with him and we don't have a choice. I certainly don't fancy a Spanish prison.' He turned to face the mountains. 'I'm not asking for any special treatment, but we need food soon and he's got to sort it.'

We lined up for a trickle of wine from the goatskin bag, mouths open when it was our turn, like schoolboys waiting for a sprinkle of sherbet powder from a tube. Pablo was last to take a swig before he slung the bag across his shoulder and waved us on. Every step brought a food memory from home: gusts of freshly baked bread, a smell of Wednesday's stew and the scrape of a knife across hot, buttered toast on Saturday night after football.

The track narrowed as we walked along a ledge near a sheer drop. A scream in front cut through the quiet. Kennedy was sliding down a slope towards the edge.

4

The voice shattered in my ears. Stones and small rocks bounced down the grassy slope. Kennedy grabbed hold of a small bush. His legs slithered and kicked – it would never take his weight. Harold edged down a couple of feet, digging in his heels. He started to scramble back up the slope.

'I can't reach him. Pass me a stick, I'll try again. Grab my legs.'

Kennedy thrashed about, clawing at the grass. 'It's coming away.' His cry cut high and scratchy like clawing fingers down a blackboard.

I threw Harold my stick and he swivelled around on his knees. Ward sat beside me on the edge of the slope. We held a leg each as Harold crawled down on his stomach holding out the stick with both hands. Pablo joined us and knelt down, wrapping his arms around my waist.

'Grab it,' Harold called.

Kennedy was a foot short.

'We're in the wrong position,' I shouted, 'they'll pull us both down.'

Kennedy lunged again. He grasped the gnarled end with one hand. I felt the pull of extra weight and began to slip.

'Other hand,' Harold cried.

Earth and scree raced past him, plunging over the edge. Kennedy had both hands on the stick now. A clump of grass came away under my feet. I pushed with my heels against firmer ground. Ward and Pablo held steady. We started to pull. Kennedy got a foothold and crawled a few feet. Harold grabbed his wrists and my stick slid to the edge, arrowing out of sight. Pain ripped through my arms and shoulders, the seconds only a marker between each new jolt and how far Kennedy had climbed from his last set of muddy scuff lines.

We lay tangled on the track afterwards. Kennedy was on his back. Harold had crawled away from the edge and Pablo brushed mud off his clothes. Ward sat next to me, head between his knees. A sound like the rushing sea filled my head and the ground began to tilt and spin.

Minutes must have passed. The faces around me still wobbled at the edges and Pablo's voice was a string of blurry words. He hauled me up.

'My guess is he's saying we're not far away,' Ward said, battling to his feet. 'Let's hope no one heard or saw us.'

We sorted ourselves into order and the path soon became wider. Kennedy took the inside track with his arm around Harold as we climbed the next hill. Were they hills or mountains? It made no difference. Pablo stopped and pointed out a farmhouse with white walls. He pursed his lips and nodded to us like a wise man addressing the crowd. Nobody spoke – nobody did anything except follow him. We reached the edge of a yard seamed with cart tracks. Birds pecked amongst the mud and tangles of rusty farm machinery cluttering approaches to the farmhouse. Pablo took a curved route around the mess and knocked on the door. The rest of us kept our distance.

'I'm so cold it's not hurting any more,' I said.

Harold gave me a sidelong glance. 'Got here just in time, I guess.'

Pablo knocked again. An olive-skinned woman opened the door. A man wearing black clothes and a beret appeared from behind the farmhouse. I wanted to believe, wanted to feel something other than exhaustion and misery, yet I already knew what had been said from the frightened faces and arm waving. Kennedy's legs had folded in front of me before Pablo was turned away.

We got him back on his feet by the time Pablo returned.

'This man is not fit to walk any further,' Ward said, firmly. 'He needs rest and food. We all do.'

Pablo looked along the valley, then anxiously up at the hill. He shook his head and spoke with occasional French words amongst the raspy dialect. His face told me danger and we must keep moving. I shuffled off with the others and took my turn to help Kennedy, but he was slowing us down.

I should keep faith: so said the creed at home and at Scouts' church parade, so said the padre, or words bandied about in bravado amongst aircrews. I'd listened to all of it, yet still saw the men vanish overnight in a totally random way. Some of those lads had a certain look on their faces. The chop look, there in a fleeting glance at quiet moments when they thought nobody was watching, there in the crew room when they put their stuff in the locker or waited for trucks to take them out to the dispersal pads. They feared their number was up, yet still clung to faith. I always told myself it wouldn't be me and never thought beyond that. Was that the same simple faith? Faith – the belief in something with no proof. Did any of it make a difference out here, except giving me the soul to keep going? Faith was no different to belief and I believed in our guides because I had to. Without them there was no hope. But hope was a dangerous thing. It sat on the crown of every hill, looking down at us like some black devil until we reached the top and saw another empty valley. I had become a walking ghost witnessing my own demise and there was a numb inevitability about it. I thought about the simple act of strolling down our street at home and knowing where I was going. The last time I'd opened the front door to our house was a surprise forty-eight-hour pass and Mum was dusting the fireplace. The instant joy on her face when she saw me had never faded from my mind. A packet of Craven "A" cigarettes sat on the mantelpiece. Dad always put his Park Drive on there. I thought we had taken in a new lodger.

'No. Your dad's had a change,' Mum said. 'The others were giving him a bad throat.'

They were giving him a bad throat. My sniggers started suddenly. Tears welled up and I choked back laughter. I fought against the shudders and swallowed my noise. That memory might have been an escape from where I was now, but not from who I was. I set my face and shoulders and narrowed the gap to the others.

Wind swept down the valley. A few pale blades of sunshine shone on the mountains. Part-hidden by a dip in the land, I caught sight of a small farm. A man wearing a beret limped out to meet us when we approached. After a long discussion with Pablo, he pointed up the slopes behind his farmhouse. The giant hills and peaks surrounding us remained distant and unreachable. Kennedy propped himself up heavily against me, so I gripped his arm to stop another fall. Harold looked close to giving up.

'He's saying something about a cabin being up there,' Ward said.

Pablo held up three fingers. Harold moved closer.

'What do you mean? Is it three kilometres… three hours?'

'Kilometres.'

'What about food?'

Pablo grinned, showing gappy white teeth. He pointed straight ahead. I'd no strength left to think about whether he understood or cared. The others had followed him past the farmhouse before I limped after them.

The impatient voice of hunger drove me on. Sunlight cast strange moving shadows on the landscape when it poked through the racing cloud. The wind stayed at our backs, buffeting us along. Skies thickened in the late afternoon and rain fell in diagonal sheets as we reached shelter. A flimsy-looking wooden shed nestled against the mountain slope. Pablo led us through the door which was grooved into a permanent half-open position. Lumps of dried black sheep manure covered the earth floor and I fell on my knees in the corner. Only relentless pain remained: pain through my body from muscle to bone, pain from skin to sinew, pain throbbing in my head and filling the empty space in my stomach. Pablo went outside.

'Someone's coming later with food,' Ward said. 'Can't be sure… I think that's what he meant.'

We had done everything asked of us, beaten off each challenge, kept going and it had come to this. The walls became a blur. I struggled to focus on the others properly. Coloured flashes flickered in my vision – the shed started to spin. I slumped back against the wall and spiralled down into a grey fog.

5

I woke from an empty, cold sleep. The journey in my dreams had taken me nowhere and food peered around every corner. It sat in lines on tables covered with crisp white cloths – slab sandwiches, ham slices fanned out on plates, cheese lined up on parade in thick blocks, tinned fruit salad and bricks of fruitcake. A coughing fit brought me fully awake. Daylight shone in through the open door, casting shadows on Kennedy's still figure on the floor. The new day carried the same grey pallor as before. Harold came in from outside.

'I've been all around. Guide's missing, gone for sure,' he said, holding on to the door. 'What time is it, Ron?'

I fished out my watch, tilting it up to the light. 'Just after twenty-past ten.'

Ward's shape stirred in the corner and knelt forward on all fours.

'Bad blisters,' he said, as if speaking to himself. Kennedy moved and groaned.

Harold stood in the middle of us. 'We're on our own, guys. Need to think about leaving. Walk back to that farm and get food… or some of us could go.' He gave a flick of his head towards the door. 'It's only three miles.'

I tried to stand up. 'Last night, the guide told Flying Officer Ward someone was coming back with food. Isn't that right, sir?'

'So where are they?' Harold gave me a thin smile. 'We've been to two places with that guy and they wouldn't keep us. We can't speak his lingo and I'll tell you something else for nothing… he's jumped ship.'

'Give it a bit longer,' I said. 'We could light a fire, just a small one. I've matches. They might have dried out overnight.'

'Squadron Leader Kennedy is in no fit state to continue,' Ward said. 'Without food and water, none of us are.'

I couldn't leave things as they were. 'Can't we wait, sir? For an hour, that's all. There's still time for someone to get here.'

Harold looked in Ward's direction. With Kennedy out of action, Ward had the senior rank.

'We'll wait,' Ward said, rising to his feet. 'I know its freezing cold here, but we can't risk lighting a fire. If no one shows up by thirteen hundred hours I'll go back to the farm. It shouldn't be difficult to spot from near here. I'll need anything you have that we can use as payment for food.'

He dusted the dirt off his clothes and walked over to Kennedy who had shored himself up into a sitting position.

'He says he's OK to continue, lads. If I have to make the trip and don't return by tonight, Sergeant Pope will assume command of the party.'

'Some party,' Harold said.

My thinking had sound logic and Ward's compromise was good. What would happen if we all struck out together now with no guides? Starving men would not think straight, they'd take risks and do careless things – walk down main roads, go to the first village or farmhouse for help, steal food or give themselves away for a meal. If left out there, we'd not stay free for long. Everything would have been for nothing and all for the sake of waiting another hour.

At first, I thought it was the wind rustling through grasses behind the shed. A figure in a woollen coat, carrying a bulky pack and criss-cross of goatskin bags, blundered through the entrance. The young man squinted at us through a flick of black hair below his large beret.

'*Ingelesa eta Amerikako zaude?*'

We managed to stand up, except for Kennedy.

'*Inglés? Americano?*'

'Yes. We are English and American,' I said.

'*Aviador?*' He pointed at the others.

'Yes. We are all airmen.'

He slung his pack and stick down near to my feet and scuffed out an area in the middle of the floor by kicking manure away. I smelt food. His two goatskin bags completed the pile and he shook hands with each of us, leaving Kennedy until last. He squatted down beside him and the handshake lingered, as if gauging Kennedy's physical state. All I could think about was a smell of bread and spice seeping from the pack – an instinctive thought rising above everything else. It came with an underlying sense of guilt, until I saw Harold and Ward staring at the same spot next to my feet.

I decided to call the young man Robert, for no reason except it was easy to remember. He spoke slowly to Kennedy in the same rough dialect as Pablo, only with more hoarse French words and mimes. Kennedy's answers were inaudible to me, yet Robert seemed to understand. He held up one of the goatskin bags like an exhibit in a court room. '*Bota*,' he said, handing it to Ward.

The *bota* reached me last. I fought against an urge to guzzle, drinking slowly to catch every drop of wine and ignoring the parched looks from the others waiting for a second shot. In the dull light, I noticed Robert as he assessed the rest of us. Words were unnecessary; reassurance came in those caring eyes. He displayed a different demeanour to Pablo, more slow and deliberate, even when handing out the oval-shaped flatbread and sausages from the depths of his pack.

He sat in the middle of the shed with his own food, so that we were gathered around him in a horse-shoe shape. We must have looked a primitive lot with our mouths full and little thought given to chewing and swallowing. If Robert disapproved it wasn't obvious. He broke off some bread and gave it to Kennedy. I couldn't forget that moment: Robert on his knees and Kennedy staring over the top of a crust into some distant place. How he had kept going defied all logic, slipping slowly towards the inevitable, before pulling himself up to cling on for another day.

Robert left him with a reassuring pat on the shoulder then

took out pairs of black canvas shoes with caulk-looking rope soles from his pack. The uppers looked similar to white plimsolls or navy-coloured yachting footwear which men wore on seaside holidays at home. Surely we were not expected to wear them in the mountains? For the first time, a hint of urgency crept into Robert's manner: the checks outside, a pacing around the shed and random fiddling with one of the *botas* as he tried to explain our next move in single words and gestures.

It took a while to remove my footwear. Blood had congealed around my toenails and blisters filled both heels. The other men were busy examining their own feet. Ward was first to put on his canvas shoes. He walked gingerly to the shed door and back, like a man in a shoe shop, trying on a pair for the first time. It was a while before we were ready. I couldn't see how the shoes would remain in one piece or keep out the cold and wet, but Robert had arrived when our spirits were at their lowest point and he knew what he was doing. There was nothing more to be said on it.

I tied my old shoes together by the laces and hung them around my neck. The others did the same.

'*Inglés Americano. Allez,*' Robert said, helping Kennedy to his feet and leading him slowly outside.

Ward's cracked soles grinned at me from around his neck as he limped out. Harold gave me an uneasy smile through the stubble and dirt on his face. I paused beside him at the front wall and took in the overcast morning.

'C'mon… we'd better go,' he said.

Kennedy held Robert's stick and used it to balance and take slow steps. Mine had fallen into the ravine when we rescued Kennedy. At least the rope soles on my shoes gripped the rising ground. I could feel every stone and ridge under my sore feet, it was like walking barefoot. Robert pushed on, often returning down our line to keep the party together. We trudged on like a funeral procession, heads bowed against the wind sweeping across hills and mountain slopes. I lost all feeling in my feet after crossing several streams. My shoes were soaked and the left side of my face and body numb. Our clothes were inadequate against the elements and it was frightening to see conditions deteriorate so rapidly when clouds covered the mountain peaks. At rest stops, Robert would pass a *bota* around as we huddled together like sheep in the corner of a field.

Mountains and hills appeared deserted, except for occasional traces of white smoke in the distance. Ward helped Kennedy while Harold moved steadily over the rough ground, his short, stocky frame holding a lower sense of gravity. With no support, the stress on my knees and ankles burst into clusters of pain. Each time I fell, the fight to catch up with the others turned into a full-scale battle. Robert always raised his hand to halt the column and check ahead when approaching a mountain summit or hilltop, which bought me time to catch up before the pattern repeated. He waited at the top of another huge slope, his fractured commentary lost in the wind. I traced the line of his outstretched arm to a house in the next valley.

The track led down to a yard bordered with woven branch fencing. Smoke rising from the chimney was instantly snatched away in a crosswind. Two wooden doors were open at ground level, exposing straw inside on the floor. The house had plaster walls and a tiled roof. I guessed at a live-in barn with windows and accommodation above. A woman with dark-grey hair matching her shawl and clothing greeted Robert at the side entrance. She led us up to a room where a black pan simmered over a fire in the corner. A fug of coffee and cooking blended with the smell of animals. We sat shivering, almost on top of the fire, while Robert chatted with her. The woman's frequent looks in our direction unnerved me. She called to someone who I couldn't see. A child with a dirty face tiptoed in carrying four small tin-plate bowls with handles. We took one each and the woman picked up a white enamel pot next to the fire. Coffee gurgled into our bowls, the bitter aroma flooding my head. For a long moment, I feasted on steam and heat by hugging the bowl close to my face before gulping the drink down as hot as I could tolerate. There was nothing more except gobbling beans off a plate and the old woman waving a pencil and paper at Ward.

'*Numero,*' she said.

'Name and number, lads,' he mumbled, through a mouthful of food.

He made a note and handed me the sheet. It was a list of names with English or American service numbers and the handwriting was different on every line. A reckless sense of comfort came from that piece of paper with its hastily scribbled list: others had passed through before. I added my details and searched for my crew. They weren't there.

Robert moved about the place with familiarity. He knew where to take his empty plate and searched a table drawer without asking the woman. I noticed him in earnest conversation with her. Whatever they spoke about was left unresolved and her glare followed him to the window. He stayed there, looking out at some distant place and shaking his head. Ward was the first to address him.

'Gibraltar... how far is it? How much further do we have to go?'

Kennedy said something. If Robert had heard either man, he didn't acknowledge them. He went back to the old woman, who turned away and busied herself with the pots. Our shoes and socks were soon lined up by the fire. Harold lit the remnants of his cigarette.

'Last one, guys.'

He took a long draw, pluming the smoke away from me before passing the cigarette around. It was a stub end, which summed up our total state. The aftermath of the journey lay stencilled on the men's faces – the same dejected look as Ken when I left the Macas' apartment in Brussels. Perhaps the burns on his hand had healed now? Maybe he was fit and travelling to Spain? I would hold those hopes in my head instead of thinking about the weak smile on his face.

The four of us withdrew into ourselves again by the fire. Had we ever done anything except that? Of course we had, we'd helped one another. Ward and I went back across the border into France to rescue Kennedy. Harold had saved his life later. What the four of us were doing now was simply wrestling with our own exhaustion and self-doubts around the next journey. But I still yearned more than ever for a bond and friendship between the group, instead of the same guarded camaraderie which hovered between discipline and duty.

Robert and the woman kept us at a distance, holding most of their conversations out of earshot. Afternoon slipped into early evening, the firelight casting an orange glow on the walls. Kennedy lay curled up in a foetal position, Ward and Harold sat, heads bowed. I must have catnapped, as the woman made me start when she lit an oil lamp in the window. I was willing her to let us stay put for the night, then I saw Robert in his woollen coat and beret, rousing the others.

We descended the stairs around eight-thirty. Robert waited at the bottom and handed us stouter, longer sticks, more like the staffs we were given by the guides when we left François. A strip of white cloth was flagged on each. When we were all outside, Robert shut the door and spoke.

'I'm sorry. I don't understand what he's saying,' Ward whispered.

Kennedy interrupted. 'Something about two hours?'

'We can't see our hands in front of our faces.' My words had stumbled out with sickening inevitability. The terrain ahead of us would only get worse.

6

When Robert turned away, I noticed a large, white square attached to his backpack. The night swallowed up the rest of him and my direction hinged again on the sound of feet ahead. A speck of light blinked on the silent, sleeping landscape, yet always the climb moved upwards into blackness. Harold was close, I heard him muttering. We scrambled higher up rock and scrub, the cold biting into my face as the temperature plunged. The shoes around my neck hung like lead weights causing me to stumble into a solitary bush close to the top, maybe nature's last stand against the bare mountain. Any stop to rub the circulation back into my legs became impossible as the man ahead of me was always nearly out of earshot.

Dustings of snow lay on the summit. Robert walked back and helped Kennedy to the top. The others huddled together against the white background. Gaps appeared in the night sky, leaving patchy moonlight as we slithered down the winding tracks on the other side. My right heel slid about in the shoe – the blisters must have burst or my feet were bleeding again. Robert halted against a black panorama of mountains and hills. Wind ripped across the slopes as he moved down our line. Ward tried to speak to him in short phrases and Robert's replies were inaudible. He mustered the rest of us together, cupped his hands and shouted in Ward's ear.

'Don't think we're far from the next place,' Ward hollered. 'We've got to get a move on. That's all I could understand. This wind's bad enough and on these paths we're right on view when there's a break in the cloud.'

The group slowed on the rocky descent. Only Robert was looking about him as he negotiated the rugged, zigzag tracks. The rest of us feathered out every step, as if tightrope walking along a narrow shelf. Ruts and dips lay hidden on the path and the edges sloped away into a murky drop. We reached the top of a ridge. A light flickered in the distance and Robert struck out for it, moving down to flatter ground. The dark shape of a house with its long, sloping roof and a barn close by came into view. He stopped us at the barn doors. The house was a dozen paces away. Restless cattle moved about in a stable area at ground level underneath its first floor. A smell of rotting manure was rising from somewhere.

Robert signalled for us to wait. He climbed an outside stairway at the left front of the house to the first of two levels. Wooden railed balconies were on both stages and in the middle of the first floor an entrance door opened before he could knock. I leaned back against the barn doors and the others did the same. We stood lined up in shadow. It was the right analogy; all of us were still in the dark.

A man and woman spoke to Robert. He replied in a faltering voice, his silhouette leaning as if trying to peer around the couple into the house. Our difficult journey with Pablo came roaring back into my head. No one was fit to continue if we were refused shelter here. The barn was closed up and silent, maybe the couple would let us sleep in there? Surely Robert would see us right?

The woman passed him something. He steadied himself against the wooden rail, swaying for a moment on the creaking slat veranda like a drunk contemplating his next step. The woman shut the door. Cattle in the stable underneath the house started braying. Robert's wobbly descent drove a stark reality home. The other guides appeared indestructible, but he was exhausted now like the rest of us. He clattered down the final few steps and walked slowly back, carrying a lighted lamp.

Once we were all inside the barn, Ward pulled the doors shut. Robert panned the lamp around above the earth floor. On the left, an open entrance led to a room with tools set out on a bench table. A wooden stairway facing us rose up parallel to a stone dividing wall.

'We're staying up there.' Ward pointed to a space at the top. 'I'm guessing at the rest of what he said. It's no lights, don't leave the barn and we'll get food later. There was something about the Spanish police not wearing uniforms around here... couldn't make sense of that. I'd say things are still pretty dicey.'

I inched up the steps. Goats and sheep bleated from the other side of the wall and a smell of cattle hung about the space. Robert dimmed the lamp as he reached the top. He called us together under a box-shaped skylight built into the sloping roof. Stars glinted above and a weak vein of moonlight shone on the layer of straw and dried leaves under my feet. His lamp was enough to reveal we were in a large hayloft with a low roof of criss-cross lattice wood supporting clay tiles. Flies crawling about the place probably came from the cattle below. Robert spoke again. There must have been a temptation for him to only address Ward, or even Kennedy, but his look seemed to take in each man as an individual before he spoke to us as one body. I admired him for that.

'He's leaving,' Ward said. 'I suggest we wait to be fed and get some rest.'

Robert shook each man by the hand before crossing to the stairs. He extinguished the lamp, and the barn door had shut before any of us could settle down in the cold and think about removing our footwear.

The noise from somebody retching woke me. It was still dark and an eerie glow slanted in through the skylight. The figure kneeling in the corner looked like Kennedy. My insides turned over. The meal promised for the previous evening never arrived and we'd had little food in three days. After Robert left, I'd removed my wet shoes and socks and fallen straight asleep. Legs and feet felt like blocks of ice now. Through the skylight, I saw the subtle fade of stars give way to dawn. It was a different sky after I joined the RAF: an unforgiving place for an aircraft, a vast space which demanded respect. The wispy cirrus clouds high in a blue sky meant fair weather, sheets of grey stratus brought overcast days and steady rain, low cumulus cloud could turn into thunderstorms, and the nimbus signalled rain, snow or hail. The weather became more than a signpost. A blue sky meant ops were certain that night. A bomber's moon was a full moon – easier to find and strike the target, but straightforward for enemy anti-aircraft guns and fighter planes to shoot us down. For an escaper travelling through countryside and mountains, it was the same double-edged sword: see where you're going and be seen.

'Listen,' Harold said. 'We've got company.'

The barn door creaked open below. Someone moved about underneath. Yellow light stroked around the gap at the top of the stairs. A middle-aged woman wearing a spotted headscarf emerged holding an oil lamp. We were fussed into a circle to sit on the floor with the woman's lamp in the middle. Any lights were at odds with what Robert had told Ward. The woman brought four large metal bowls from the loft corner and by the time she came back with a jug of hot water, we had all taken turns to hold the lamp and examine our feet again. My soles were covered in patchy red skin, a blister on the right heel looked split and my toenails remained a bloody mess. Everyone had started to scratch themselves. Maybe they were suffering from the same rash as me, or lice. I was last to immerse my feet painfully into a bowl. The other faces were already in different stages of grimace or relief.

We didn't have long to wait before the woman brought a meal of mutton and beans on metal pie plates. Goats and sheep were driven out later from underneath the hayloft. Sawing and hammering went on below throughout the day, and around mid-afternoon a patter of steady rain sounded on the roof. Nobody put their socks or shoes back on, and none of us tried walking barefoot except to visit a bucket in the corner. We sat or lay on the straw in a silent world until daylight slipped away. Only rain and a symphony of drips remained, which finally drew me into a long and fitful sleep.

Another overcast day showed through the skylight. Rain was still falling and nicks of light crept through gaps in the roof tiles. Voices came from outside, then a sound like an army tramping up to the hayloft. Kennedy and Harold were awake. Ward was straight to his feet. Four men in soaking clothes shuffled in.

'Skipper,' Ward called out. He hobbled across barefoot and shook hands with the first man. I hadn't seen him before, but the slim figure alongside was Bob Clements, the Canadian I'd stayed with at the Macas' apartment in Brussels. Beads of rain trickled down his weary face. Johnnie, the chap with a Northern England accent, was with him and the smaller, thickset figure of Mills the American hung back behind them. They had been in the farmhouse near Rumes where we changed our papers, and at the policeman's home after we crossed the border into France. The new man introduced himself as Squadron Leader Passy. The others didn't venture beyond a nod or tired hello.

In the furore I hadn't noticed the other two men in dark clothing at the top of the stairs. One was wringing out water from his beret, the taller figure muttered to him and they left us. We helped the new party to remove their coats and lay them out on the floor.

'Best we can do, chaps,' Ward said. 'There's nowhere to hang these and fires are not allowed, I'm afraid. We've been here for two nights and turn our coats over if we can find a dry spot on the straw.'

Passy looked suspiciously at the steady drips falling from the roof. He sat down with Ward. Mills joined Harold, Clements went to Kennedy and Johnnie stayed alone, curling up in the corner. He was the only one from the new party who kept his canvas shoes on. I guessed that Passy was Ward's pilot, so it was natural they would stick together. The Americans had paired up and so had the Canadians. In an instant, the national kinship and rank had swept away any flimsy connection which might have existed in our original group.

Ward soon slipped into a whispered conversation with Passy. The two of them were just within earshot of me and Ward addressed him as Skipper again. I doubted there would be any relaxation of protocol with the rank and file here, such as Clements had initiated with me at the Macas' apartment in Brussels.

'Any news on what's happened to the others?' the Skipper asked.

'Only Geoff,' Ward said. He explained how they left the crash site together and reached Paris.

Geoff was obviously Flying Officer Madgett.

'We were taken to this posh block of apartments and up to the second or third floor,' Ward said. 'A lad, must have been about eighteen, invited us in. He introduced us to a middle-aged woman, a pleasant sort. She was his mother and had a younger son and niece with her. She told us we'd be staying with them for a while and we introduced ourselves. The place was like a palace, with expensive furniture, there was even a piano. My schoolboy French isn't too clever, but Geoff speaks it reasonably well, so we all managed fine. Some drinks and a meal... got a good night's sleep too.'

His pause for breath was no more than an instant. 'Strolled up the Champs-Élysées quite often, dined out at various well-known haunts. I was told not to worry as we were in good hands. The underground provided all the money and the head waiters were fully aware of who we were. Quite a lot of visitors came to the apartment too. Nobody bothered about that sort of thing. Eventually Geoff got told he was leaving. Why they picked him I don't know. He went first and then...'

His voice dropped. 'Kennedy over there arrived. He was with me for a few days and then we left together by train for Bordeaux.'

'And all the while, I was stuck in not much more than a damn cupboard,' the Skipper said.

I only caught snatches after that. The Skipper stayed in Paris at an old woman's place in rough conditions and each evening went to another house to sleep. I thought I heard him say it was in the middle of a park but couldn't be certain.

'I'm not sure what you're complaining about, Skipper,' Ward said. 'You went out every night.'

I could almost see the smile on his face.

The Skipper had met Clements near the rail station and caught the night train to Bordeaux. They joined Johnnie and Mills at Dax. The rest of his story sounded similar to our group until they reached the Spanish leg of the journey. He said nothing about that part.

Ward's Paris excursion had been another world from mine. I understood the relief at meeting his pilot and an officer's trust between them, except it was like listening to a different person. Maybe Ward was condemned by his higher rank to say certain things to me in order to keep that distance. He had opened his shutters for the first time, even if the Skipper was the only one meant to hear. I still didn't know Ward's first name.

The farm stayed quiet apart from the spat-spat drips through the roof. Our gallery of unshaven faces weighed each other up through the morning light. The new arrivals looked in better shape than us. They soaked their feet in the same bowls we used earlier, whilst the man and woman from the farm brought a breakfast of tortillas, blood sausage and a hot drink which tasted of aniseed. I slept and rested all day until twilight when the two guides who had brought the Skipper's party returned. He spoke to them in smatterings of Spanish.

'Any pukka gen?' Ward said, getting to his feet.

The Skipper grimaced. 'Two more nights of walking. They say it's still dangerous to travel during the day, so we're leaving in fifteen minutes. I'll make sure everyone's in the picture.'

Exhausted men traipsing through mountains in the dark without getting arrested, or worse, should have been worry enough, but my physical state had dulled everything down to simply staying upright and surviving.

The others left the barn in the same pairs they formed in the hayloft. Rain had stopped and the wind began to drop as the last daylight traces disappeared behind the mountains to the west. At the first rest point, Johnnie and I stayed away from the group near some bushes and mossy rocks on the slope.

'So nobody in your party brought their old shoes,' I said.

'No. A guide told us we wouldn't use them again. These darned things are splitting and my feet are soaking wet and freezing.'

'So are mine. Trouble is, we won't get far without them on this ground.'

'How come you brought your old ones?' he said.

'We all did. I figured we'd need them after crossing the mountains. Never expected things to be this bad though.'

'Can't have been as rough as the other night. That was the worst weather yet and I've been travelling since September.'

I was about to latch on to his reply when the Skipper joined us.

'Keep your voices down, lads. I've just had another ear bending off one of them, there's supposed to be no talking. Anyway, we're ready to push off in a minute. Taller chap says we'll stop again in a couple of hours then move on to another place before it gets light.'

Johnnie was shifting his feet cautiously on the spot. 'Did he say how much more of this we've got? It feels like we're going around in a circle.'

'I've asked him,' the Skipper said. 'Not sure my French and attempts at Spanish stretched that far, or he just doesn't know… or won't say. It's certainly off the beaten track here. Let's hope we're getting close.'

Close to what? I doubted any one of us knew, least of all Kennedy who was being helped to his feet again by Harold.

7

The guides grew frustrated with our slow pace at the back. I reasoned they must be farmers, shepherds or more likely smugglers. Each one knew the tracks and turns, every danger and where to look out for Spanish patrols or quislings. They were a living part of the hills and mountains and treated those giants with respect. This was not a time to be held up by stragglers.

Hours passed between each rest stop. The long reach of night was endless. Our path through miles of dead and thinning bracken levelled onto an even stretch with a bank sloping down on one side. We halted suddenly and were pushed down the slope into undergrowth. I lay amongst the wet and a smell of decaying vegetation. A rustling sound came on the wind, slowly drawing nearer. A line of five men carrying packs and bundles passed by on the ridge. When our guides reappeared, I literally crawled up the steep bank along with the two figures nearest me.

We walked. The black hills and mountains stacked up ahead like some giant rollercoaster. I couldn't take the pain and exhaustion or stay on my feet. Past and future ceased to exist and it was a relief when the present began to fade. Figures around me became ghosts drifting in front or appearing at my side. I rested with them at some indeterminate point during the night, squashed in the corner of a derelict sheep shed. Time existed only in coughs and groans which broke my stupor until Harold tugged my arm and helped me to stand.

Dawn crept along the valley as we approached the back of an isolated house near a road. A wiry-looking man escorted us inside, chattering to himself in French, lighting lamps, and gathering the party together in a large live-in kitchen. Smoke from the beginnings of a wood fire blew out from the hearth when he rushed past to hang a blanket on two nails to screen the front window.

The men sat strewn around the floor. I was closest to the back door. The Frenchman found some cigarettes which he cut in half at the table and handed around, poking the last one between his lips. My brain was drugged with exhaustion – body and soul screamed they couldn't do this anymore. No matter what had passed before, or how near I was to freedom, the will and fight had run out.

Someone lodged a cigarette behind my ear. Johnnie's distant voice brought me back.

'I used one in Paris. Two shapes on the floor like feet, a hole in the ground and when you pulled this piece of string you got a darned footbath.'

I must have only dropped out for a moment. A mesh of tobacco smoke hung above the men. I sniffed the rich smell. I'd smoked cigarettes like those in Maison Blanche when we landed there after bombing Friedrichshafen on the first shuttle raid. The room sharpened into focus. Ward and the Skipper sat under the window talking to the Frenchman, who broke off to pull at the blanket and check the view outside. No Germans would be down the street. Apart from that, little else had changed for us. If I did make it back home, seeing someone look out through a window would never feel the same again. None of us shifted off the floor to occupy the two wooden chairs at the table. Johnnie soon stopped talking and the others dozed or stared at their cigarettes. I didn't see our guides leave.

After a meal of vegetables, beans and white cheese, I slept again until a rapping came at the back door. Two men in their thirties with granite, gangster features came in behind the Frenchman.

'*Vos convoyeurs sont arrivés, mes amis,*' he said, looking around the room.

'Guides have arrived,' the Skipper said, as if we all needed his translation. Both wore the mandatory thick coats. One man had his unbuttoned, revealing a navy waistcoat with large buttons, a white shirt and neckerchief. Their berets were bigger than ours, fitted level and high on the forehead so they hung over at the edges. Both spoke in some sort of Spanish and both carried a *bota* and bulky, brown leather bag.

'Pay attention, chaps. It'll be nightfall soon,' the Skipper said. 'We leave in ten minutes. They say this is the last jaunt. It'll be a good few hours and there won't be much time to stop.'

The men listened with vacant faces and red-rimmed eyes. Kennedy looked as if his worst nightmare had just crawled out. Only the Skipper and Mills were ready.

The Frenchman dimmed the lamps then held the back door open until we recovered our sticks and assembled outside. Stars littered the black sky and a rising moon shone above the hills and mountain peaks. Some of us took in large gulps of air as we moved off. I slotted in the middle of the column with Johnnie and could clearly see where my feet were treading. All of us would be visible from the hills. It didn't seem to matter anymore.

These guides were slower and even more cautious than the others, with one man scouting ahead before the other moved us along. The upper slope on the first hill had a thin covering of snow, so I stepped into the powdered footprints: only one set, large and heavily deformed where others had walked in the lead guide's tracks. Footmarks intermittently veered off in skid lines where someone had slipped. Wet clung to my frozen feet and the cold pecked at my toes. The men ahead leaned hard on their sticks, panting out plumes of frosted breath as our shadows followed us down tracks and gullies on the other side. I rehearsed each step in my head like some novice dancer. Johnnie took an awkward fall and not long after, Kennedy tripped. Near the base, we rested by a stream. I knelt down, drinking the icy water. From the moon's position, we must have taken more than two hours to climb over that hill. Johnnie sat rubbing his ankle, Harold and Mills prodded at their footwear. None of us would see this out with our feet intact. The canvas uppers on my shoes were coming away from the soles. I still had the elastic bands Dinah had given me in Belgium during my early days with Denise. They fitted around perfectly.

The guides patrolled our line again. They knew how to ask for money: rub thumb and forefinger together, hold coins out in their hand; it was a universal language. The Skipper tried to explain we had nothing. A thought stole into my head. Somewhere about my person were the French banknotes, but I couldn't feel my hands or fingers and the simple act of searching through my clothes now was some mammoth, impossible task. Both guides stood away from us, took long swigs from their *botas* and ate bread.

After each valley, another hill loomed – less steep now. At every stop the hassle for money started again. When someone asked how far to go or how much longer, the lead man always pointed ahead. His friend stayed at the rear, moving us on as we tried to keep a tight line. If anyone fell, or stumbled, whoever was behind would help them. The expletives uttered did more than break a rule of silence. At least the tracks were wider in places and foot placement became easier. I spotted the shed when we rounded the edge of a ridge.

The place had a cold smell of disuse. The lead guide struck a match to make a sweep of the inside. Some wooden slats on the back wall were splintered or missing. I huddled into a sitting position and slept.

Gentle warmth licked over my face. I squinted at the dancing light from a small fire. *Hope is to see the light, in spite of all the darkness.* Did the padre say that? Or was it the headmaster at school assembly? Wherever the words came from, I understood their meaning: we were going to get through this.

Broken slats must have been used to make the fire. Most of the group lay sprawled on the earth floor closer to the heat and some were snoring. The lead guide squatted down near the Skipper, poking at the fire with a sliver of wood. His rusty voice cut above the crackle and flames.

'What does he want now?' Ward whispered. 'Arguing about lighting that fire again, or is it the old spondulicks line?'

'No,' the Skipper said calmly. 'They're taking us down the mountain before it gets light. Car will meet us at zero seven-thirty. He says we're going straight to San Sebastian. I'll wake the men later and tell them.'

I wanted to be the first to answer him, wanted to share it, but knew my voice would betray the emotion welling up inside. The next thing I remembered was being shaken hard and Ward's voice yelling, 'Get out. The bloody place is on fire.'

8

I blinked through the smoke. The back wall was a sheet of yellow flame. For a lunatic moment I lay still, drawing in the precious heat. Fire leapt across the roof. Men blundered past me coughing, hands wafting around their faces. I careered after them. The guides ran out and corralled us down the slope as we stumbled blindly through the dark. My eyes were still smarting – how long had I been out of it? I found myself near the front as the Skipper pushed past and blocked the way. Spanish voices hissed in angry whispers before the lead man disappeared into the night.

The Skipper mustered us together. 'You can see a fire of this size for miles. We must get clear before half the Spanish army descend on us.' He quickly ran through the plan. 'It's mostly downhill. One of the guides has gone on ahead. We'll reach the rendezvous in about an hour.'

The remaining guide waved impatiently and the party moved off. At least half an hour must have passed before he halted on top of a ledge. A steep cutting disappeared into the blackness. We inched down the slippery path and stopped later to pick up the lead man. He slung a *bota* off his shoulder and threw it to Kennedy. The Skipper was the last to take a drink.

'Listen, everyone. They've said it's safe for me to talk for a moment.' The Skipper pointed into the void below. 'Car will be down there around seven-thirty. I suggest we just let them get on with it and wait for the word. The main chap told me it'll be four out at a time.'

He looked at Ward. 'That's your party first. The rest of us will follow later.'

'Bit like the buses, eh?' Ward said. 'Another one will be along soon.'

'How soon?' Johnnie asked.

We went on ahead of the others with the lead guide in front. Ward kept close to him, Harold helped Kennedy and I stayed at the back. My feet were thawing out. Only my toes stayed numb to the pain in my heels and arches. Darkness thickened around us on the descent. No noises behind me now. We stopped. Both sides of the cutting stretched up to the sky. The guide crunched onto what sounded like a dirt road then disappeared on the opposite side. Two whistles. We scurried over to join him behind some thickets.

'Where are the others?' It was Harold. 'And who the hell are we supposed to be meeting?'

The troubled, reedy voice had sounded nothing like his. I missed Ward's answer – we were all beyond our limits.

A pale, damp mist persisted. When daylight came, the morning would be cold and still. The guide finally stepped on to the road and waved us forward.

'Azkar.' His voice snapped through the dark. 'Jarrai nazazu.'

We broke cover. An engine snored in the distance. Two yellow fingers of light probed the mist. Headlamps. A single flash and the car crawled towards us.

'Itxaron… attendez,' the guide said sharply, placing his hand firmly on my shoulder. The car stopped about five yards away. Headlamps went out. A red dot appeared inside the car, glowed then dimmed. The guide hurried us to a dark saloon. An interior light came on. He bundled the others into the back. I finished up on the front passenger seat looking straight into the driver's face, a swarthy man with a gappy smile and pack of Lucky Strike cigarettes in his hand. He tossed them over his shoulder along with a box of matches, lit a smoke from his own cigarette and passed it to me.

'Si bueno,' he said, gripping the steering wheel as if it was going to fly away. The interior light went out and the car spluttered off with the man saying nothing through a veil of smoke, except we were going to San Sebastian, we were Inglés and we were Americano. The others spoke quietly in the back. I was glad of a chance to stay with my own thoughts. I searched for emotions I feared I would never feel again. They were still missing, but the mountains were in the past and if we could patch up our damaged bodies, a lesser challenge waited.

A blue dawn showed in the east. We turned onto a main road. I saw my first Guardia Civil standing on a bridge, smart and upright in his flat, triangular hat and green uniform. He paid no attention to us. Roads were empty apart from cattle and farm carts. We dipped over a hill. An ice-blue sea and waves shimmered in the early sunshine and the medieval buildings of San Sebastian clustered around a bay. I didn't know what to say or feel. The car rattled down to the town, turning on to an empty promenade with tram lines. For the first time in years, I saw the break of waves on a beach with no barbed wire or tank traps. My heart missed a beat in the same rush of excitement I had experienced as a boy at the first sight of sea and sand.

The bay curved around to rocky headland where houses clung precariously to a steep hillside. A line of white, hotel-styled buildings and grander structures hugged the seafront, with the rest of the town lost in a tangle of rooftops. The car turned into a side street of dingy, four and five-floor tenements with makeshift washing lines hanging between windows. Men idled on the corners, while children stared at us from alleys or played in the dirt. Within minutes we were on to the main roads amongst the brown buildings and bleach-white apartments which reminded me of Paris, except the Guardia Civil were about, patrolling streets in pairs. The driver pointed to the right before muttering something.

'There's a bridge across the river, which splits the town, apparently,' Ward said from the back.

'God damn it,' Harold exclaimed.

A black, German staff car was parked kerbside amongst a small line of vehicles. Wehrmacht soldiers wandered along in casual groups.

Ward wound up his back window. 'They must be on leave. This place is only an hour from St Jean de Luz on the French side.'

We had walked for days and circled right around only to return close to the Spanish side of the border with all its risks. I was beyond thinking about why.

The cinema newsreels at home showed ruined Spanish cities and how Hitler had bankrolled the Spanish fascists, yet San Sebastian appeared intact. The car turned slowly into a litter-strewn passage no wider than a large alley. Sun-bleached backs of houses with rows of windows and small vestibule yards lined both sides. We stopped outside an open gate. An upright, elderly man appeared at the doorway of a brown stone building which matched his suit colour. He rubbed his hands together and ventured out past some dustbins towards our car.

'Ve rapido, rapido.' The driver waved his hand urgently as if swatting away a fly. I doubted he was entirely Spanish. The few English words he had used were too well formed, even with an applied accent. He was probably working for the British and listening in on any chat in the car. His side of the vehicle was next to a wall so the others piled out at the back through a single passenger door.

The elderly man watched us with anxious eyes and had the kind of ruddy complexion which came from too much sun. As soon as I got out, the car sped off.

'Follow behind me, gentlemen.' He glanced up at the windows opposite. 'We mustn't be out here for long.'

The old school tie voice sounded out of kilter with his face. I devoured every sound and texture of those plummy, English words. We crowded after him into the yard. The warm smell of decaying rubbish vanished once we walked through a white tiled kitchen and down the corridor to a reception hallway. He cleared his throat.

'I was wondering where you chaps had got to. Anyway, welcome to San Sebastian.' He pointed to the stairs. 'Onwards and upwards and we must be quick about it. I'll show you to your rooms.'

Pain still cut through my body at every step. I tried to catch his long sentences which tailed off when he disappeared from sight up the next staircase. He waited for us on the second-floor landing. A smell of disinfectant hung in the air.

'The others in your party should be along soon,' he said, feeling in his trouser pockets. 'You can get a bit of a wash and then it's breakfast later. Let me know if any of you could do with patching up.'

'What day is it?' I asked.

'Thursday,' he said, handing me a pencil and an old envelope. 'Just need your names now.'

'Do you want my rank and number?'

'Good Lord, no. Not in here.' His face had turned a puce colour. I thought he was about to have a seizure. How was I supposed to know? All of us had been asked for that information before. Kennedy started talking. The man interrupted him.

'Gentlemen, some important rules, please. There won't be anyone here for about another half hour. Despite that, you are all still at risk. Whilst in the hotel, on no account must you leave this floor, or speak to strangers or staff. If by a miracle you've still got cigarettes, don't flash them about, they're often sold singly in Spain. Make no mistake, things change here by the day. Every one of us could be arrested unless we're on diplomatic soil.'

He paused, as if waiting for some sort of response. 'Oh... and someone from the British Consulate will be arriving later. He'll tell you what will happen next.'

We wrote our names on the envelope. The man took it from Kennedy and led us down a short, carpeted corridor with doors on either side. A makeshift dining area and a bathroom were at the end. Ward and I were shown into the room nearest the toilet facilities and the hotelier left us. Ward went straight out. I leaned back against the door, absorbing the fresh, airy smell. A fan hung from the ceiling like a still propeller. Sunlight rippled on the floorboards through a gap in the curtains. The single bed was only a fold of cool, white sheets and a pillow away from me.

They would have soap and towels here, water, proper food. My throat felt like sandpaper, yet the pictures of a gargantuan English breakfast wouldn't leave my head.

The first hint of tears came, turning the dappled sunshine into prisms of light. The remembering did that. All the bad memories suddenly seemed like moments ago. They were there in stark colours, resonant sounds and voices with no distance or fade. *It will be alright in the morning*: Mum's words were a comfort once, but since the start of my war, I grew to know what must happen first during the night before the cycle started all over again. On this journey I'd sought refuge and comfort in the past, but had that shelter gone? What about the future? There was nothing more frightening than the not knowing. My mind had nowhere to go now.

Ward would be back soon. He couldn't see me like this. I wiped a sleeve across my face, reached the bed and sat on the edge. Earlier, while we hid in the cutting to wait for the car, I had untangled the shoes from around my neck and carried them. Keeping the things in the first place felt like a good idea at the time. That depended now on whether my damaged, swollen feet would fit inside them, or how much walking lay ahead. I untied the laces and let the shoes drop onto the floor. The canvas ones came off my feet easily. My rubber bands were long gone and when I pulled the right sole, it separated from the upper. I wriggled out of my raincoat and jacket. They ended up on a chair next to the dresser. When Ward returned I was plucking up courage to try and unroll my socks.

'The moment of truth,' he said, joining me.

The socks stuck to my feet with dried blood and gunge. As I peeled them back, tracks of raw and dead skin came away. Some blisters were split. Others had a deep redness around the edges with a yellow crusting on the top. I would say nothing to the hotelier – someone from the British Consulate was coming and if we were leaving, I had to be on that journey.

Ward put his socks and shoes back on. The intense itching all over my body returned with a vengeance. I unbuttoned my shirt.

Whatever was underneath would also be on my lower half. A rash of small red spots and blotches covered my waist and underarms.

'We're all literally lousy,' Ward said, scratching at his midriff.

I hobbled barefoot across to the window, pulling the curtains back as far as they would run. San Sebastian sprawled out under a blue sky and people walked along the street below me without an upward glance. I absorbed every detail from the view, trying to recall the last time I looked through a pane of glass without feeling fear or guilt. I turned to face Ward.

'Do you think it's nearly over, sir?'

'I don't know sergeant.' He looked away. 'I really don't know.'

PART FOUR

Spain Two

1

I held a nervous hope all might be well. It was something I wouldn't share with Ward or the others. At the window, I'd become caught up in the moment: a surge of warm sunshine, the clean hotel room and hearing the King's English again. But no real safety existed until we reached the nearest British Embassy, wherever that was.

A tap came at the door. The hotel man brought in a carafe of water and two glasses on a tray. Ward and I gulped the lot down before he returned carrying two rolled-up white towels.

'No hot water this morning,' he said, from the doorway. 'Have to make the best of it for now.'

Ward flinched as he got up from the bed and tiptoed cautiously towards him.

'What's the latest on the war?'

'Papers are censored here,' the man replied. 'There's been some sort of pow-wow with Churchill, Stalin and Roosevelt. Good things, I think. Wireless can't always pick up the BBC here.' He handed us the towels. 'I should find out more today from the vice-consul. Careful… soap and razor are inside.'

His nose twitched. 'Can't do much about your clothes, I'm afraid.'

He walked out and then poked his head back around the door.

'I'll give you the word when breakfast's ready. Please take on board what I said earlier about this floor. And keep away from the window. Last thing we want is a visit from the police.'

My skin felt sore after the shave. Minutes earlier I'd been ankle deep in the bath, trying to soap myself down. The cold, black water was still in there. I knelt at the side, pulled out the plug and my last five weeks spiralled down the hole. Nothing would be left behind: no dirt, no trace of the journey, no looking back. I turned on the tap, furiously scrubbing my fingers against every trace of scum inside the bath. Pain shot through both feet again, a dizzy heave hit my stomach and my arms weakened. I got up, grabbing at the sink. After two or three minutes I managed to ease my singlet back on. Dirty clothes smelt even worse on a clean body. Best get dressed and return to the room.

The hotel woke from its slumber. Doors shut and movement sounded on the floor below. About half an hour later, the Skipper arrived with the others. I sat barefoot in the chair listening to their voices in the corridor as the men went for their ablutions. Ward lay asleep on the bed and only stirred when a call for breakfast came from the hotelier. I was last to the dining area. The door was missing with only screw holes left in the frame. Shafts of winter sunshine flooded through a large skylight. The escapers sat crammed around two circular café tables under an umbrella of cigarette smoke. Packets of Lucky Strike with a red circle stamp were on both tables. I latched on to what the hotelier had said about not flashing cigarettes around. The only vacant seat was between Johnnie and Mills. Harold had parked himself opposite. The Skipper sat with Ward, Clements and Kennedy at the other table – the officers' table. I tried to disguise my limp and Johnnie gave me a cheery wave as I crossed to the empty chair.

The two groups had resumed their alliances from the mountains. They weren't cliques; it was just the natural order again. Johnnie and I seemed out on a limb, yet he was sociable enough, just a lot older than me. I reckoned on him being in the RAF from the early part of the war and probably a flight sergeant, but it was guesswork as he hadn't given much away. Mills said something to Harold and they both laughed. I hadn't heard either man do that before. Mills still listened more than he spoke and remained constantly stiff and tense around his neck and shoulders. I thought about the two of them standing together at Lucie's house like a couple of sailors staring out to sea. How much had they changed since then? Was that question irrelevant now we were over the mountains and one step from the next leg to Gibraltar?

Any incidental talk faded on our table. I looked at the officer's group where the Skipper was holding court. Kennedy rubbed his face. I still couldn't believe how he made it here when all of us had reached a point in the Pyrenees when we were ready to give up. Every man kept him going and he was brighter now. If only Ken could have travelled with me from Brussels. The thought drew me to the rest of my crew again. What the hell happened to them? I lit a cigarette and blew the smoke upwards.

Bottles of spirits and glasses clinked into the room on a hostess trolley pushed by a teenage girl with black ringlets down to her shoulders. To a chorus of muted calls, she blushed and arranged glasses at each table next to the whisky and gin. My slug of Scotch burned – too much too soon. I filled the glass with soda water while the others were knocking back a second measure. The girl returned a quarter of an hour later with platters of ham, cheese, olives and salad on the trolley. Colours and smells swamped my senses. 'Drum it in,' someone called, rapping the table. Laughter rose as the girl laid out plates, then scuttled away. The chatter began to fade inside my head, like the volume slowly turning down on a wireless. Our salad led me back to summer days, cricket and newly mown grass. The smell of ham and cheese could have been Simpkin and James, the posh grocers at home, or our last family Christmas tea before everything changed.

We finished with a bowl of bananas, oranges and grapes. There was real coffee and a gnarled, green fruit I'd never seen before. Everyone spoke more in their own group than with others and occasional restrained laughter bubbled over in the smoke. Each man let off his own steam, whilst still hiding behind the exchanges.

The Skipper said he had found it difficult convincing some helpers he was genuine because of his French and German. I heard nothing more of interest, as the conversations taxied along in safe zones. Gibraltar was mentioned and a hush followed as if it was still a forbidden word. Johnnie and I must have looked adrift from the rest. No one was ill-mannered or rude, we just had to pick our moments to chip in and keep afloat.

Thoughts slipped back to parts of the journey. My mind avoided filling in any blanks and I imagined the worst possible things around the fate of friends who had helped me. I poured another glass of whisky and drank it straight down.

The buzz stopped when the hotelier walked in. 'Gentlemen. Please pay attention to the noise.'

He paused in the sudden hush. 'Someone from the Consulate will be arriving just before one o'clock. He'll tell you what happens next. Please make ready to leave straight after he has spoken to you.' His ruddy face darkened. 'And remember what I've said about the noise. I trust you've all enjoyed your breakfast.'

The atmosphere fell with a crash after he left. Pauses grew longer as the euphoria of alcohol faded. Peripheral noises grew louder in the silences: a glass placed on the table, the creak of a chair. Cigarette smoke floated around the static ceiling fan. The airmen's faces were tired, distant and marked by their ordeal. Caught in the sunlight, they could have been old men lost in rocking-chair moments, their minds slipping back across the seas to home.

2

The tall man standing in the doorway wouldn't have been out of place at Royal Ascot or Henley. His double-breasted suit was Savile Row and the raised chin made him look down his nose at us.

'Good afternoon,' he said briskly. The polished shoes squeaked as he walked in. 'I work in the British Consulate. In twenty minutes we'll leave for Madrid in a diplomatic car.'

He tugged at his shirt cuffs. 'Journey will take about seven hours.' His voice quietened. 'The first four men who crossed into Spain will be first to leave. The rest follow tomorrow night.' His gaze steadied on us, as if waiting for a question or dissenting voice. He checked his watch and stepped back to the door.

'Excellent. I'll see the lucky ones back here in ten minutes.'

I returned alone to our room. Voices came from the corridor. I sat on the bed, passing my tiny cardboard box from hand to hand. Its sides were bowed and the lid sat on top like an ill-fitting hat. Razor and soap had long gone, I should have thrown it away days ago, but like the crucifix and other items, the box had become a part of me. A mottled tidemark stained the cardboard where the wet had seeped through my raincoat. I imagined the shape as the map of an island – some special place where my future was safe and the past never followed.

Time to leave and Ward still hadn't returned. My raincoat would have to stay behind. It was covered with mud and other things: the ripe smell had hit me after I returned from the ablutions. I'd already transferred everything else to my jacket when the room door finally opened.

Ward sat down beside me on the bed. 'I shan't be coming with you,' he said, untying his laces. 'I've decided to stay with my skipper. We'll travel in the next party.' He coaxed off his shoes. 'The American's taking my place.'

'Do you mean Mills, sir?'

'Yes. I'll see you in Madrid.'

It came as a surprise not a shock, as the Skipper was Ward's pilot. I hurried to the dining room where Kennedy waited with Mills and Harold. The Consul man loitered behind them, fidgeting with his shirt cuffs.

'OK, chaps… decide where you'll be sitting in the car. There's room for one at the front and three in the back. Give me five minutes' start then go out through the kitchen at the rear. I'll be waiting, engine running.' He adjusted his shirt cuffs again. 'It'll be berets on, heads down and get straight in the passenger side. You must keep a low profile until we clear the town.'

This man had no air of a subordinate, he *was* the British Consul. We put on our berets and had sorted out seating positions before his footsteps faded out of earshot.

Mills led us down the stairs. I noticed Kennedy had changed his trousers. The hotelier was in the kitchen. He gestured to a flask and packs of sandwiches on the table.

'For your journey, gentlemen. He's ready. All the very best to you.'

A black American Packard waited outside of the yard. I slid onto the front seat while the others dived in behind. Kennedy was last and sat at the back of me. The interior had a strong smell of leather upholstery and stale tobacco.

'Keep your faces away from the windows,' the Consul said.

The car manoeuvred out of the alley and on to a road with shop awnings and empty pavements.

'Bad show,' he said. 'Not ideal. It's still siesta and we're right in view.' I noticed him glancing in the mirror. 'We'll get well clear of the town and manage with a couple of stops before Madrid.'

He swung the car onto a narrow street of taller brown buildings. Two Guardia Civil were sharing a cigarette at the next corner. Above ground level, the buildings made it easy to imagine a San Sebastian before Franco, when apartments and hotels looked down on crowded pavements, where the drip of old money drove the traffic hum and clanking trams. I was in no mood for that mirage; I just wanted to get clear. The hotel had been an oasis, but I'd seen enough of Franco's world in the cinemas and newspapers to know he had ripped the heart out of Spain and left behind an empty shell. The country was under the kind of black cloud which hung overhead when nothing would be the same again. I thought about our bombed cities at home, the families and lives torn apart, the people I'd left behind to fight on in Belgium and France. The world was scarred in every direction.

We climbed away from the town on deserted roads. Harold and Mills spoke about their meal. The Consul had withdrawn into himself, eyes fixed ahead, face sewn up tight. My spirits wavered again. What kind of life waited for us after this bloody war? Cooped up in safe houses, there had been wastelands of time to think about it, yet I couldn't recollect when that single thought had pushed in front of my own worries about capture for more than a few seconds. It had been too dangerous to look into the future.

The sea glittered for a final moment before we dropped below the hilltop. Four years had passed since I last saw colour and sparkle like that. Lowestoft summers had been special, carefree times throughout my childhood, with the whole school holiday at Aunt Beat's, where the sun shone over sands and water. The storm was gathering in that final August before war, as I walked with Gordon past the Victorian hotels, lawns and flowerbeds on the North and South Parade. We lived several doors apart at home and had grown up inseparable pals. In early 1941, the train journey with him to RAF Cardington for aircrew selection had been a compartment full of excited young faces – all lads going to do their bit. Gordon and I passed the tests and interview and were put on reserve. We got called up separately and he went to the Middle East as a ground wireless operator. He had hardly entered my mind for months. If war forged new friendships for some, it chipped away at old ones. I hoped we could pick up again as true friends did, except what would we be picking up? When five weeks of black water had disappeared down that bath plughole in the hotel, the last traces of my youth vanished too.

The Consul stopped on another gritty road and got out. A ripple of grey hills covered the horizon. He crunched around to the bonnet, produced a small Union Jack flag and tied it above the radiator grill.

'That's the ticket,' he said, getting back into the driver's seat.

'So... we're in the clear then?' Harold said.

The silence pressed down through my body, anchoring my feet to the floor.

'There's a little way to go yet.' The Consul smiled. 'Let's just say things are looking better.'

The Union Jack fluttered. We picked up speed past undulating brown and green scrub. Dust billowed by my window as a Spanish army truck passed from the opposite direction. A thread of bony cattle dawdled along the roadside. People stared at the car as we drove by them: old men with craggy faces, a woman in black carrying bundles of straw, and two boys struggling with a donkey and cart.

I drifted in and out of sleep.

'Hey, will you take a look at that,' Mills said. His voice had woken me. The landscape was dotted with burnt-out trucks and armoured vehicles.

'Parts of Spain are still full of remnants from the civil war,' the Consul said.

I expected him to elaborate. He didn't. The dusty miles took us through villages of rough brownstone buildings, white houses and a church bell tower – there was always a church tower. The conversations mumbled on. Kennedy chattered about some mountains in Canada, before his voice merged into the drone from the engine. We passed the edge of a town with city walls and red roofs. The car pulled off the road after a long climb.

'Five minutes for a leg stretch,' the Consul said. 'Can't hang

298

about I'm afraid, it's pretty high up and we're half parked on the road.'

I joined the others, gazing at a range of purple mountains silhouetted against the twilight.

'How long to Madrid?' Mills asked.

'I'd say a little over three hours, including a quick stop for petrol.' The Consul folded his sandwich bag into neat quarters. 'We should arrive around eight o'clock. Busy old place. Not an easy billet though, it's crawling with spies and Germans. We're often tailed. Not to worry, they won't see anything tonight.' He slipped the bag in his suit jacket pocket. 'It shouldn't bother you chaps. You'll be on your way before you know it.'

He wiped his hands on a handkerchief. 'Right… this won't get the baby a new frock. Let's get back in the car. You can drink whatever's left in the flask and eat the rest of your sandwiches as we travel.'

The dashboard instruments glowed in the dark. I finished the coffee and tracked the bounce of beams from the car's headlamps on the road before sleep swept in again.

A sudden lurch woke me. I felt a nudge against my arm.

'Madrid coming up.'

Dots and twinkles of yellow light patterned the scene below: single spots, daisy chains, straight lines, triangles and circles. They were any shapes my mind wanted to make. The sheer beauty of a city with lights made me rub my eyes and stare. It had been so long.

'Time's seven fifty-two,' the Consul said. 'We're nearly there. Keep away from the windows, just in case Jerry is cooking something up in the building opposite the embassy.'

The world grew bolder and brighter. Light shone from signs and windows; people strolled along pavements. We drove under a stone archway. Vehicles had parked away from the kerbside in a snaky trail. The narrow backstreets had a seedy yellow glow, doors to the bars were open, women loitered on corners, and dead-end alleys waited between buildings.

The car shot forward as if breaking cover and drove through an open gateway into a large courtyard with buildings on three sides. The engine stopped. A tick of hot metal below the bonnet broke the stillness. The Consul turned off the headlamps.

'This is the embassy. We are now on British soil.'

3

I limped across the courtyard with the others. One step from Gibraltar: the ridiculous simplicity of it circled around in my head. Nobody could touch us here. A young man in his twenties waited under an outside lamp near a short flight of concrete steps. His three-piece suit made him look like a tailor's assistant; only the tape measure around his neck was missing. He acknowledged the Consul as we approached.

'Welcome, gentlemen. My name is Watkins. Do go straight up and wait for me in the lobby.'

He shut the door noisily once we were all inside. The Consul winced and touched the knot of his tie. 'If you'll excuse me, there are matters which I must attend to. I will bid you all goodnight.' He passed a note to Watkins and with a polite nod, retraced his steps and went outside.

'Yes,' Watkins said, reading the note. He wafted the paper about. 'Just a list of your names, that's all.' His voice rose. 'I'll show you where the cloakroom is, and then take you through for drinks. Unfortunately the ambassador isn't here tonight.'

Minutes later, we entered a small anteroom with double doors facing us. A soft hum of conversation came from the other side.

'There's a small reception committee. It's important when chaps like you arrive. You're the nearest we get to the real war.'

Watkins moved nearer to us. 'It's not only that.' His voice dropped to a whisper. 'Keep Spain neutral and happy, that's the top and bottom of it.'

I gave a sympathetic smile. The others kept quiet. He looked young for His Majesty's Diplomatic Service, but what did I know?

The doors opened. A man with a pencil-thin moustache and brandy glass peered out. 'Ah there you are, Watkins.' He waved us across. 'Come in, come in. You chaps must have had a hell of a time. I'll introduce you as our latest guests and we'll go from there, it usually works best. Now, what'll you all have?'

I wanted a bed and sleep. The others eyed him with heavy expressions. He turned to go back inside. Our clothes looked filthy against his Whitehall pin-striped suit. The dirt was still ingrained in my fingernails and I'd missed the man's name. He would be Mr. Barrington for the moment.

The rum warmed my chest. We stood on a woven carpet in a room with gentlemen's club furniture and the smell of beeswax and old books. All four men around Barrington were embassy staff with a jumble of names. They chatted to us, juggling their glasses and cigarette cases with practised ease.

'Gitanes,' a man with greying hair said to me as he killed his lighter flame and hot smoke cut into my throat on the first draw.

'Doctor will see you all before you get cleaned up and turn in,' Mr Barrington said. 'And Miss Green will be along in a moment to see about some different clothes.' He grinned. 'She has a good eye for measurements.' He slipped away before any of us had a chance to reply.

Miss Green was stoutly built, with an inquisitive face and a curled smile. A matching blue skirt and jacket gave her a hospital air as she marched across the room.

'I think we can help here,' she said, after the pleasantries. Her eyes were always on the move, trawling up and down my body, darting along the rest of our line.

'If anyone requires new shoes, you must say so now.' She turned to Mills. He was the only man still wearing the remnants of his canvas mountain ones.

'I could do with a new pair of feet,' I said. She laughed politely and moved on to the rest of the men, like an officer inspecting a parade.

'Thank you boys, I think that's everything for the moment.' Mills got another glance as she left.

I huddled in with the others. The reception committee stood a distance away, weighing us up over their drinks and small talk. When I checked again, the men were placing their empty glasses on a tray. They came over and wished us well.

'Just put those on the table, chaps,' Mr Barrington said to us. 'Someone will see to them later.'

'Excuse me, sir,' I said. 'Are you able to get a message to our families?'

'Not my bag, old boy. It'll probably get passed on to the air attaché. I'm not going to beat about the bush. You've got some way to go yet.' He pointed to a fan of documents on the table. 'You'll have to read and sign those first. Then, if you'll follow me please. Once the doctor's done, someone will take you across to the dorm.'

The papers had a section for identity details, a question about where I'd crossed the Pyrenees and a declaration not to talk about my journey or helpers. I filled it all in and I was going home, whatever Mr Barrington might have thought.

4

We lined up wet, naked and shivering on a tan-coloured stone floor away from the showers. The doctor was all prod, peer and cold stethoscope; a man with a pointed chin and lank, black hair plastered flat against his head.

'I see,' he said, scrawling through my hair. 'Thank you.'

He moved down our line without a pause as if we were one linked package, until he reached Kennedy. They spoke in low voices. The doctor's heavily accented English slowed his sentences. My feet throbbed and smarted. I picked up the towel, hugging it close around my body. Standing about starkers with the others, I should have felt exposed and undignified. Getting in a clean bed was all that mattered.

'I will give you something for your headaches,' the doctor said to Kennedy. 'Please tell the medical officer about them when you arrive at your destination.'

'Can we get dressed?' I asked.

'Not yet,' the doctor said, walking over to the sink. 'Not in those.' He waved at the four puddles of clothing on the floor.

'The two of you with rashes,' he said, drying his hands. He looked at Harold and me. 'It is scabies. I think you have this from your clothes or bedding. I cannot be sure with the rest of you. There are the possible signs and we must treat them. You all have the lice on your body. I see bite marks.'

He walked along the line. 'You must wash and shower every day. I have one more task.'

He reached into his medical bag, lining up four shaving brushes and jars of ointment on the table, as if he already knew before we arrived what treatment was required.

'For three days, you must spread this over your body after the shower.' He picked up a shaving brush and mimed the action. 'And you will start now, before dressing in the different clothes.'

He walked to a table in the corner and scribbled on a notepad. 'Please excuse me, while I discover what has happened to your clothing. When I return, I must examine your feet.'

We were still looking at one another when he turned around at the door.

'Please continue with the ointment. No one will enter this room while I am away.'

It was a relief to know we had some privacy from the outside. I imagined Miss Green barging in with an armful of clothes and seeing more of our measurements than she expected. A strange interval followed where we spoke about anything except our predicament and state of undress. The barriers between us briefly vanished in a reek of ointment. Harold helped Mills apply it between his shoulder blades. I teamed up with Kennedy and smelt hospitals, antiseptic and vinegar. His hair had lost most of its brown colour and was almost completely fair. He must have dyed it at some point during his escape.

The doctor returned after a long delay. 'Your clothes will arrive soon.'

I was last to sit in the chair by the table. 'There is no infection,' the doctor said, gently winding a gauze bandage around my left foot. 'I will also cover the blisters on your other foot, and we can see again in two or three days. They should heal soon.' He smiled at the others. 'No frostbite. You are all very lucky.'

He left us when Watkins and a couple of ancillary clerks struggled in with three military-style kitbags. Watkins blushed as the clerks slipped away.

'Shirts and trousers, etcetera are in the first two bags. Underclothes and the remainder are in the other. There's also a pair of shoes somewhere.' He sidled to the door. 'Soap, toothbrush and shaving kit are inside a towel on your beds in the dorm. I'll collect you in ten minutes. The doctor says to leave your old clothes on the floor.'

The notion of searching through bags with only a towel around my waist and a small table to lay out the garments was like being at some peculiar rummage sale. We sorted ourselves a set of indoor clothes, jacket, braces and underwear. Mills had a pair of ill-fitting trousers, but did get his shoes. The smell and sensation of a clean shirt against my skin felt contaminated by the ointment. I transferred everything except the handkerchief to the replacement jacket. When Watkins returned, we were ready in a line of assorted shades and styles.

'In case it's not been mentioned, there are two important things in here,' he said. 'Don't go outside the embassy unless you have permission and are escorted. I'm afraid that we can't let you exercise in the courtyard or go anywhere near the front gate at the moment as its vital you are not seen from the buildings opposite.'

We would see little of Madrid and that suited me. As Watkins led us from the rear of the building, I caught a rich smell of freshly lit pipe tobacco. It was another slice of home.

The makeshift dorm was across the courtyard in a long, low building near the garage where the Consul had parked earlier. It was the size of a hall with around twenty army camp beds lined in opposite rows like a hospital ward. Some of the ceiling lights had been switched off, casting chequered shadows. Three men sat playing cards at the far end. A bundle opposite them was entangled in the blankets. Four beds closest to us were made up. Most of the others were stripped, as if their crews had failed to return from ops. Watkins' words grew distant. I ran my fingers along the nearest bed, lay down and slipped into the black corridor of sleep.

The dorm had simple cornice work around the ceiling edge. I turned over, relishing a proper night's sleep again. The towel and accoutrements were still next to me. Kennedy sat on the next bed.

'If you want something to eat, we'd better go.'

I struggled to sit up. 'Go where?'

'The dining room or whatever you call it. That fella last night said it was near here. Don't you remember?'

'Yes,' I mumbled, in a way which said I didn't.

'Come on. We'd better follow the others,' he said.

Harold and Mills had already left the dorm. Strains of their cheerful conversation echoed from next door. Kennedy hobbled alongside me. He still seemed distant and unsteady on his feet but said he was OK. That was the most I would get out of him. As I reached the dining room door, three things had lodged in my thoughts: he still had big problems with his headaches, the distance between me and the Americans was growing, and that particular issue was becoming irrelevant.

A range of assorted wooden tables were set close together for breakfast. Somehow the staff had found white cloths to fit them. The three card players from the dorm were farthest away, with one sitting directly underneath a dartboard. They acknowledged us, although I got a sense from their huddled conversation they preferred to keep things as they were. On the far side, a fresh-faced man sat stirring his tea, next to a miniature billiard table. Kennedy sat with me at a table adjacent to Mills and Harold, who said they weren't much for darts or billiards. That was the limit of our chat before the kitchen staff served up orange juice, porridge and toast. The crust crunched between my teeth and a drip of warm, salty butter slathered into the corners of my mouth. Only a hot cup of tea was missing. A white china pot arrived moments later.

I stayed behind to finish my tea after the others had left. We were being looked after exceptionally well. The faint metallic chatter of a typewriter came from somewhere in the embassy depths. Areas around the dorm and dining room were not at the working end – I had noticed that on my way back from seeing the doctor the previous evening. Locked rooms and half-open doors with a skeleton of furniture inside were all part of the mystery around here.

A strong smell of ointment hit me before I reached the dorm. The four men from the far end were missing. I picked up a shaving mug and went to get some water. Watkins had left us some decent kit – even a small mirror. The doctor arrived around ten-thirty and handed Kennedy a brown paper bag.

'Please only take these as we have discussed. You know what I said about seeing the medical officer.'

I settled into the long reach of the day, dozing or joining in on snippets of talk with the others. There was a stupor in our smiles and words, a reminder of how close to the edge we had been in the mountains. The four blokes from the far end hadn't returned and were absent from the dining room for twelve-thirty fish and chips. The embassy staff referred to the midday meal as lunch. I'd always known it as dinner.

Watkins intercepted us on our way back into the dorm and addressed the Americans.

'A visitor is here to see you both.'

'Bet it's their ticket to Gib,' I mumbled under my breath as Watkins led them away.

All four beds at the end of the dorm had been stripped. A pack of cards lay on Harold's pillow. I wandered down the room while the Americans were away and spotted a copy of the *Daily Express* under a bed. It was days old, with parts blacked out by the Spanish censor. War news was vague: Canadian and Indian troops were on the offensive in Italy, a large force of RAF aircraft had bombed Berlin at night. I devoured every column of a British newspaper again – even the Phyllosan and Wrigley's advertisements. When the two Americans returned, I'd no need to ask them the obvious question.

'Saw a Major,' Harold said. 'Should be outa here pretty soon.'

'British?'

'Nope. Major Clark, United States Army Air Force.'

His words still sounded so slow and matter of fact, as if he were rubbing them in. I knew that was not his way. Harold had always been direct and plain-speaking with no time for periphery, but underneath I saw a decent and straightforward man just trying to get through this war.

'That's great news, chaps,' I said, trying to swallow my own disappointment.

Only four places were set for the evening meal. The Americans were more convivial, with general chat about the dorm, food and embassy. Neither of them spoke about their meet with Major Clark. Most of us had lit cigarettes when the coffee came with cream and sugar, or side-arms as Harold called it. Kennedy took that as his cue to turn in early. He had picked at his food and was the only one not smoking.

'Headaches,' Mills said, after Kennedy left. 'The guy's still struggling.'

I spooned in the sugar. 'The doctor told him to go to the MO as soon as he gets to the next stop… Gib, I suppose. All being well, he won't be waiting around too long, let's hope none of us are.' I waited for a reaction. Mills gave me a thoughtful nod and excused himself.

Harold stirred his coffee. Silence fell over the room like a blanket, except for the quiet pulse of the city outside.

'I was like a ghost out there.' I'd thought out loud with the first thing entering my head.

'What?' He placed his spoon carefully on the saucer.

'On the mountains. Sometimes, I was just waiting for my own slow death.'

'Guess you weren't the only one.'

'No. Perhaps I got too wrapped up with my own destiny and fate instead of just staying on my feet and forcing one foot in front of the other.'

He stared into his cup.

'Can I ask you something, Harold?'

'You've asked a lotta things.'

'I haven't. I wanted answers when we were together in Paris. That was all.'

My words had tumbled out again. A myriad of unanswered questions and unfinished business had been in my head for the whole journey and most of it had to stay that way. One question had parked itself weeks ago in the back of my mind.

'Do you remember after we'd got into France and left the policeman's house?'

'Yeah.' He straightened in his chair.

'Just before the sandy-haired guide told us to keep quiet, you said you might have finished up in Paris after your kite got damaged by fighters on a bomb run in Germany. You told me you helped fly it back.'

'Maybe.'

'I never forgot what you said that night, Harold. You were an engineer and gunner, not a pilot. You'd only done a few hours' stick time.' I took a long drink. 'You said it was another story. So, what happened?'

He tapped his cigarette over the ashtray. 'Why do you wanna know?' His voice stuck on the words as if they had an acid taste to them.

'You'll be leaving soon. Whatever's happened between us, we've been through a lot together. This might be my last chance to—'

He cut in. 'We started the bomb run. Four bandits attacked from twelve o'clock... shot up the cockpit and nose. One top turret gun was KO'd. I fired the other.'

His cigarette end glowed. 'They kept coming back, ripped the kite apart... tried to finish us off. I shot one down, damaged another. Oxygen system was kaput. Pilot dived low under the main formation, made for scattered cloud before turning west. Navigator had lost an eye and was bleeding badly. We were still being attacked when I got to the cockpit. It was a helluva goddam mess.'

He looked away. 'Pilot and bombardier had bad wounds to the head and body. Shell went through the co-pilot's chest near the shoulder and exploded as it hit the armour plate on his seat.'

'There's no need to say any more, Harold.'

'Yes there is. And you're gonna hear me out before Don Mills gets back.' He ground his cigarette in the ashtray.

'Co-pilot was in a bad way. One of the waist gunners and me got him outa the chair. He cashed in his chips a coupla minutes later. We got the nav into the seat and he helped the pilot, who kept passing out. Waist gunner did his best with the first aid. I went back to the gun turret. We lost the fighters and I salvoed the bombs low over the Channel. The gear was damaged, so I had to wind the doors manually. Then I took over the controls from the nav and helped land us at some RAF fighter base in the south of England.'

He shook his head. 'Gave me a medal for that. Didn't bring the co-pilot back, did it? Yeah… life's all about surviving, but how many times before your luck runs out?'

I struggled to reply. Any words would sound trite and empty. I fudged it and asked about the injured crew. They did recover. He added nothing more and Mills returned just in time. Harold picked up his cigarettes and I was left on my own in the room again. When I got back to the dorm, four more beds had been made up.

Voices woke me. Light shone on the floor near the dorm entrance. The Skipper, Ward, Clements and Johnnie crept in with Watkins, who switched on the main lights to groans and curses from the Americans. It was just after seven-forty and still dark. The new arrivals had clearly been through the bags of embassy clothing.

The men were still in their beds when I returned from breakfast with Kennedy and the two Americans. We had sat together as the first glimmers of day stole through the dining room windows. After the previous evening, I couldn't predict what to expect from Harold. I listened, stayed in the background and spoke occasionally, trying not to think too much. Our future beyond the embassy had prompted enough questions already, with too much time to search for answers. The hour passed with cordial chat and stares into the middle distance. Nothing had changed between any of us and that was some sort of relief. My time with Harold since Brussels had been like picking at a roll of Sellotape and never finding the start.

The Skipper and his party surfaced before the mid-morning meal. Ward sat on the next bed to me, lathering a shaving brush around his chin.

'We left before dark. The journey was all bumps and humps but managed to get some shuteye though. I didn't see much at all, except some lights here and there.'

Johnnie walked by us, a towel over his shoulder and toothbrush between his teeth.

'We had to see the doctor, or whoever he was,' Ward said. 'Didn't realise how bad a state we were all in until I got cleaned up. But it seems like we'll be looked after very well here.'

'You will, sir,' I said.

The razor scraped down his cheek. We spoke about the embassy and I gave him the form and routine in the place. He pondered for a moment and acknowledged the Skipper who had returned to the dorm. I left them to it and wandered across to the Canadians who were poised to make a move for lunch.

The staff moved some tables back after our evening meal, so we could play billiards and darts. A wooden cupboard had cards, dice and a few board games, which passed a couple of hours before I wandered back to the dorm with the others. A shift in the mood between us had emerged during the afternoon, despite the men sitting in the same company as at the hotel in San Sebastian. In the impromptu games room, I saw more signs of chat and smiles between the groups.

The dorm was in darkness when we returned. I flicked the switches so that only the lights above our beds came on. Night and day, dark and light had governed my world since I landed in Belgium. Would it be reading or playing cards next? I joined Clements and the Americans. The others were turning in for the night, so we found some chairs and used Harold's bed as a table. My Gin Rummy hands slipped past with brief interest. Only the cards resonated with me. I pictured the different pack in Paris and saw Joseline sitting with Charlotte and the Painter, waiting for the next rap on the door.

The days stretched out ahead. Except for a visit to the doctor, our time outside the dorm revolved around meals and then games after evening dinner. An unspoken ritual developed between us, with newspapers, books and magazines flung from bed to bed without word or warning when we'd finished with them. Anything to be discarded worked its way to a chair next to Harold. I flicked through a *Signal* magazine in Spanish, with the usual German propaganda photographs. Speech bubbles drawn in pencil emanated from some of the figures, whilst other rude doodles made it obvious what was on the artist's mind.

I saw much of my own self in the other men. Their euphoria after the embassy gates closed had disappeared after a first full night's sleep. The new arrival woke to a more measured relief, his shelter a fortress and with it a first sense of real safety. He spoke in quicker, vibrant tones through his tired face, before a gradual change brought in the long train of idle thought and a sense of being in limbo. The moment dawned when he realised he was only suspended in a larger, more pleasant bubble than before and still remained reliant on others. For a while that was a better place to be because bad things might still be waiting on the outside. In the mirror, his nervous smile reassured him that we were all still in it together.

As time passed, it was easy to spot a man on the brink. He stretched out on his bed staring at the ceiling, missing that extra card game until someone poked him in the ribs. He moved about in slow motion, tiptoeing from the dorm to the toilet, drawing out every second. Each day had inevitability. Each day he longed for that summons to the embassy inner sanctum, or for Watkins to walk in with a date for his departure. Each day, no news was bad news. In weaker moments, instinct took over and turned into nervous anticipation as, hands in pockets, he paced the aisle between the beds and hid between his past and future.

5

'Sorry to interrupt your lunch,' Watkins said. 'The old man wants to see all three of you.'

I clunked my cup down on the saucer.

'I'll take you all across in a minute,' he said, looking at Kennedy and Clements first. We walked after him in single file, as if no one wanted to make eye contact. Watkins cut across the courtyard corner and up a flight of stairs to a short corridor of offices.

A man in a light grey suit sat writing at his desk. His hair had receded on the right side of his forehead, leaving a triangular bare patch. The window behind him looked down on the courtyard, where a rainy daylight gave the room a drab, sombre aspect. He didn't look up.

'Thank you, Watkins. That will be all.'

Three chairs were in a line in front of his desk. A vase of flowers stood on an occasional table next to a bookcase. The man stopped writing and rose to his feet.

'Please… take a seat, gentlemen. My name is Creswell.' We shook hands with him and the chair upholstery sighed as we sat down on it. He turned his paperwork face down.

'The air attaché would normally be here, but he's been otherwise detained. The three of you will leave for Seville within the hour.'

His words hit me and were swept away in the moment.

'That's great news, sir,' Clements said. 'Next stop Gib.'

Kennedy's eyes shone for the first time since I'd met him. The Canadians' faces were like schoolboys with books on prize-giving day.

Creswell coughed. 'One moment. I haven't quite finished yet.'

He waited for the chatter to stop.

'It's not that straightforward. You'll be staying for a while at an address in Seville. That's all I can tell you.'

The room instantly felt cramped and airless. A car started up in the courtyard.

I sat forward. 'Have you any idea how long we'll be there, sir?'

'When will we get to Gibraltar?' Kennedy's voice had a faint quiver.

Clements gave him a stern look. Creswell interrupted softly.

'Gentlemen, please listen.' He picked up the fountain pen, screwing the top on. 'I can't give you any more information.'

He stared at the pen. 'Please understand that things are, at best, sometimes very delicate. Circumstances change by the day. We are doing all that we can.'

Kennedy wiped his forehead. 'There were four guys here when we first arrived. I haven't seen them since. And the Americans told us days ago they were leaving.'

Creswell nodded. 'Yes, but that's the Americans, and they're still here. We don't ship everyone out at the drop of a hat. This is a working embassy, not a casualty clearing station. I'm afraid it's out of my hands at the moment.' His voice was polite but firm. 'You must follow instructions. I'm sure you're used to doing that.'

'We are, sir,' I replied. 'I must apologise, you've looked after us very well. It's just that we're so close and only a journey away.' The words felt heavy. My fingers locked together. 'I thought I was finally going home.'

He smiled. 'And you will. It might take a while longer, that's all.'

He rose and walked around his desk to the door. 'Someone will be waiting for you at two o'clock. Get yourselves ready. I wish you all the best.'

No one spoke after we left the office. A confusion of thoughts were written on the Canadians' faces: relief at moving one step nearer to Gibraltar, anxiety at leaving sanctuary and a fear of the rigours of yet another journey and safe house.

The dorm was deserted, except for Watkins.

'Have they gone to lunch?' I asked.

'No. The Americans have another visitor and the English lads are in the main building with a grandee who comes here. He's some sort of Spanish Duke. Pro-British, probably made his money in sherry. I don't get to find out these things... it's wheels within wheels and all that.'

He moved closer. 'Seems to think it's his responsibility to entertain some of our guests and show them the sights and reputable places in Madrid... and the disreputable ones.'

'You're joking, right?' Clements said.

Watkins smiled. 'Of course. They don't tell me anything in this place.'

He walked to the door. 'So, are you fellows leaving?'

'Yes. At two o'clock,' I said.

'I'll try and see you before then.'

Kennedy sat down heavily on his bed. 'What the hell was all that about?'

I thought about our clandestine journey to get here, the arrival and the restrictions.

'I haven't a clue and I'm not going to try and find out.'

None of the missing men returned to the dorm. Clements had wandered off to try and find them so we could say our goodbyes. Kennedy threw his magazine down on the bed.

'We'd best get ready.'

My razor, packet of blades and shaving brush went into the cardboard box. I'd almost ditched it again in San Sebastian.

Clements brought a short, angular man with black hair and bushy eyebrows into the dorm. 'They're not in the dining place or washroom. Raymond here says we've got to leave.'

With the embassy protocol, I wasn't sure whether it was his first or last name. He shook my hand.

'Don't know where your pals have got to, but we must look sharp now, the car's waiting.'

He handed us each a packet of Gitanes and some paper money.

A rush of disappointment came at not saying goodbye to the others. So much had been left unsaid, yet leaving in this way seemed a fitting epitaph to my time with them. Raymond led us to the side of the garage where the Consul had parked on the first evening.

'Stay here for a minute. We're out of sight from the gates.'

Watkins was walking in that direction through a veil of drizzle. A black saloon reversed slowly towards us. Raymond opened the rear doors and we climbed in. Clements took the right-hand seat and Kennedy the middle, whilst I sat behind the driver. The sliding glass screen behind him was open.

'Heads low until you hear the word,' Raymond said, clambering in the front. 'You know the drill.'

We ducked down. I felt the car swing out from the embassy and rumble over cobbles.

'You can sit up now,' the driver said, eventually.

His blue-grey suit could have passed as a chauffeur's uniform. We were on a wide city centre road of tall department stores and offices with cars or trucks parked outside.

'We'll get to Seville between nine and ten tonight,' Raymond said. He looked at the driver who nodded.

'So what happens after we get there?' Clements asked. 'They haven't told us anything.'

'We drop you off at an address, make sure everything's alright and that's our bit done,' Raymond said. 'Don't worry, it's all in hand.' He peered at the driver again, as if waiting for confirmation. The driver kept his eyes on the road ahead.

I would never get used to the not knowing. I thought of asking about Watkins' story around the Spanish Duke and his tour of Madrid for the British lads. Best left alone unless the Canadians spoke about it.

'You'll catch some of the scenic route,' Raymond said.

He left the glass screen open, pointing out sights and jumping into any spells of quiet with a chatter which had none of the diplomatic ring I heard in the embassy. Away from the centre,

Madrid was a jigsaw of cobbled avenues, flanked by brush-top trees and stately buildings of brown limestone with large, oblong windows. Grander façades had a small, leaded dome or mock Spanish bell tower as a corner feature. In the narrow streets a regal past persisted amongst the ornate stonework. Occasional signs of the old regime were still present with men in smart suits and women showing off their finery, whilst the masses wore sullen clothes or overalls. Cars were early thirties with their American sedan shape, narrow bonnets and bulbous headlamps. A horse and cart waited kerbside, another moved slowly between traffic and tram lines. The Guardia Civil were everywhere again.

We drove by an arched monument fronting a park and lake. A black Mercedes Benz with its Nazi flag fluttering on the front approached from the opposite direction.

'Look left, everyone,' Raymond said.

The Mercedes slowed. Its driver stared at us.

Raymond jeered. 'We often give each other the evil eye.' He laughed as though it was some kind of game.

The suburbs were a mirror of San Sebastian, with decayed apartment blocks and barefoot children. The difference here was the heaps of rubble on overgrown bombsites. A shadow had fallen across this area and the sooner we got clear of Madrid the better.

Raymond had more than a hint of a London accent and his talk lightened my mood. The driver would let him speak for a while then shoot a serious look. Miles of thirsty brown and green countryside slipped by before the game began again. Neither man mentioned their role in Madrid. I guessed at Raymond being a messenger, maintenance man and occasional driver.

'So, what were you lads doing before the war?' he asked.

Before the war? There it was again. Back then, he would have looked just the part in a London taxi or holding court with the other cabbies over a cuppa at a mobile tea shelter.

The Canadians began to talk more. It was all safe ground but Raymond worked hard to keep the conversation moving.

'I was a Chartered Accountant before volunteering,' Clements said. 'I guess when this is all done I'll go back home and pick it up again.'

Raymond raised his eyebrows. 'Where's home?'

'Stockholm. It's in Saskatchewan, same spelling as the place in Sweden. Pretty small really, some houses, a crossroads and that's about it.' He looked through the car window. His gaze was a long way from Spain.

Kennedy skimmed over an answer. He lived in Fort William, Ontario on the edge of Lake Superior and had worked for the railways. He never mentioned his father. I thought back to the comment Ward made to me in the Pyrenees about Kennedy telling him his father was vice-president of the Canadian Pacific Railway. When my turn came, I sketched in some of Leicester and my printing job.

A line of hills in the northeast broke the flat land. It had stopped drizzling by the time the car hit higher ground. The land fell away on one side then rose again, dotted with small trees. When the car finally halted on a level stretch of road, I'd seen more carts and mules in the last four hours than vehicles.

The driver topped up the tank from two jerry cans and we left after sandwiches and flasks of tea. Full sunshine burst through in the final hour of daylight. The valley floor looked rich and fertile, lines of orange trees crowded up to the road, vines were silhouetted in rows against the last embers of day and warmer air blew in through the car window. I had a sense of anticipation again.

Raymond called out from the front. 'Are you awake back there?'

We all answered.

He twisted around. 'Not far to go, lads. Seville's a busy river port, so we'll have to be careful.'

The car crawled along for miles, its headlamps picking out potholes and pits in the road.

'We could be in luck,' the driver said suddenly. 'There's a power cut.'

I peered out and saw nothing but night. Raymond wound his window down. The breeze smelled of mud and river. Dim shapes of buildings were looming out of the dark. We stopped with a lurch. The driver killed the engine and lights.

'This is it,' Raymond said. 'I'll check the coast's clear. Get out when I tap the window. You won't be able to see much, so stick close by me.'

The door closed with a quiet clunk. Kennedy wriggled around to squint through the back window.

'I can't see anything.'

The driver started the engine. 'Get ready. We're on a corner here, so I'll have to shift, pronto.'

Two taps came at my side window and we were straight out onto the cobbles. A ship's horn cut through the night. Raymond turned a street corner, hastening towards the light coming from a window on the opposite side. A shadowy figure waited in the doorway and I followed the others into the house.

The glow had come from an oil lamp on a table. Someone shut the front door and brushed past me. Kennedy's heavy breathing was near my shoulder – Raymond and Clements were close. The lamp brightened, yellowing the plain plaster walls. I caught a whiff of smoking oil and a woman's face wavered in the light. She smiled and moved her head, rippling the jet-black hair on her shoulders.

'The journey is good for you?'

'Yes,' Raymond said. 'And it's a nice warm night too.'

The woman wore a pleated black skirt and white embroidered blouse which had a parchment tint when it caught the full lamplight. She slipped into quieter Spanish words and his stumbled replies forced a laugh. He handed her an envelope.

'We speak English now,' she said, smiling again.

Raymond cleared his throat. 'Driver will be waiting. Have you everything you need?'

She nodded. 'Please… you must go now.'

'Usual thing, lads,' I heard him say. 'No going outside and the rest of it.'

'We know what to do,' Clements replied. 'Had enough practice.'

'Fair enough. I'm sorry fellas, I haven't introduced you.'

The lamp dimmed. 'There is not time,' the woman said, urgently. She went to the front door and Raymond left in a hurry.

'*Bueno*. At last,' she said. 'We will sit in my kitchen.'

She turned up the lamp again. I could see the others clearly now. The room had a panelled sideboard, large sofa and four woven cane chairs around the circular table. We walked past a steep staircase and through an arched entrance. A stove, sink and kitchen table with four chairs appeared in the sweep of light.

'There is no *electricidad* in Sevilla. Tomorrow… yes.'

She apologised and placed her lamp on the kitchen table, explaining about power cuts during the last two evenings and coffee in the pot being over two hours old.

'Would you drink brandy? I have some.'

She lined up a bottle and four wine glasses from a cupboard I hadn't noticed. We politely declined as there was barely enough left for three shots. She insisted and the moment became difficult.

'I have cigarettes, Ma'am,' Clements said. 'Would you like some?'

He offered the packet.

'*Gracias,*' she said, taking one. 'I have friends, but Gitanes, *cigarillos*, we cannot buy them. I will smoke it later. Now you must eat *tapas*.'

The Gitanes had lightened things, although I wasn't sure if we had created a problem. I knew little about the Spanish way of life – Franco or no Franco. Did that matter? Normality had finished when the war started. The woman spoke in brief sentences as she prepared the food. It passed as easy conversation and we sat at the table answering her questions. Sometimes she would face us and tilt her head as she listened, drawing in each word. I tried to guess her age. It was impossible; the smile chased away every line on her face.

'So,' she said, serving up the small plates. 'You are *Ingles, Americano* and *Americano*?'

'No, we are English, Canadian and Canadian,' Clements said, pointing us out.

We gave her our first names. The woman smiled with a polite nod each time.

'*Ingles, Canadiense* and *Canadiense*. *Excelente*. And later I show you all your beds.'

She borrowed my matchbox and left us while we ate cheese, olives and small squares of dried, salty meat. The ceiling creaked when she moved around in the rooms above us.

No one made a move to smoke. Clements put his fork down.

'I've got some questions. They'll keep till later.'

'She didn't give us her name,' Kennedy said. 'What do we call her?'

'Señora,' I replied. 'There's a ring on her finger.'

Both the Canadians laughed. It wasn't intended to be funny; I'd travelled and stayed with a string of people with no names, it was natural to look for clues. I would always address her in that way.

The Señora returned carrying a smaller lamp and led us up the stairs. Two beds were crammed in a small box room.

'For you,' she said.

In the light, I saw my own reflection from a dresser mirror in the room opposite. The only other door was further down the passage. She waited until we were descending the stairs before I heard her open it.

I woke during the night for a second time without knowing why. We had drawn lots before turning in, to decide who slept on the sofa in the front room. I was happy to bunk alone, as the day had overtaken me. The curtains puffed in and out in the breeze and the room had a chill, so I got up to close the window. The street was in darkness. Every place I'd stayed in had its own set of creaks and groans and I came to recognise them. This house had a mysterious stillness of its own – a hesitant quiet. I listened by the window. Then I heard it. Movement in the room above and a string of muffled sobs.

6

A cart woke me, rattling past on the cobbles. The scent of hot oil and tortilla strayed into the front room – I recognised the smell from the embassy. Clements and Kennedy were sitting at the kitchen table when I arrived. The Señora looked up from the stove. She had tied her hair back.

'*Buenos dias*. Please sit.' She turned the pancake. I pulled out a chair opposite the Canadians.

'Sleep good?' Clements whispered to me, above her gentle humming.

'Not too well. Kept waking. Somebody was moving about in the room above. I heard crying. It wasn't the Señora. Didn't you notice anything?'

'No. I slept all night. It must have been *her*.'

I said nothing more. It was bad manners to whisper and I would choose my moment to pick up that conversation again.

'Do you know how long we'll be staying?' Clements asked her.

'No.' She served up the tortillas. '*Alguien visitará pronto...* a man will visit soon. Today the sun is good, so you can sit on the roof at the back of my house. You will see across the town. Now, I make us drinks, so please smoke if you wish.'

She stayed busy about the kitchen until we had finished breakfast.

'Señors. I must speak with you,' she said, sitting down with us.

Her eyes glistened. I pushed my cigarettes across the table. She fumbled one into her mouth and drew off the flame from my match.

'My daughter also lives here. She is in the bed upstairs.'

'I heard somebody moving about last night,' I said.

'I am sorry. My daughter is ill. This happens often with the night. It is best that she always stays in her bedroom. Yesterday was many busy things for me and today it is good that I speak. Now you are certain where I go and what I do.'

She waited for us to light a round of cigarettes. We had never seen her husband either. Perhaps she would tell us about him? Clements spoke first.

'How old is your daughter?'

'She has fourteen years.' She took a drag on the cigarette and opened her mouth to swallow the smoke. Her face was suddenly bleak, the voice a whisper. 'It is difficult. *Medicamentos*, the medicine... also the food. There is never enough. When the ships arrive, it is possible to wait and try to buy... if you have money.'

'I've seen queues in every country since I began my journey,' I said.

She looked down at her hands. 'Yes. Many wait a long time and they still have nothing to give their families. But the Generalissimo is kind. We have soup that is water and there is also a piece of bread.' It was a statement, and she had put the question into it.

A tear escaped. 'The bread is for one day, but the people eat as soon as they are given. Señors, if you walk on the streets of Seville, you will not see the dogs or cats.'

She placed her cigarette carefully on the ashtray. The Canadians fidgeted in their seats and an ache grew inside me like a blackened bruise. I'd seen enough of fascist Spain festering around the tenement blocks and alleys or begging in the gutter. The Señora was another victim.

'I have some money,' I said. Clements gave me an approving nod. 'We all have money. It's not much—'

'No Señor.' A shadow crossed her face. 'That is not what I am saying.'

She rose, picking up the plates. I was an intruder in someone else's world, a world I could do nothing about. She battled through every day and now we were another problem for her. I wanted to push those thoughts on one side. Hers was a separate war.

I looked across the city from the flat roof. Stucco white buildings lined the narrow streets and red tiled rooftops stretched away to a distant Moor bell tower. Sunshine warmed my face and it was strange to feel a gentle heat after what had happened in the Pyrenees. Kennedy sat alongside me with his back against a border wall: we were out of sight from the front of the house. He unfolded a foil sheet of aspirins before slipping them hurriedly away again.

'Doc reckoned there'd be enough to get me to Gibraltar. We've been here four days,' he said to himself.

I pretended not to notice. He only had four tablets left.

My worries hadn't disappeared and we were used to waiting, but the nag of anticipation around a visitor arriving with news niggled like a toothache which was always worse at night. Today was going to be the day and that drove us on through the routine: a frugal breakfast, another small meal in the evening – burrito, tortilla and chorizo, the Señora had taught us the words. Her daughter would often call out and the Señora stayed with her for long periods. We sat on the roof until late afternoon, or mooched about the front room, as there was nothing in English to read, only Spanish novels and a pile of *ABC* newspapers in the corner.

The church bells rang out again: three rings, a pause, three more – sixteen, seventeen, eighteen. Midday was the urgent call to worship and the same at six in the morning and evening.

'Franco gives much back to the Church,' the Señora had said after our meal the previous evening. 'They have power again, the most for two hundred years. The Church say their enemies are the communist, the liberals and Jews, but we are all afraid. During the civil war they are with the Nationalists. It is the crusade.'

Religion and politics in Spain were welded together the same as in Italy. A Catholic chap on the base at Bottesford said the Italian surrender to the Allies would make no difference to the Church in Rome – nothing would.

'Another Mass?' Kennedy said, shading his eyes against the sun.

I scratched at my midriff. 'That bell only tells the time for me. After what we were told last night, it's best not to think about any

326

of it. The Catholic Church is right at the front with Franco. No one's safe.'

I imagined the people being drawn to prayer and made to spill out their secrets at confession. Someone could get suspicious about the Señora at any time and inform the Guardia Civil.

'Think about how you felt at home when a church bell rang, and how you feel now,' I said to Kennedy.

'Don't go that deep, myself. Just gotta get to Gib. Just want to feel better?'

I stood up and stretched. 'Best I go and see where Bob has got to.'

Kennedy gave me a desperate look. 'Ron, we're only about a hundred and twenty miles away. That's three or four hours in a car. I still haven't worked out how they'll get us across the border.'

The Señora was absent when we got down to the front room. Clements paced around and the bells rang again. They sounded softer inside the house, less menacing. In low moments, a flimsy sense of sanctuary did exist downstairs. I pictured Mum setting off for church on a misty Sunday morning and Dad already hard at work in the garden. I was back at Saint Barnabas church parade in Scout uniform amongst the Woodpigeon Patrol – innocent, unscathed and with no concept of real fear.

The next morning, the Señora called us down from the roof. A dark-haired man in a navy, chalk-striped suit greeted us in the front room. His trilby hat was hanging from one of the cane chairs at the table.

'Good morning. My name's Montgomery. I'm the British Vice-Consul in Seville.'

He had the same headmasterly air and practised handshake as all the diplomats, his gaze shifting to the next man in our line, as if ticking off some mental list.

'Been sunning yourselves?' he asked. 'Bit breezy up there, isn't it?'

The Señora brought in four cups of coffee on a wooden tray.

'Ah gracias,' Montgomery said, gesturing us to sit at the table. He waited until she had climbed the stairs.

'She's a jolly decent type, actually. But first things first. Sorry it's taken so long to get to you. I trust everything's been tickety-boo here?'

Clements glossed over our last few days. He avoided mentioning the daughter. Montgomery listened, chipping in with small talk about Seville and the recent war news. This world was not open or candid; conversation stayed with trivial observations and generalities. Nobody asked him the obvious question. I sipped my drink and waited. I wasn't going to be the first to tempt fate.

'Do you think it's still possible Franco will pitch in with Hitler?' Kennedy said.

Montgomery raised his eyebrows. 'I don't think Spain is ready to fight another war… not for a while anyway.'

His face wrinkled. 'Gibraltar's vital, so we still have to be careful. Make no mistake, the British are not popular in large parts of Spain, whichever camp you're in. Seville is fiercely nationalist. Franco's got to stay in power that's for sure, as we can't have the Left back in. You don't need a crystal ball to see what will happen in Europe with the Russians after Germany loses the war.'

'You sound pretty optimistic,' Clements said, sarcastically.

'More realistic, to be fair.' Montgomery gave him a condescending look. 'You can't fight a war on two fronts. Hitler's discovered that. And now the Italians have thrown in the towel…'

He glanced at his watch. 'I digress. There's a British merchant ship docked in Seville, picking up a cargo of oranges. It's about nineteen hundred tons. They're pretty small here because of the size of the river. You'll be smuggled on board tonight. She sails for Gibraltar tomorrow.'

The rest of his sentence faded. I saw the mouth move and heard nothing. Montgomery placed his cup on the table.

'Capital. I'll be back at eight-fifteen sharp. It'll be dark enough by then and you must be ready to leave on the dot. The Spanish guard the ship and, without going into detail, things will happen at a certain time and we must be there.'

He took his hat. 'I think that's all. Is there anything more you would like to ask?'

Now that the moment had come and gone, I'd a numb indifference to the news, as if suddenly drained of all emotion.

'Can you tell us anything about the Señora's daughter?' Clements said. 'We've not seen her. She stays shut away in an upper room.'

'Catholic families are very strict in Spain,' Montgomery said in a voice that sounded as if we should have known. He raised his eyebrows again.

'A young girl of that age in a house with three men, it's not the acceptable thing.'

Clements nodded. 'OK. She says the girl's ill. Do you know what's wrong with her?'

Montgomery glanced in the direction of footsteps coming down the stairs.

'Tuberculosis.'

'Ah, Señora.' He switched on a smile. 'If I may speak with you for a moment and then I will leave by the back way, if that is acceptable.'

He put his hat on, touched the brim at us with a forefinger and disappeared with her into the kitchen. The Canadians shouted out and embraced. In the distance, I heard the church bells ring again.

Later, we sat around the kitchen table. Clements had a cigarette in his mouth. He patted his pockets for the matchbox. The Señora stood at the sink washing plates after our final meal. Her sparkle had gone. I'd noticed it disappear slowly over the days and watched her spirits fall. I imagined her waiting at the docks for black market food or slipping away to a snatched meeting with some shady profiteer. Where did the small amounts of fresh food come from? She never left the house. Perhaps she did go out, or a friend called while we were up on the roof? The nervous circuits in my brain were overthinking again.

She joined us at the table. The room became gauzy with smoke as she forced out a story. Not about herself or her family, only of Spain and how the nation really was. The Monarchists hankered for a return to days before the abdication in 1931. The Republicans, even in defeat, were still full of squabbling splinter groups, leaving the way clear for a corrupt fascist state to bulldoze the country along by force.

'The killing is every day,' she said, lighting another cigarette. 'Many thousands are in prison, some say half a million... women also. What have these people done except stand with their families?'

She talked about the prisoners' children, swallowed up in orphanages or forced into barracks for education and drill, in the Falange way. 'Later they march through the streets in uniform.'

I listened, although my thoughts had moved onwards to the next few hours. She began to laugh, yet the sound had no humour in it. I braced myself for more politics.

'You are ready to leave this house, Señors, all of you. I understand. Soon you will be free and safe.' The smoke clouded around her. 'You are also asking some questions. I know this.'

She turned her head away from us. 'Where is *mi marido*... my husband, you say? I will tell you. My husband is in the prison.'

She stubbed out her cigarette and rushed upstairs.

7

Montgomery arrived promptly via the back door, dressed in a belted black raincoat with matching trilby in his hand.

'Good evening. It's a little chilly outside tonight.'

He followed the Señora to the kitchen table. I decided it must be a British diplomatic trait to speak about the weather before anything else: a manoeuvre to open a door for small talk while he got his bearings.

'Been here six months,' he said to us. 'I was in warmer climes before this. Right, gentlemen, if everything's on the top line, we'd better go.'

We said an awkward goodbye to the Señora. I wished her earlier words had remained unsaid. Montgomery spoke in Spanish and shook her hand. He gave a little bow before putting on his hat and leading us to the back door. The kitchen light went out.

'Right, chaps. Next stop, SS *Tudor Prince* and keep close to me. Some streets have no lamps, so for God's sake keep an eye open for the gutters, there aren't always drain covers. You'll break a leg, for sure.'

We walked in pairs. The smell of sewers hung under my nose. A man and woman passed under a street lamp opposite. At night the footfall always came before the figure. Montgomery stopped abruptly, herding us into a gap between two buildings.

'Damned business,' he hissed, looking up and down the winding street. 'Had a tail on me when I first arrived in Seville. They're not so frequent now, but we can't be too careful.'

'Germans?' whispered Clements.

'No. Mostly Spanish Foreign Department.' Montgomery looked out again. 'Come on, we're not far away.'

A breeze blew up the side street. We passed a bar with its door open. I caught the drift of voices and stale wine. The street ended in blackness where the buildings finished. Montgomery waited at the corner by a brick warehouse.

'I can't see a darned thing. At least if anyone's following, they won't spot us.'

We rushed across a wide road, stepping into the dock area through the gap in a wall alongside the pavement. A series of dim lamps shone from the tops of tall poles.

'Keep low, everyone. We don't want to be seen from the road.' Montgomery waved us down behind a wooden hut. He looked tired and top heavy in his hat and raincoat.

'This is the tricky bit. Our ship's about four hundred yards ahead.' He peered around the side wall. 'It's the one in the middle.'

Three vessels were moored in the distance along the quayside, vague black shapes with a single funnel each. Lights dotted the far bank and the air carried the same smell of wet mud. A shudder moved down the nape of my neck and across my shoulders as if I were standing in an icy draught. The port was far too quiet.

'Make for the back of that brick building,' he said, pointing to a low, oblong shape around a hundred yards away. 'Watch where you're going, it's easy to fall over something.'

I went to move. An arm blocked my way. Montgomery's breathing laboured against my racing heartbeat. Men's voices echoed near the road. His hand clamped on my shoulder, then eased its grip as the noise faded.

He tapped his watch. 'Can't see the time.'

My hands were trembling. 'Almost eight-fifty.'

He pressed up close against the wooden hut. 'This is it. Go.'

We crossed railway lines set in the concrete and weaved a path through a shanty town of crates, wooden barrels and tarpaulins. The brick building had a line of small windows. This time we stood upright. I saw the ship, its dark hulk moored near an open metal shelter with a roof of three curved arches.

'We must get nearer,' Montgomery said, with a shake in his voice. 'I don't see the guard.' He gave a long sigh. 'Damn risky. We might be spotted.'

Seconds passed. Doubts crept into my mind – he was a diplomat not a spy. I looked at the others – Kennedy glancing nervously around, Clements, leaning hard against the wall. A tarpaulin flapped and the scrape of boots sounded nearby. We all dropped down on the ground, except Montgomery who was crouching. He angled his head towards the noise then fiddled with his hat.

'We'll have to chance it. You must be on board at nine. Make for those crates over there… and for God's sake, keep quiet.'

With a huge gulp of air, he lurched out and we followed.

I peeped through a gap between rows of wooden crates. The ship was moored about twenty-five yards away, near a small loading jetty, jutting out from the quayside. Light from the bridge sketched out the king posts and deck. A Spanish guard stepped under the lamp a few paces from the gangplank. Scuffing his feet, he turned back to shuffle through the same manoeuvre on the other side. A tiny, red dot glowed at the top of the gangway then moved slowly down to the wharf. The guard stopped and waited until the outline of a man stepped on to the quayside. Their faces flickered for an instant in the flare of a match, before the two figures walked slowly together along the dockside into the night.

Montgomery's hand clapped on my shoulder. 'Go straight up the gangway Ron, and don't stop.'

About thirty paces to the ship. Water slopped against the wharf – a fishy, rotten smell hung in the air. Cold rails against my hands – footsteps on the gangplank. I reached the top as a man in a black, woolly hat emerged from the shadows.

'How many more of you?'

My mind stalled for a moment. 'Two.'

'Good. That's what the captain said. Hide here till I've got the others.'

I squatted next to the deck rail. Kennedy arrived, then Clements.

'Welcome aboard, gents, I'm the mate. The guard will be back any time now. I'll put you in the forepeak, it's the safest place. River police come on board tomorrow and search the ship. They'll be around until we leave the estuary.'

He set off towards the bow. 'We sail at midday.'

I crept after him with the others and stepped on to the raised upper deck.

'Hang on here for a minute and keep low.' He pulled open a hatch, climbed over the coaming and disappeared down a dark hole. Seconds later a whistle came from below. His flashlight revealed a ladder.

'Take care with your footing, and go straight to the bottom. Make haste.'

I climbed down into a cold space, smelling of oil, damp rope and tar.

'You'll be in the bow against the hull and anchor chain lockers,' he said. 'It's a bit cramped, unfortunately.'

His voice had a metallic ring under the low ceiling. The torch beam danced around the bulkheads and floor. Standing room was about twelve paces square. Rusty anchor chains were visible in two adjacent steel compartments behind a four-foot high bulkhead stretching across the width of the bow. On the port side, a plated wall ran floor to ceiling along the hull up to the left chain compartment. The mate trained his torch on it.

'There's a narrow space between the bulkhead and hull. You'll have to climb over the anchor chain and turn around to get in.'

His light swung around to the back wall which was lined with paint tins, rags, pieces of tarpaulin, and rope. 'Once you're inside, I'll pile some of this rubbish in the corner, it'll help to disguise the gap.'

He handed a smaller flashlight to Clements. I caught a quick sight of the mate, a thin man in a navy coat and white round-neck sweater. The woolly hat looked welded to his head.

'Don't use the torch unless you have to,' he said. 'I'll guide you in. Canteens and sandwiches are halfway down and a bucket's in the corner. Not many of the crowd know you're down here, so stay absolutely quiet. I'll be back tomorrow once the police and river pilot have left the ship and we clear the estuary.'

The mate shone his light on a mass of coiled, rusty chain. We clambered over the bulkhead. Clements steadied Kennedy. They climbed up and disappeared from sight. The chain was covered in dirt and oil. I crawled on top of it on my hands and knees, turned about and dropped into the narrow space. Kennedy held our torch steady. A bucket was at the other end. Canteens and four small parcels wrapped with newspaper were stacked where the mate said they would be. The hiding place measured about three and a half feet wide, barely enough space to sit singly.

Both sides were tight against my arms. I slid to the floor, pressing my back against the chain compartment wall. The mate had started shifting junk against the other side of the bulkhead. The two Canadians sat cross-legged facing each other next to a pile of blankets. Clements rolled one up and threw it to me. We were all gasping in the stuffy air. The mate's boots clumped up the ladder, our flashlight went out and the hatch door banged shut. I wiped the sweat off my face and pulled the blanket tight around my shoulders. In the thick blackness, it was pointless opening my eyes.

The ship groaned in the water. In the dead quiet of the early hours, I listened to sounds above: a metal door closing, noises on deck from men who would be breathing in fresh air, men who could look up at an open night sky. The cramped conditions made it impossible for us to get comfortable or sleep. We tried to stand under the low ceiling, flex our legs and shuffle around in our own tight circles between the hull and bulkhead. I had to cross my arms against my chest to make a turn. The space behind Kennedy was just enough for me to kneel, bend forward and stretch my back.

'What time is it?' Clements asked, flicking on the torch.

A circle of light settled on my arm, turning the creases in my jacket into furrows, hills and canyons.

'Somewhere after one o'clock. Can't see properly... could do with the torch,' I said.

'I need the bucket,' Kennedy said.

'You heard what the mate said about noise and moving around.' Clements' voice came with a crackly whisper. 'We must get organised. There's at least another ten hours until we sail. I'm sitting next to the bucket and you've both got to climb over me to use it.'

We formed a routine for everything: no talk or noise unless essential, take timed slots on listening duty and each sentry to take the torch and my wristwatch. Canteens and sandwiches were put against the bulkhead wall. We had a couple of five-minute breaks to eat and drink together. Only one man at a time could stand. I gave up my blanket to cover the bucket which had the same strict controls, yet even with a handkerchief pressed against my mouth, the fetid air made me gag.

How would we get out if anything went wrong? Most of my previous hiding places had an exit. Paris had been different but this dirty hole was something else. Night passed somewhere between lucid thoughts and trying to sleep. In the soupy state of my mind, neither was possible.

Clements had crawled back from the bucket when I heard the noise.

'Someone at the hatch,' I whispered, turning off the torch and squirming away to squash up against Kennedy.

Spanish voices chattered above. The deck hatch crashed open and a thin ray of daylight fell on the anchor chain visible in the gap. Someone climbed down the ladder. A torch beam stroked along the hull, hovering near our entrance. Slow footsteps paced the floor – boots against the bulkhead, boots about to climb on the chain. I stared into the dark. The thump in my chest grew louder. Kennedy's breathing sounded rapid and shallow then I realised it was my own. A circle of light held steady on the hull above me. Bile rose into my mouth, the deepening quiet swelled inside my head and I tried to hold my breath. A loud curse and clatter shattered the quiet as tins hit the floor. The boots moved away, climbing the ladder, lighter and quicker now. I counted time until the deck hatch shut.

'God, that was close,' Clements said. Neither of us answered.

Just after twelve, a low vibration and throb started from the ship's engines. Water splashed against the side – we had cast off. No one had spoken since the hatch shut. I kept any thoughts to myself. They would remain unsaid, because we had passed the penultimate test and nothing must tempt fate to alter that thin line of status quo between the ship sailing and reaching the estuary. A long-forgotten childhood memory came into my head. If I walked to school and didn't step on the gaps between pavement slabs, everything would be alright.

The foul atmosphere smothered any sense of smell and taste. My head felt ballooned to twice its size and we all had nausea. I took a slug of water from the canteen, trying to force down some Spam sandwich. The texture was as unmistakable as the feel of hardtack biscuits inside the paper bag next to me.

'What happens if we're torpedoed?' Kennedy said, above the beat of the ship's engines.

Clements tried to stand up. 'What? On the bloody river?'

Sniggers and coughs sounded. 'Quiet,' he panted.

Our safety valves shut off. I heard the top unscrew off a canteen.

'No. I meant while we're sailing down the coast.' Kennedy's voice tailed off.

'One thing at a time,' I said. 'Let's get to the estuary first.'

It began as a dull scrape below my feet. The ship juddered. A grating roar came like the tide drawing back on shingle. The rubbish stack outside our hiding place collapsed. Tins rolled across the floor. Noises on deck and below became busier – shouts more urgent. In the airless space it was like trying to breathe through a straw. Fear rose inside me like floodwater – the engines kicked into life again. With a tortured groan, the ship moved then stopped. Feet trod across my shins; an arm struck me in the stomach. I fought a way up to a standing position. We were all on our feet now and squashed together. The rushing noise below became a waterfall.

8

A hand gripped my arm from behind. 'Steady. Stay where you are.' Clements' words came in a heavy whisper. 'We've run aground, that's all. Ship was going too slow to get damaged.'

The hand let go. 'They might be emptying the ballast tanks,' he said. 'We sit tight again and wait.'

'We can't do much else,' I said. My cheeks burned. 'And I am steady. It was instinct to get up and go for the gap... we all did it. And don't you manhandle me like that again.'

'Quiet... both of you.'

Kennedy's words sounded like something between a whisper and a cry. They brought me to my senses and I instantly regretted the outburst. The rushing water stopped. Noises around us became more measured and the ship settled. I chose my moment to apologise. Each of us did. *I'm sorry,* were two words to break a silence, two words that needed no qualification or mitigation. A line was drawn under what had happened and we moved on.

I turned everything over in the quiet of that afternoon; it stopped the walls from closing in. The ship had not taken on water, the mate could get us out and we'd try again to re-float. I'd passed through the line of panic now, only fear remained. Nothing showed in the dark, yet I imagined the Canadians' faces with the same bleak look as in the safe houses and mountains. We were still blind and totally reliant on others. Daylight would be fading outside. Surely all the ship was waiting for now was the tide?

The deck hatch opened. The first few steps down the ladder caught against the rungs before the hatch banged shut. A clunking noise came with the slow descent, then muttering – English muttering.

'Are you gents alright in there?'

The mate's silhouette showed in a splash of torchlight as he climbed onto the anchor chain with three water canteens strapped across his chest. The beam probed our hiding place.

Clements shielded his face. 'What's going on?'

'I'm sorry, couldn't get to you before. Ship's stuck on a mud bank and the Spanish river pilot is still on board. I've had to wait until dark to sneak down here.'

I cut in. 'Is there any damage?'

'No. The ship's fine.'

I forced myself to stand and try to rub the cramps from my legs. The mate knelt down gingerly on the anchor chain.

'Hold this.' He passed me his torch before unslinging the canteens.

I shone the light as he struggled to pull out paper bags from his pocket.

'Sandwiches again,' he murmured, peering past me into the black hole. 'They'll keep you going for a while and we should be off the bank on the morning tide. I'll get you out myself once we reach the estuary.'

'How long will that take?' Clements asked in a dry, precise voice.

'A couple of hours, once we can re-float. Steady as you go gents, we're not far off now.'

I returned the torch. 'Can we climb out for a bit and walk around the room? It's getting pretty rough in here.'

'No. It's too risky. Climbing on the chain is out of bounds too. I had to shut the top hatch when I came down, we can't take a chance that any light or noise reaches the deck. Give me your empty canteens and I'll swap the bucket.'

After he closed the hatch, I switched on our torch, flicking it idly around. The battery was low and I'd gone against orders. Kennedy sipped slowly from his canteen and Clements lay in a curled-up position with his back facing me. I killed the light and didn't bother to check my watch. In the stifling dark space, the inner tide of my body could no longer put a time on things. I tried to focus on Gibraltar. The frozen stiffness in my back and cramps knifing through my legs wiped away any other thoughts.

I woke with a pounding headache. The ship's engines churned – there was no contented pulse, no steady rhythm. Noise and vibration hammered down the hull, drilling me straight between the eyes. A grating shift came, then a shudder and short burst at half ahead speed.

'We're moving. We're off the bank.' Clements' voice disappeared in the din.

Kennedy shone the torch against his wrist. He wriggled over and shouted in my ear.

'It's almost nine-ten. Your shift in twenty minutes.'

As if on cue, the engines settled and water sloshed against the hull.

'Pass me my watch, I'll start now,' I said. 'Sounds like full steam ahead. The mate reckoned on two hours to the estuary. You get some rest.'

Two hours. That would be about the limit of how much more we could stand. My thoughts turned in swirling circles on how the biggest things could still hinge on the smallest of details. A second made the difference between life and death on bombing raids. A fraction earlier or later to the target meant a whole aircraft length, a distance for flak and cannon shells to hit or miss, for men to die or live. If the ship had steered several yards to port or starboard on the river, we could have been on the open sea by now, or in Gibraltar. We were seconds from disaster when the search in the forepeak was abandoned. One move in the wrong place could still change everything. My journey remained balanced on a tightrope and the bad memories reached out again with long, black fingers.

The escape had changed me irreparably. It proved how easy it was to spend so much time with people and know so little about them. I doubted I would ever observe folks in the same way again: the man standing outside Leicester railway station, workers waiting for their trams in Humberstone Gate, and the two youths who had followed me from Halford Street to the Market Place. I would view any stranger with suspicion.

The engines stopped a couple of hours later.

'Nearly there, guys,' Clements said. 'Just a short wait until the Spanish have left the ship.'

I fell into the sick excitement of that moment: a thought of daylight and fresh air, the afternoon outside, a cloudless blue sky and seaward horizon beyond the estuary. I willed the hatch to open and to hear the mate's boots clumping down the ladder. The anchor chain moved suddenly. A deafening rattle filled our space and the bulkheads seemed ready to split apart. Nothing had been said about dropping anchor. When the noise stopped, I waited for someone to ask what the hell was going on. All that came back was a ringing in my ears and the steady rock from the ship.

The mate arrived after dark with more water and sandwiches. We didn't stand up or crawl to the mouth of the hole. His monologue droned in and out of earshot. The swell was too bad on the open sea, so the ship anchored in the estuary and the river pilot had stayed on board.

'If all's fair, we sail on the noon tide tomorrow,' he said.

I threw our empty canteens to him and didn't hear his response. He left without changing the bucket.

9

'They've gone. You can come out now,' the mate called from the other side of the bulkhead. 'Sorry you've had such a rough time. Anyone need a hand?'

He covered the chain with a tarpaulin. 'Captain said to wait until we'd hit the open sea before fishing you out. Hatch is open so you can get used to the daylight before we go up on deck.'

We climbed over the bulkhead and crawled across the chain. A column of grey light flooded in from above. The Canadians struggled across the floor to the ladder, their unshaven faces giving them a lank, shabby appearance.

'Nearly midday. Captain will see you after you've had a chance to get cleaned up,' the mate said.

He gave us a couple of minutes to acclimatise. 'OK gents. Take your time. I'll be right behind you. Follow me once we're all on deck.'

We buttoned our jackets and struggled up the ladder in stages. I had to squint against the glare as we neared the top. An able seaman helped me through the hatchway.

'You can clear up down there now,' the mate said to him as he emerged.

I reached the deck rail, gulping in fresh air with the others. A low thread of coastline ran parallel off the port side.

'We're sailing close to Spain,' the mate shouted above the wind and sea crashing against the ship. 'Neutral waters… the safest place. There's still some rough stuff further out to sea.'

We walked towards the ship's bridge. A cold wind and the smell of salt air began to clear my head. I noticed three figures observing us intently through the bridge windows until we passed out of view below.

Kennedy sat with me later in the crew mess room on one of the 'L' shaped wooden benches screwed to the wall. The showers had been cramped and tepidly warm – enough to coat the surround with a thin film of condensation. Two and a half days of dirt had swilled off my body in a string of shivers. By the time Clements and the mate joined us, I was used to the smell of stale sweat and muck on my clothes again. The mate looked at us doubtfully. 'Right gents, the captain is ready to see you now.'

After a shave, we were still a mess. The Canadians brushed at their shoulders and sleeves as if trying to cover up the problem.

'This isn't the normal thing,' the mate said with a thin smile. 'Bridge is usually out of bounds.'

He moved as if to make for the door, then stopped. 'New broom, I suppose, he's not been with us long. Our Captain Clare passed away suddenly while we were at sea.'

The ship cut through the waves as we walked a short distance along deck. I climbed some metal steps, watching the wind snatch away smoke from the funnel. The mate escorted us onto the bridge, then left. A sense of calm and order filled the compact space: a quarter master steady at the wheel, the captain looking out over open sea on the starboard side and an officer scanning the coast through his binoculars.

'Passing Cadiz in fifteen minutes, sir,' the officer said, switching his field of view to the open water.

'Thank you, Mr Mitchell.' The captain turned to face us. 'Welcome, lads. You'll be alright in here for three or four minutes, it's quiet at the moment.'

He was a lean man in his late forties, with soft features and quizzical eyes.

'Captain Wiles, Master of the *Tudor Prince*,' he said, shaking our hands. 'I'm sorry about your berths – not even steerage, eh?' He smiled, observing the ship's bow dipping in the water. 'We couldn't take any more risks. Weather's still a bit lively, but you lads seem to have found your sea legs alright. You must have sailed before.'

The Canadians told him how they had reached England by ship. The nearest I had come to that was rowing on Abbey Park boating lake in Leicester. 'I haven't been to sea, but the flying has helped, sir.'

My gaze strayed across the slate-grey water. The rise and fall of the waves and whitecaps had a hypnotic effect. I had tried to join the Navy twice, yet I stood on this bridge as an outsider. Fate was giving me a glimpse of the path I never trod because others intervened. Fate controlled everything. Life was mapped out and the choices you had were not choices at all, only a course already plotted in. Final outcomes were pre-determined; the escape had convinced me of that.

'I was worried when the Spanish searched the forepeak,' Clements said. 'They came down the ladder, poked about a bit and left.'

The captain nodded. 'It was the last place they checked. We were going to try and bluff it out if things got tricky.'

'I thought we were in trouble when the ship ran aground,' I said. 'The noise was terrible.'

'Always sounds worse below deck on a ship of this size. The Guadalquivir is a pretty shallow tidal river and the mud banks shift. We certainly jumped through some hoops to get afloat.' He gazed out to sea again. 'Then we had to drop anchor in the estuary because of swell. My apologies, lads… over sixty hours down there is not for the fainthearted.'

I looked along the bow then realised he was studying me with interest.

'Yes. We are armed,' he said. 'It's a twelve pounder and there's a four-inch gun at the stern too. We've got some MRA lads on board to sort those out.'

I knew there were armed merchant ships, but not on smaller vessels.

The officer still had his binoculars trained on the water. The captain turned to him.

'Mr Mitchell. Increase the lookouts and inform me immediately if there's anything unusual, anything at all.'

'Aye aye, sir.'

'I will be in my cabin with our extra passengers.' There was a hint of mischief in his voice. 'I'm sure they'll appreciate something other than sandwiches and water. I'll return within the hour before we reach Cape Trafalgar.'

Mitchell kept his focus straight ahead and the captain led us off the bridge. He shouted into the wind, scanning the sea and periodically glancing back at us.

'You'll have a decent hot meal and then we're only hours away,' he called, ducking off the deck and through a doorway.

We clattered after him down the metal stairwell and crowded into a corridor. It was a relief to get away from the weather. He waited for us to settle.

'I'll be quite straight with you... we're not out of the woods yet. You must stay vigilant. Once we get near the Straits of Gibraltar, there's a risk of U-boats. Ships have been lost. They often track vessels down the Spanish coast.'

I thought back to Kennedy's comment on the river, about being torpedoed. It wasn't funny now. The nagging uncertainty bubbled up again. We stopped outside a cabin door.

The captain rubbed his hands together. 'Not to worry, we'll do our best. Now it's brandy first before anything else.'

'Aye, aye sir,' Clements said.

The cabin had a neat wood shine with brass trimmings of authority. We crammed around the small table for a meal of meat, potatoes and two veg – piping hot English food. I'd eaten well at the embassy in Madrid, but this came with a simplicity and appetite from the sea air. The captain talked warmly, avoiding the war, and throwing in small talk when the pauses came. We spoke a little of our homes again and life on sunny normal days. It felt so distant and artificial, when all I could think about was reaching Gibraltar. I sat forward at the table to show some interest. It was the least I could do.

'When I've a few minutes to myself in here, it's good to think about the old times.' He wiped his mouth with a large napkin. 'Helps, you know. I'm just trying to get through this lot in one piece like everyone else.'

Clements put his glass down. 'How long have you been in the Navy, sir?'

'Been at sea since I was a boy.' He slid the brandy bottle across the table and sailed off to a chain of places I'd only seen at the cinema and in newspapers.

'I remember approaching New York. Ship was the *Celtic Prince*... wasn't much more than seventeen. Never forgot the sight... it's a special place.'

I waited for more, but he pulled himself back, squaring his shoulders.

'And so is Gibraltar. You'll see the coast of North Africa too, it's pretty close.'

New York was another unanswered question; the escape had been full of them. I swilled my brandy around the glass. Harold had berated me in Paris for asking too many things. How many times had I thought about that? I rarely got the answers. Sometimes it was better that way. We never saw the Señora's daughter. I knew each of us had a picture of that poor girl in our heads, yet they would all be different. There wasn't a single photograph of her in the rooms we visited in the house. The Señora loved her daughter and I had never asked to see a snap, a framed picture, or one of those fancy colourised works. I spoke with the Canadians about it when we sat on the roof one afternoon, and that was where the matter stayed. Best not to ask questions they reckoned, because the Señora would tell us if she wanted to. They weren't being hard; it was what we had all got used to doing. I pondered whether she had been waiting for us to ask. I wondered if her daughter would die.

'Well gentlemen, alas, duty calls.' The captain glanced at his overcoat hanging on the door. 'We'll be passing the Cape of Trafalgar soon. You can sit in the mess room or go on deck for a while. If anything happens, just stay where you are and await orders.'

He raised his brandy glass. It was only the second time I'd seen him touch it.

'A toast to better times and the future.'

10

The Canadians went below and left me on deck. Lookouts had increased, key vantage points were manned and men in duffel coats stared out to sea from behind the guns. The smudge of Spanish coast grew smaller and a sharp chill came with the wind. I looked across the grey waves at an empty horizon, thinking about what lurked below the surface.

I missed Cadiz. We had been dining with the captain, and now Cape Trafalgar had slipped past with no sense of being close to history. I walked along the deck to lean on the port rail near a lifeboat. It was suddenly there in the distance: a grey shape tacked on to the end of the coastline, jutting out proud and upright. My heart raced. I would tell the others. Kennedy and Clements had spotted it, they were standing behind me. We knotted in a huddle for a full half hour gazing into the distance, oblivious to the cut of wind and water. But the Rock was getting no nearer.

Spokes of sunlight poked through the cloud, making patches of emerald green on the sea. The Spanish coast looked more than a thin, black trail now, the rise and fall of land clearly textured and defined. The Rock waited for us – a purple shape in the distance.

'It's getting a bit blustery,' the mate said, moving up beside me. 'Captain says get yourselves inside for a while. Catch up on a bit of shuteye and I'll pass the word when we're close.'

We returned to the mess room and I sat on the benches with the others. Clements spoke over the throb from the engines. My gaze wandered around the contours of the cabin, absorbing none of its detail. Kennedy started to pace around the small space. We were all listening out for the mate or the thud and explosion of a torpedo. The waiting would be no different right until the end.

I must have dozed off. The light had dulled in the cabin when the mate called us.

'We're in the Straits of Gibraltar, gents.'

We went up on deck with him. The wind had dropped slightly and a hint of orange sun to the west coloured the sea.

'I'll leave you to it,' he said. 'Watch out for the coast of North Africa.'

A wave of grey hills sat behind the rocky edge of Spain. Clements sighted the African coast first. We sailed into the Straits proper. Both sides were no more than seven miles from the ship and the Rock loomed in the copper glow of late afternoon, its upper slopes crusted in patches of green, like lichen. The ship slowed and stopped near the harbour before dropping anchor. In the distance, a small service launch bobbed towards us, frothing a widening trail of wash. The Canadians leaned on the rail observing the boat's approach. A mix of emotions engulfed me. For the first time in the voyage I felt queasy with apprehension and euphoria at almost reaching safety, yet still being in danger. The sense of home was there to reach out and touch, yet it still felt misty and distant. For the Canadians it would only be simple relief. They were half a world away from their own firesides.

The launch stopped before coming alongside. I wondered how we would manage to get on board. Two divers swung themselves over the side, splashing into the water.

A crewman must have noticed my puzzled expression. 'They're checking for limpet mines on the hull before we can sail into harbour.'

The divers disappeared below the surface. Pin pricks of light were already showing on the Spanish coast as evening approached. Gibraltar stood, blacked out and surrounded. The divers had checked the hull on both sides and returned to their launch before the ship's engines started again. We slipped into the harbour with the onset of twilight – warships, tankers and an armada of smaller vessels silhouetted against the Rock. Enough visibility remained to manoeuvre along the wharf next to another freighter. The gangway went down. It was almost six-thirty.

I sensed no one wanted to be the first, no one wanted to actually say it. Nobody did. The three of us just shook hands – words were meaningless. A huge lump rose in my throat and I was thankful for the dark so no one could see me. The first few stars glinted through gaps in the night cloud before they misted in front of my eyes.

The captain came down from the bridge.

'Good luck lads, and all the best to you. I'm sure a reception committee is waiting down there.'

We thanked him and the mate led us onto the gangway. A shadowy figure waited at the bottom.

'Have your documents ready, please.'

The mate stepped onto the quayside. Questions were asked. A masked light stroked his face. Another torch joined in – two dim yellow circles dancing to the conversation. We waited on the gangway in a kind of no-man's-land between ship and British soil.

The figure's voice grew more agitated. I followed the Canadians down to the quayside, making a semicircle with the mate around two men. In snatches of flimsy torchlight, they might have been Gibraltar Security Police, the Corporal of the Guard or probably harbour sentries. I really didn't care.

The mate moved between us. 'I'm sure your next billets will pass muster.' His voice picked up. 'Wherever you're bound for, have a safe journey, gents.'

I turned around for a last look as he disappeared up the gangway.

'If you'll step over here, please,' the nearest sentry said.

We held our ground. The mate's footsteps halted at the top of the gangway, his dark shape the same as when I first saw him at Seville. A sense of closure came at that moment. I knew the Canadians felt it too.

Neither sentry asked questions apart from the usual name, rank and number. Two soldiers arrived and led us through black, narrow streets to a barrack hut and buildings near the harbour. I heard no vehicles, only chatter and the clump of service boots. The taller soldier reported to a gate and soon escorted us to what resembled a guardhouse.

'Wait there,' he said. 'The RAF will make arrangements for you to be collected.'

I felt like a commodity.

We were escorted by two Snowdrops (RAF Military Policemen) through a camp built on flat land next to the harbour. I couldn't see much in the dark until we approached a two-storey building and were shown to a small orderly room walled with filing cabinets. The wooden desk was clear apart from some empty wire trays, a telephone and notepaper. An RAF corporal replaced the receiver. He studied the sheet one of our escorts had given him.

'This all seems to be in order.'

Our escorts had reached the door before he had finished speaking.

'Someone's coming across soon, gentlemen,' the corporal said in our direction. He made some jottings on the sheet. 'After checks are completed, you'll receive further instructions tomorrow to report here for temporary identity cards. Then it will be a trip to stores for uniforms and footwear. I'm afraid that will all be dependent on what they have available.'

The door swung open and an RAF captain entered. 'Are these the chaps? Excellent,' he said, hardly giving the corporal time to finish his salute or answer. 'I'll have the list now, please.'

I heard him repeating our names under his breath as he looked down the sheet. He was the adjutant for certain, as his next action was to separate me from Kennedy and Clements.

'A word before we get down to business. This is an RAF barracks, but outside we have thousands of Spanish who enter Gibraltar every day to work here. They have to leave by twenty hundred hours, so I don't need to remind you to be very careful what you say anywhere on the Rock. And that means at all times.'

After what we had been through, I was surprised he had mentioned it. He told me to wait and I would be escorted to the Sergeants' Mess. Kennedy and Clements followed him out of the room: destination, no doubt their Officers' Mess and accommodation. The division of rank had asserted itself again, except it had never left my group from the moment we all met at Lucie's house near the French border.

The next morning, I was given a message at breakfast to be ready by eleven-thirty for an appointment with an army officer. A man wearing a beige flannel suit waited outside my accommodation block and handed me a security pass.

'The Major will see you at midday. If you're up to it, we've plenty of time so I'll make a slight detour on the way.'

Earlier, it had felt strange and uncomfortable eating my breakfast in the Mess without a uniform. No one appeared to notice me; maybe they were used to it. The previous evening, I had fallen straight into a deep sleep and recalled little except someone entering our quarters around midnight. A ship had come adrift from its moorings and everyone was to get down to the harbour immediately. Some of the other chaps roused themselves. I told the bloke to clear off, but after the room had emptied, sleep would not return. My eyes stayed open, pinned back by the strain of darkness. So much of the journey had been at night and memories invaded my thoughts again with a string of pictures in panorama: the value of small things in my pockets, the simple kindnesses given by helpers and the risks they took for complete strangers. The very least I could have done for them was face up to my own doubts and fears. I gave myself another mental shake. Was it nearly over? I had asked Flying Officer Ward the same question in the hotel room at San Sebastian. Now for the first time I dared to believe I really was going home to see my family, but feared jinxing the outcome by thinking too far ahead or reflecting again. Sailing out of Gibraltar was doubtful, so I guessed on a long flight to a destination somewhere in southwest England. The aircraft would have to fly west into the Atlantic to clear the airspaces of neutral

Spain and Portugal and then stay well out of range from German fighters on the inward route.

In daylight, it was easy to spot how close the barracks were to a long, concrete airstrip positioned at the end of an isthmus between Gibraltar and Spain. The man in the flannel suit sauntered alongside me, making polite conversation. The same grey sky as in the mountains hung over the Rock. Tight-packed streets in the old town echoed with noise: jeeps weaving between pedestrians, thin alleys with granite steps always climbing upwards, and sandstone buildings on the Rock trailing almost down to the sea. I saw my first British policeman amongst the throngs of service personnel on a good old-fashioned English street with pavements, a General Post Office and shops with awnings.

The army building had a fortified appearance with its white block-stone wall and a soldier guarding the entrance. It could have been built during the Napoleonic wars. More than a century had passed since then and the British were still protecting the gateway to the Mediterranean. The soldier checked our passes and my escort led me through to a tree-lined quadrangle with a line of doors along one side.

'We're right on time,' he said. 'I'll let the Major know you've arrived. Then I'll take you back to the barracks later.'

Inside the nearest window, an army sergeant sat at a desk, flanked by trays stacked with paper. We walked past to one of the doors further down which was slightly ajar. My escort tapped on it and looked gingerly inside.

'Sergeant Morley, for you, sir.'

A man in army uniform looked up. He was around mid-forties with dark bushy eyebrows and a five o'clock shadow.

'Come in and shut the door. Take a seat. I'm Major Darling.' He waited until I'd settled.

'Well done for getting here, sergeant. You can tell me about your journey in a moment, but we'll start with your name, number and details of your aircrew.'

A few tired Christmas decorations hung across the office walls.

There was a small printed sheet on his desk. I could hear the typewriter clattering next door.

As we worked through the details, it struck me the Major had an unfortunate name for an interrogator.

'Actually, its temporary sergeant, sir,' I said, after giving him the initial information.

He looked at his sheet.

'No. It's definitely sergeant... flight sergeant in fact. According to this, you've been promoted. It must have been while you were posted as missing.'

I felt no instant elation, as if it was some distant thing which belonged in that other world.

'Your family will have been notified. But they won't know you've reached Gibraltar.'

The printed sheet went inside a file on his desk. He took some blank foolscap paper from the drawer.

'When we've finished and you're sorted out, get down to Main Street and send a telegram to your folks. It'll probably arrive quicker than the one from the Air Ministry. Just tell them you've got here and you're safe and well. Don't put anything else.'

He drew a line with his fountain pen across the middle of the paper.

'I'd like you to start at the beginning, from the time your aircraft took off. Tell me everything you can remember, no matter how insignificant. Even the smallest details can be vital, especially the names of anyone who helped you and their addresses if you can recall them. We keep a record of what these people have done for the Allies, for obvious reasons. I'm also interested in anyone you had contact with who was also evading or escaping.'

He frowned. 'You didn't write anything down, did you?'

I said nothing about my pencil note in Denise's pocket book. It was not what the Major meant and I'd made no other jottings. My story spluttered at times like petrol in a blocked carburettor. Details flowed then stalled. Parts of my escape became shrouded in a mist of vague dates, places and darkness. I needed time to think. It felt like an interview, when things which should have been said were always remembered later.

The Major listened intently – scribbling notes in the two halves and stopping me to query answers or press quietly when the facts grew sketchy. He prompted me for descriptions, often nodding his head as if he knew the people I'd spoken about. When I was struggling, he would describe them and it was often correct. He asked more questions, wrote down a long screed about my time prior to Antwerp and always put his pen down before querying something, which gave me a moment to set my mind. Perhaps that was part of his questioning technique but I had no inclination to puzzle over any of it.

'I need to cover one or two more things,' he said. 'Arrangements will be made to get you flown home as soon as possible. It might take three or four days to schedule. In the meantime, once you have a uniform and temporary identity card, you're more or less free to move around places that are not off limits.'

He placed his notes inside the file. 'You've just signed the disclosure form, so this is a last reminder to say nothing about your journey until debrief in London. I'm afraid you'll have to repeat all of this again.' He paused. 'If anybody asks what you're doing here, you're an airman passing through from North Africa. It's Christmas Eve tonight and Gibraltar's already spilling over with service personnel. Go out and enjoy yourself, but don't get drunk.'

I caught his solemn look again, not authoritarian or schoolmasterly, just a reminder of the importance of what I knew. I thought about the 'Be like Dad keep Mum' poster above my bed in the barracks and the 'Walls Have Ears' bills pasted everywhere back home.

'Is there anything you would like to ask me?' he said.

'Have you had any news about my crew?'

'Only your navigator, Garvey, and you gave me that.'

I'd banked on something, however remote or flimsy. Perhaps the rest of the boys were prisoners of war or escaped by another route.

'You might find out more when you get home.' His voice sounded sincere, even though he must have repeated the same phrase numerous times.

'May I ask a last question, sir? Those chaps I escaped with. Do you know if any of them have passed through Gibraltar yet?'

'Unfortunately I can't help you there.'

I felt sure he gave me the slightest of nods.

'I think we'll have to leave it at that,' he said.

'Oh… there's one last thing.' His face broke into a smile.

'Happy Christmas, Flight Sergeant.'

EPILOGUE

Ron returned to the RAF barracks after his meeting with Major Darling. The time taken to issue a temporary uniform and identity documents delayed a visit to the main Gibraltar Post Office until well into the afternoon. His parents received a telegram late on Christmas Eve and the message read: *Arrived safe and well. Home soon. All my love Ron.* The Air Ministry had sent them a letter dated 20 December 1943 advising an unconfirmed report had been received from a reliable source that their son had reached a neutral country. This was the first his parents knew that he was alive, but they could only speculate as to his location. Major Darling was correct to assume Ron's telegram would reach his home before the official one from the Air Ministry. Their message arrived on 28 December informing his mother and father their son had reached Gibraltar.

Kennedy, Clements and Ron left the Rock in a Dakota aircraft bound for Whitchurch Municipal Airport near Bristol on the evening of 28 December. They arrived early the next morning and the men were taken under escort by train to London and directly on to the requisitioned Great Central Hotel in Marylebone where MI9 carried out individual debriefings of escapers and evaders. The main interviews took place on the same day, followed by questioning to establish events and circumstances around the loss of their respective aircraft. Ron was released and sent home on leave on New Year's Day 1944.

George Ward and Harold Pope had reached Gibraltar by road on 13 and 17 December respectively. Ken Garvey was sheltered by the Comet Escape Line until his burns healed sufficiently for him to travel. After an exhausting journey over the Pyrenees and detention by the Spanish police in Irun, he reached Gibraltar and was flown back to England to be debriefed on 18 January 1944. All the evaders Ron met on his journey eventually arrived safely in the United Kingdom. He had no further contact with any of them, except for Garvey. Denis Vanoystaeyen wrote to Ron after the war ended. They remained friends for life, corresponding regularly and finally meeting again in Belgium in 1986. 'Denise' was his alias (birth name Dionysus) and he adopted the English spelling and pronunciation of Denis after the war.

Ron never returned to bombing operations. In early 1944, Bomber Command's policy remained largely unchanged in not sending aircrew back over occupied Europe if they had evaded capture there and returned safely to the UK. An airman's knowledge of Resistance and escape networks could severely compromise those organisations if he found himself in enemy territory again and was captured.

After six weeks' leave and medical treatment for the effects of crossing the Pyrenees, Ron was assigned in February 1944 as a staff wireless operator and instructor to RAF No 10 Observers Advanced Flying Unit at Dumfries. In August 1945 the unit was renamed No 10 Air Navigation School and moved to RAF Chipping Warden until relocation at RAF Swanton Morley in January 1946. Between February 1944 and 4 June 1946 when he was released and demobbed, Ron made 227 flights, virtually all of them in Avro Anson aircraft.

He had married Mary in April 1945 and the war in Europe ended whilst they were on honeymoon in Llandudno. After leaving the RAF, his printing apprenticeship remained unfinished. Work in a factory with its noisy machines, oil and chemicals bore no comparison to the fresh air and open spaces of an aerodrome. He joined GPO telephones on the pole gangs, and most of his working life was in telephony. Mary and Ron had two sons and three grandsons and in the mid-1960s became regular attenders at their local church before joining the choir there. Ron died in January 1999 and had never been inside an Avro Lancaster since the night of 3 November 1943.

Lancaster 111	'U' Uncle	467 RAAF
No JB121		Squadron

3 November 1943 **Take off: Bottesford 17.03** **Target: Dusseldorf**

Crashed in an open area between Kleinstraat and Dikstraat, called at that time the Heikens which was near Klein Vorst in Belgium.

Eyewitness accounts stated that the pilot successfully avoided the centre of the village as the aircraft still had a full load of bombs and incendiaries on board. The impact created a large explosion and crater. Two houses near the crash site caught fire.

Captain and Pilot	Squadron Leader W. J. Lewis D.F.C.	'Bill'	★KIA
Navigator	Flight Sergeant K. Garvey	'Ken'	Evaded
Flight Engineer	Sergeant C. E. Stead	'Eddie'	POW
Wireless Operator	Sergeant R. C. Morley	'Ron'	Evaded
Bomb Aimer	Sergeant A. J. Scott	'Scotty'	★KIA
Mid Upper Gunner	Sergeant G. P. Baylis	'Curly'	★KIA
Rear Gunner	Flight Sergeant J. H. Mallin D.F.M.	'Jimmy'	★KIA
Second Pilot	Flight Sergeant J. W. Evans	'Evans'	POW

★Killed in action

Sergeant Stead's injuries from the flak explosion gave him little choice except to surrender. His liberation report states he was captured at Hagen, Holland on 3 November. He received no medical treatment until his arrival at Stalag 1VB on 15 November, where he spent the next ten weeks in the camp hospital.

Flight Sergeant Evans received minor wounds including a small piece of shrapnel in his stomach. He was sheltered by a Dutch farmer, but the man's children saw him. Evans made a decision to leave and give himself up to the enemy to avoid putting the family in danger.

Squadron Leader Lewis baled out of the aircraft. He died soon after landing as a result of his wounds.

The bodies of Sergeant Scott, Sergeant Baylis and Flight Sergeant Mallin were found in fields the next morning.

AUTHOR'S NOTES AND SOURCES

Where known, the personnel involved in this evasion are named. Some were identified by descriptions given in official reports and individual accounts. For obvious reasons, it was rare for helpers to give their real identities to escapers and evaders. Aliases were sometimes used, or no information at all, hence the names Morley adopted to remember them by.

Key for Main Sources & Author's Notes
RCM – Ronald Morley

DV – Denis Vanoystaeyen

MISQFH – Military Intelligence Services Questionnaire for Helpers

US E&E – US Military Intelligence Service Escape & Evasion Appendices plus handwritten Stenographer Reports

MI9 E&E – British and Commonwealth MI9 Escape & Evasion Appendices

ORS (BC) – Operational Research Section (BC) Report on Loss of Aircraft on Operations

POW Lib Report – Questionnaire for British/American Ex-Prisoners of War MI9 & MIS-X

Name or Alias Stated by Morley	Identity	First Location	Main Sources & Author Notes
Old man and woman at the farm	Unknown	West of Geel and south of Morley's landing point which was northwest of Geel and the Bocholt Kanaal.	
'Steff'	Staf de Bruyne	Field, then his home in Oevel.	DV, RCM. Met Morley again in 1986.
'Victor'	Antoine Heylon	Field.	MISQFH-*Heylon, Van Hoof & others.*
	Jozef Mertens	Unknown.	MISQFH-*Mertens & Heylon.* Not seen by Morley. Likely the lookout and scout when Morley moved from the field.
Man at Steff's house	Gustave de Bruyne	His home in Oevel.	DV, RCM, MISQFH-*Van Hoof.* Gustav was Staf's father.
'The Blacksmith'	Jules van Hemelin	His home in Oevel.	DV, RCM, correspondence to Morley post-war.
'Old man by the fire'	Unknown	His home in Oosterwijk.	DV.
'Belgian Policeman'	Dionisius van Hoof	Home of Gustav de Bruyne then his home in Voortkapel.	DV, RCM, MISQFH-*Van Hoof & others.* Deputy Village Gendarme. Provided civilian clothes & disposed of RAF uniform. Arrested 17/06/44. House ransacked by the Gestapo. Imprisoned.

'Maurice'	Louis Schoonheydt	His home in Voortkapel.	DV, RCM, MISQFH-*Van Hoof & others*, letter to Morley post-war.
'Denise'	Denis Vanoystaeyen	Home of Louis Schoonheydt.	DV, RCM, MISQFH-*Van Hoof, Vanoystaeyen, L Smolders & others*, MI9 E&E 1682, regular correspondence with Morley after the war. Met him again in 1986. Secret Army White Brigade. Resistance activities. Assisted sector SOE agent François Beckers, who arranged Morley's path into the Comet Escape Line. Enlisted in the British Army, Rifle Brigade after Belgium was liberated on 02/09/44. (First name of Dionys used on files)
'Jos'	Joseph A.van Roosbroeck	His home in Achter Olen.	DV, RCM, MISQFH-*Vanoystaeyen, Van Roosbroeck, w*rote to Morley after the war & sent photographs. Wife was Delphine.
'Dinah'	Dinah van Roosbroeck	As above.	DV, RCM, MISQFH-*Vanoystaeyen*, author's meet & conversations with Dinah. Jos's daughter. Attended some Resistance arms drops.
'Peter'	Petrus C. Peers	His home in Boechout.	DV, RCM, MISQFH-*Vanoystaeyen*. Local farmer. Secret Army White Brigade (Sector Ranst).

'Girl at window'	Maria Pelegroms (later Vanoystaeyen)	Her home on the edge of Boechout.	DV, RCM, author's meet & conversations with Maria. Married Denis after the war ended.
'Louis'	Louis Donckers	His home in Ranst.	DV, RCM, MISQFH-*Donckers*, *M Chardome*, Geheim Leger Armée Secrète & White Brigade file. Secret Army White Brigade (Reception & Shelter).
'The Chief'/'Marcel'	Marcel Chardome	Louis' home in Ranst.	DV, RCM, MISQFH-*Donckers*, MI9 E&E 1682, *M.D.N. Fiches de Renseignements*. Group Commander Antwerp Section (Shelter). Liaised with area SOE agent François Beckers who arranged Morley's path into the Comet Escape Line. Spoke Flemish, English, French & German.
'Rupert'	Rupert Chardome	Parents' home in Ranst.	Noted on a list of Belgian SOE agents (National Archives, Kew). Marcel's brother.
'Jeanette'	Marie-Joseph Erkes	Her home at 146, Chausee de Malines, Antwerp.	MISQFH-*M.Chardome*, *Erkes*. Correspondence from Madame Erkes' nephew Jean Erkes. She provided shelter in Antwerp.
Young blonde female guide in a green coat	Unknown	Opposite 146, Chausee de Malines, Antwerp.	RCM, MI9 E&E 1682.

Male guide, dark suit & carrying a raincoat	Unknown	Near a tram stop in Brussels.	RCM.
'Lily'	Aline Dumon Known as 'Michou' in Comet. Often used the name 'Lily' to evaders.	Home of Hélène Camusel.	MISQFH-*various*, RCM, MI9 E&E 1682 *& others*. US E&E *various*. Allied documents & reports of interview, author's correspondence with Mdm. Aline Ugeux (née Dumon) & original Comet docs. Group Dumon. Met evaders in Brussels area & led them to safe houses in the city. Escorted evaders to railway station for the next leg of their journey. MISQFH-*'Became a legend among the airmen who had safely returned to England.'* Left Brussels on 5 Jan 1944 as sought by the Gestapo. Operated in Paris from Jan 1944 and went to Madrid via the Comet Escape Line. Left Madrid 3 March 1944, resumed operations in Paris & made five trips to Spanish border with evaders. Now 'burned' as an operator, she returned to Madrid in May 1944 & reached the UK on 22 June 1944 via Gibraltar.
'Mademoiselle'	Hélène Camusel	Her home at 160, Rue Marie Christine, Brussels.	MISQFH-*various*, RCM, MI9 E&E *various*, US E&E *various*. Apartment used as shelter, assembly & dispatch point for evaders. Also kept a store of clothes for a time. Aline Dumon was hiding there from 01/09/43, but she had to leave urgently, as a Comet agent was arrested on 10/12/43 & they had Camusel's address written on a list. Camusel arrested by Gestapo 24/12/43. Released 08/01/44.

'Georges'	Eli Miroir Known as 'Canard' or 'Rio' in Comet. Also used 'Georges', mainly to evaders	Home of Hélène Camusel.	MISQFH-*Miroir & others*, RCM, MI9 E&E *various*. US E&E 280 & *others*. Head of Group Miroir. Set up & arranged IDs, photographs, civilian clothing, food & lodging. Arrested by Gestapo 23/01/44. Deported to Germany 6/05/44 & to Buchenwald, Ellrich & Belsen. Liberated 15/04/45.
'Bald man with deep-set eyes'	Pierre Lucien Rene Pirart K/A 'Rene'	His home at 8, Rue des Tournesols, Anderlecht, Brussels.	MISQFH-*Pirart* MI9 E&E 1606, RCM, Audio tape & correspondence from George Ward. Pirart was a forger for Comet & assembled false documents in Brussels. The background in Ward, Madgett & Morley's ID photos is identical & not on any other Comet photos. Ward & Madgett both state they were sheltered at a house & had their photographs taken there. Ward noted that they watched the man they were staying with make up their false identity cards. Pirart states he sheltered Ward and Madgett.
Photographer 'Another man, all head and shoulders'	Raymond Vignoble	8, Rue des Tournesols, Anderlecht, Brussels.	MISQFH-*Vignoble*, letter from Aline Dumon, RCM. From Aug 43 to Aug 44, 'photographed 200' for Henri and Marie Maca, Aline Dumon and Eli Miroir at his home or other locations. Also lodged six evaders and took them to the railway station to be handed over to Aline Dumon or Miroir. Surprised by the German Abwehr while carrying out a mission. Escaped, but all his photographic equipment was destroyed by them.

'Henri'	Henri Maca Known as 'Harry' in Comet	His home at 31, Avenue Val d'Or, Brussels.	MISQFH-*H.Maca, M Maca*, RCM, MI9 E&E 1682, 1657 & 1709, US E&E 280 & *others*. After arrests of Comet helpers in Jan 44, he took over responsibility for lodging airmen in Brussels. Went into hiding in Schaerbeek. Arrested 27/05/44 by Gestapo. St Gilles prison. Deported. Passenger on the infamous Nazi Ghost Train from Brussels Sept 1944. Liberated by Allied troops Sept 1944.
'Marie'	Marie Maca Known as 'Germaine' in Comet	Her home at 31, Avenue Val d'Or, Brussels.	MISQFH-*M.Maca, H Maca*, RCM, MI9 E&E 1682, 1657 & 1709 & *others*, US E&E 280 & *others*. Sister of Henri Maca. When the main Comet guide in Brussels was forced to leave in Jan 44, she took over that role. As the Gestapo net closed around her, she left on 25/01/44 to meet a contact at a rail station in the Ardennes. Eventually escaped to Switzerland.
'Madame', the neighbour	Jeanne Vantuykom	31, Avenue Val d'Or, Brussels.	MISQFH-*Vantuykom*, RCM, MI9 E&E 1682, US E&E 280 Lived at 2, Rue Martin Lindiken, Wolwe St Pierre, Brussels. House & garden backed on to the Macas' apartment building. Arrested 31/07/44 by Gestapo & imprisoned. Liberated from Antwerp prison by the Allies 03/09/44.
'The Stranger'	Unknown	En route to the cinema in Brussels.	

'The Gunman'	Unknown	Likely to be a storeroom inside shed one at the tram station, Avenue de Tervueren, Woluwe–Saint Pierre, Brussels. In 1941 the back was converted to accommodate a mess room, offices, workshop, and stores for maintenance of rolling stock.	
'Pretty girl at Rumes station, no more than 18'	Amanda Stassart Known as 'Dianne' in Comet	Rumes station and then to the home of Nellie & Raymonde Hoël, Rue de Sartaignes, 'Bachy Nord' in the buffer zone between Belgium & France. Then to the home of Maurice Bricout in Bachy, France.	MISQFH–*Stassart, Bricout & others*, MI9 E&E *various*, US E&E *various*, official & personal reports & declarations. From end of Oct 1943, guided evaders across the Belgium border into France and on to Paris. Worked on five separate passages until the Comet arrests in January 44. Planning new routes with other operators when arrested by the Gestapo on 18/02/44. Deported to Ravensbrück 22/04/44, then Mauthhausen 01/03/45. Liberated 23/04/45. Her mother, Louise, fed & sheltered evaders at her home 10/10/43–15/02/44. Arrested 15/02/44. Deported 25/02/45.

'Small girl with her hair in a bob'	Henriette Hanotte Known as 'Monique' in 'Comet	As above.	MISQFH-*Mathys, Dumon, Stassart, Bricout & others.* US E&E 124, 187, 223 *& others*, MI9 E&E *various.* Official & personal reports & declarations. Author's meet & conversations with 'Monique'. Visited Rumes with her to retrace the railway station to Bachy route she used with Morley. From 1940 worked with her family on escorting Allied evaders and escapers across the border and into France. She became one of Comet's main guides. From Aug 1943 to Jan 1944, she escorted evaders from Rumes station across the border into France then on to Lille and latterly Paris. From Jan 1944 acted as liaison between Brussels & Paris. Reached England in May 1944 via France, Spain & Gibraltar. Volunteered to return to Belgium to continue her work. She became a second lieutenant in the Auxiliary Territorial Service of the British Army, but damaged her leg during parachute training. When she recovered, the Allied advance and liberation had made her return mission unnecessary.
'Lucie'	Raymonde Hoël	Home of Raymonde & Nellie Hoël at Rue de Sartaignes, 'Bachy Nord' in the buffer zone between Belgium & France.	MISQFH-*Michiels, Hoël.* The farmhouse on Rue de Sartaignes in the buffer zone between Belgium & France was used by the evaders during the crossing to surrender their documents & money in exchange for French replacements. Maurice Bricout then arrived to lead the evaders across the border along with their guides, to his house in Bachy. Raymonde's sister Nellie was not seen the evening Morley was there, but may have been in the house & unwell.

| 'Sandy' | Unknown. Possibly Emile Roiseaux, known as 'Emile le Plombier' in Comet. Possibly Raymond Itterbeek. A member of three secret organisations | Hoël's home at Rue de Sartaignes, 'Bachy Nord' in the buffer zone between Belgium & France. Then to the home of Maurice Bricout in Bachy, France. | Emile Roiseaux – Comet guide from July 1943, before being sent by Comet to the Ardennes to prepare the Marathon camps for fugitives. Raymond Itterbeek made various crossings as a guide over four different passages, including Rumes. Arrested 04/01/44 with two evaders en route to Lille by train. Death sentence given in Brussels. Various prison transfers. No orders were received for his execution. Liberated by US Army in April 1945. |
| 'Bernard' | Georges Arnould

Known as 'Albert le Pâtissier' in Comet | As above. | MISQFH–*Arnould, Michiels & others.* US E&E 280.
Comet guide between Brussels & Rumes, before being sent by them to the Ardennes to prepare the Marathon camps for fugitives. Physical description suggests he was one of the two men who changed the evaders' identity documents at the Hoëls' farmhouse & escorted them over the border. It was not the usual Comet protocol (apart from Albert Mattens) for the Brussels to Rumes guides to take part in a Rumes to Bachy crossing. Harold Pope states in US E&E 280 that the two French lads who escorted them across to Cysoing had changed their passports for them. Although Belgian, 'Sandy & Bernard' would speak French as their native language. |

'The French Policeman'	Maurice Bricout	Hoël's home and then to his home in Bachy, France.	MISQFH-*Bricout, Michiels & others*. RCM, MI9 E&E 1606,1642,1664,1657,1679,1682 *& others*. US E&E 280 *& others*. Lieutenant Customs Officer, described by evaders as a Border/French Policeman. Comet Mar 1943–July1944. Worked on Rumes to Bachy passage in Nov 1943. Its lifespan was a few weeks. Worked on this route in collaboration with colleague Albéric Houdart. Bricout guided evaders from Nellie & Raymond Hoël's farmhouse to his home in Bachy. Evaders were fed & stayed overnight there before being escorted by guides to Cysoing rail station, then on to Lille & Paris. Bricout's dog, Cocquette, often gave early warnings of approaches to the house. Continued to shelter and pass on evaders until forced to go into hiding with the Resistance in early July 1944. The Gestapo raided his home on 28/07/44 when he returned to look for some linen. He escaped through a back window.
'Rachel'	Rachel Bricout	Bricout's home.	MISQFH-*Bricout, Michiels*. Maurice Bricout's wife. She fed & lodged the evaders overnight. On 28/07/44 when Bricout escaped from his house, the Gestapo arrested & imprisoned her. Liberated from Lille prison 03/09/44 in poor health after being found abandoned in the prison hospital.
'The young boy'	René Bricout	Bricout's home.	MISQFH-*Bricout*. Bricout's son. Sometimes accompanied the guides escorting evaders to Cysoing.

| 'Pierre' | Albert Mattens

Known as 'Jean Jacques' in Comet | Bricout's home. | MISQFH-*Mattens, Michiels, Hanotte & others.*
Original chief of guides in Belgium. Became Chief Guide of the Belgium to Paris Sector. Organised convoys of guides & evaders from Brussels to Paris. Also acted as a guide, carried funds between Paris & Brussels & delivered instructions between the two locations. In addition to Rumes to Bachy he created five additional escape passages from Belgium into France.
Arrested at Mons 06/01/44, carrying false identity papers & 500,000 francs for Comet. Imprisoned & deported. Liberated from Amberg by US Army 27/04/45. |

| 'The Chief' | Jacques Le Grelle

Known as 'Jérôme' in Comet | Paris, Gare du Nord rail station. | MISQFH–Le Grelle, Mattens, A. Stassart & others. RCM, US E&E 279, 280, 281 & others.

After the original Comet Escape Line suffered a series of arrests of main personnel by the Abwehr & Gestapo, agent Le Grelle was charged by London to reorganise a new Comet line. The Allied bombing offensive over Europe predicted big losses & increasing numbers of airmen parachuting & landing in occupied Western Europe. It was vital to return as many of them as possible to England to continue the fight. Le Grelle contacted survivors of the old Comet line & met Jean–François Nothomb, the sole surviving key operator. They agreed to work together, but on Nothomb's terms that the new line operated with no British control. Activities were centralised in Paris along with intelligence & admin. Le Grelle organised & operated the Paris section, which received evaders from the Belgium group. Evaders were then escorted to Bordeaux where Nothomb took over.
Arrested 17 Jan 1944. Imprisoned, interrogated & tortured by the Gestapo. Transferred to St–Giles prison, Brussels, where the cycle was repeated. Death sentence given 26/07/44. Deported. Various German prisons. Liberated from Amberg by American forces on 13 May 1945. |

Code name	Name / notes	Location	Details
'Madame Black'	Fernande Onimus Known as 'Rosa' in Comet. Named by some of the evaders as 'The Little Lady in Black'	Paris, Gare du Nord rail station.	MISQFH-*Onimus, M.Lami, Verhulst & others. RCM, US E&E 280 & others, MI9 E&E-various, The Pilot Walked Home – Dennis Hornsey, The Comet Connection – George Watt.* Organised safe houses in Paris after recruiting volunteers. Responsible for getting photographs taken of the evaders for documents. Obtained clothing & cigarettes. Guided evaders to lodgings around Paris & delivered them to their guides, ready for the journey south. Arrested 18/01/44. Deported. Died Ravensbrück 23–24/04/1945.
'Madame Blonde'	Germaine Bajpai Known mainly as 'Hautfoin' in Comet	Paris, Gare du Nord rail station.	MISQFH-*various US E&E 281 & others, MI9 E&E-various, One of Those Days – J. M. Elliott.* George Ward audiotape & correspondence. Operated in a separate Paris sector to Onimus. Similar responsibilities. Arrested 18/01/44. Deported. Died Ravensbrück 04/02/45.
'Joseline'	Odile M. Verhulst	7, Rue de Cher, Paris.	MISQFH-*Verhulst, M.Lami, RCM, MI9 E&E 1682, US E&E 280, 281 & others.* Lodged & fed evaders July 1943–Jan 1944, helped by her daughter, Mariette Lami. Arrested 18/01/44. Told the Gestapo her daughter knew nothing of her activities. Deported 13/05/44. Died Ravensbrück 20/02/45.

'Charlotte'	Mariette Lami	7, Rue de Cher, Paris.	As above. Arrested 18/01/44. Imprisoned until liberated by the Allies.
'The Painter'	Vassili Lami	7, Rue de Cher, Paris.	Mariette Lami's husband. Worked with his brother in the Verhulst's internal decorating business. Helped with looking after evaders staying in the apartment. Also involved with Resistance work. Went into hiding. Arrested 27/07/44. Deported & became a victim of *nacht und nebel*. May have died in a camp as a result of Allied bombing of Lunebourg, or at the end of March 1945 as he was reported to be on a train transporting sick prisoners to Neuengamme when it was machine gunned by the SS. Witness & friend Robert Maileet was on the same train & never saw him again after the incident.
'The grey-haired old man'	Albert Verhulst	7, Rue de Cher, Paris.	MISQFH-*Verhulst, M. Lami*, RCM. Husband of Odile Verhulst.

| 'Susanne' | Marcelle Douard

Known as 'Marie Louise' in Comet | River Seine embankment, Paris. | MISQFH-*Douard, Witton & others*. MI9 E&E *various*. US E&E 280 *& others*, 1946 testimony from E. Perroy & R. Gaillard. Identifiable, as she was only approx 4ft 8in tall. Comet guide from July 1943. Usually escorted two evaders on the Paris to Bordeaux train, often three times a week. Rolande Witton (known in Comet as 'Rolande') operated on the same journeys with her two charges, but the guides were not known to one another. They always travelled in separate parts of the train, alternating their journeys between 2nd & 3rd class.
Douard also occasionally relayed orders in Paris from Chief Le Grelle to Onimus & Bajpai. Arrested 18/01/44. Imprisoned Fresnes & Romainville. Deported to Ravensbrück 17/04/44. Liberated by US Army at the end of the war. |
| 'Max' | Marcel J. Roger

Known as 'Max' in Comet | Bordeaux rail station. | MISQFH-*Roger, Nothomb, De Greef, Ayle & others*. MI9 E&E *various*, US E&E 283, 285, 322, 359, 361 *& others*.
Some liaison work from July 1942 between Paris & Brussels. From June 1943, guided evaders from Bordeaux, Bayonne or Dax to the meeting point with Basque guides who would take them into Spain. In Feb 1944, arrests caused interruption in activities. Went to London at request of the British. Returned to France & continued passage of evaders in May 1944. Trips made with a second guide to the south of France with parties of five men. Hunted by the Gestapo & forced to return to England via Spain in July 1944. |

'François'	Jean-François Nothomb Known as 'Franco' in Comete	Outside Dax rail station.	MISQFH-*various*, MI9 E&E *various*, US E&E *various*, RCM. Operated on the original Comet line. Organised the new line with Le Grelle. Operated journeys with Marcel Roger from Bordeaux to the Pyrenees & link with Spain via border crossings. Arrested in Paris 18/01/44. Death sentence given 28/07/44. Liberated from Bayreuth camp by American forces 07/05/45.
'The young woman cyclist who joins François'	Denise Houget	En route on bicycles through foothills of Pyrenees.	MISQFH-*various*, RCM. Personal accounts, *Reseau Comete –Remy*. Accompanied Nothomb/Roger (or both), cycling with the evaders on routes from Dax to Bayonne & others.
'The middle-aged woman at the restaurant'	Jeanne Marthe Mendiara	Inn/restaurant outside of Bayonne	MISQFH-*various*, MI9 E&E *various*, US E&E *various*, RCM, *Comete Alternative Passages* – Geoff Warren, Cheryl Padgham & Philippe Connart. Ran the Café/Restaurant Larre in Sutar where evaders were hidden overnight & fed before leaving by bicycle for the Pyrenees via the Saint-Jean-de Luz passage, or the later eastern routes of Larressore & Souraide. Bicycles were abandoned and hidden on the last leg of the Larressore route and collected by Martin Garat, the local baker. Evaders were escorted to a barn (*borda*) located between villages of Larressore & Espelette (Mandochineko borda.). Mme. Mendiara's husband was a POW in Germany. Middle-aged man helping her is unknown.

| 'Pierre' and the guides through Spain | Baptiste & Pierre Aguerre, Pierre Etchégoyen, Jean Elizondo and, on occasions others in the later legs of the journey | Mandochineko *borda* barn located between villages of Larressore & Espelette. | M19 E&E 1630, 1631, 1657, 1658 *& others*, US E&E 279, 280, 281 *& others*. RCM, George Ward audiotape & correspondence, *Comete Alternative Passages* – *Geoff Warren, Cheryl Padgham & Philippe Connart*. Guides were recruited by Pierre Elhorga who had worked in the first Comet line, assisting with the feeding of evaders. He was tasked by the re-formed line to find & secure guides for three new eastern routes. Pierre Etchégoyen, Baptiste & Pierre Aguerre & Jean Elizondo had a detailed knowledge of the mountain area. All came from Espelette but were in hiding from compulsory work service and wanted by the police. At dark, a combination of the four guides led the evaders on a six-hour journey through the Pyrenees to the Spanish border. On occasions a replacement joined the group at a given point along the route. They avoided the village of Espelette, followed the Latsa valley and climbed rising ground before walking along a pass between the mountains of Mondarrain & Atxulegi. After navigating down Larreko valley, they followed the Haizagerriko brook upstream to the planned border crossing point, where they climbed a hill. The first safe house was at the Jauregiko *borda* farm, 200 metres inside Spain. The Morley group crossing did not go to plan. |
| 'Bald headed man in doorway of the first farm in Spain' | Jan Mihura | Jauregiko *borda* farm. | The occupier of the *Jauregiko borda* farm. After resting overnight, the evaders were escorted south around or over the mountains of Gorramakil and Gorramendi, and on to the Mortalenko borda farm, located close to the gap of Ispeguy in Erratzu. From there, they reached San Sebastian by varied routes taking two to three more days. This journey also did not go to plan for the Morley group. |

			Names of other embassy staff are unknown, so pseudonyms and descriptions have been used.
'Creswell'	Sir Michael Creswell Attaché British Embassy, Madrid Codename 'Monday'	British Embassy, Madrid.	
'Montgomery'	Edward E. Montgomery British Vice Consul, Seville	Home of Spanish civilian, Seville.	MI9 E&E 1657, RCM Appointed British Vice-Consul at Seville 05/06/43.
'Captain Wiles'	Captain Alfred Lumley Wiles	SS *Tudor Prince*, Seville.	RCM. Also a letter from M. H. Bland & Co. Ltd dated 9/12/43, requesting the Captain of the Port in Gibraltar to sign on Capt. Alfred Lumley Wiles as Master of the SS *Tudor Prince* in lieu of Capt. Y. N. Clare who passed away during the previous voyage to the UK. SS *Tudor Prince* was sailing to Gibraltar with a cargo of bitter oranges.
'Major Darling'	Donald Darling British Secret Service Cover role as Civil Liaison Officer of the Chief of Staff Codename 'Sunday'	Gibraltar.	RCM, US E&E 280.

The Evaders

Name Stated by Morley	Identity	First Location	Sources & Author Notes
'Clements'	Flying Officer Robert S. Clements RAF 57 Squadron	31, Avenue Val d'Or, Brussels.	MI9 E&E 1657, ORS Report K113. 2nd Pilot, Lancaster. Op Dusseldorf 3/11/43. T/O East Kirkby 17.10. Shot down by night fighters.
'Ken'	Flight Sergeant Kenneth Garvey RAAF 467 Squadron	31, Avenue Val d'Or, Brussels.	MI9 E&E 1709, ORS Report K1154. Navigator, Lancaster. Op Dusseldorf 3/11/43 T/O Bottesford 17.03. Shot down by flak.
'Harold' (First introduced by 'Georges' as Sergeant Pope)	Temp Sergeant Harold L. Pope USAAF 100 Bomber Group 349 Squadron Air Medal Two Oak Leaf Clusters	Gare Midi rail station, Brussels.	US E&E 280, M. Pope & *The Onida Watchman* newspaper. Engineer/Top Turret Gunner, B17. Op Gelsenkirchen 5/11/43. T/O Thorpe Abbots 10.30. Engine hit by flak. Unable to keep up with formation & losing height rapidly. Bombs jettisoned. Order given to bale out. Aircraft reached England with pilot & co-pilot still on board.
'Flying Officer Madgett'	Flying Officer Geoffrey E. A. Madgett RAF 138 Squadron	Train from Brussels to Tournai then Rumes rail station to Hoël's home at Rue de Sartaignes, 'Bachy Nord'.	MI9 E&E 1606, ORS Report K106. Navigator, Halifax. Special Mission Belgium 19/10/43. T/O Tempsford 00.05 on SOE parachute drop mission for two Dutch agents, Jan Van Schelle ('Apollo') & Johan Grün ('Brutus'.) Flying low. Hit by flak over Herenthals, Belgium. Crash landed.

'Flying Officer Ward'	Flying Officer George Ward D.F.M. RAF 138 Squadron	Details as per Madgett.	MI9 E&E 1607, ORS Report K106. Rear Gunner. Other details as per Madgett.
'The Scottish chap, Jim'	Flight Sergeant John Harkins RCAF 428 Squadron	Hoël's home at Rue de Sartaignes, 'Bachy Nord'.	MI9 E&E 1642. Pilot, Halifax. Op Frankfurt 4/10/43. T/O Middleton St George 17.30. Shot down by night fighter over France.
'Mills'	2nd Lieutenant Donald O. Mills USAAF 96 Bomber Group 413 Squadron	Hoël's home at Rue de Sartaignes, 'Bachy Nord'.	US E&E 279. Bombadier, B17. Op Duren 20/10/43. T/O Snetterton Heath 11.25. Bomb bay doors would not open on run to target. Pilot released via salvo lever. One engine not functioning fully. Fell behind bomber stream. Aircraft alone on return leg. Shot down by fighters.
'Man with the North of England accent' (Johnnie)	Flying Officer Edward C. Johnson D.F.C. RAF 617 Squadron	Hoël's home at Rue de Sartaignes, 'Bachy Nord'.	MI9 E&E 1639. Bomb Aimer, Lancaster. Op Dortmund-Ems Canal 15/09/43. T/O Coningsby 23.55. Low flying to the target. Hit trees on a hillside whilst waiting turn to bomb. Two engines damaged. Order to bale out. Landed NW of Almelo, Germany. (Dambuster. Took part in Operation Chastise on German dams 16–17/05/43.)
'Tennessee'	Temp Sergeant Hank C. Johnson USAAF 388 Bomber Group 563 Squadron Air Medal	Hoël's home at Rue de Sartaignes, 'Bachy Nord'.	US E&E 281. Engineer/Top Turret Gunner, B17. Op Gelsenkirchen 05/11/43. T/O Knettishall 10.00. Hit by flak near target. Engine damage. Pulled out. P47 US fighters cover until they had to return due to lack of fuel. Shot down by enemy fighters.

'Henri'	Henri A. Neuman SOE Saboteur & cofounder of Groupe 'G' Codename 'Jérôme' or 'César'	Train from Brussels to Tournai.	US E&E 280, 272, 273, *Avant qu'il ne soit trop tard: portraits de résistants – Henri Neuman*.
'Sergeant Watt'	Staff Sergeant George Watt USAAF 388 Bomber Group 563 Squadron	Hoël's home at Rue de Sartaignes, 'Bachy Nord'.	US E&E 281, 282. Right Waist gunner/Assistant Engineer. Report as per H. C. Johnson's, *The Comet Connection –George Watt*.
'Squadron Leader Kennedy'	Temp Flight Lieutenant James L. Kennedy 24 RCAF Operational Training Unit	Outside rail station, Dax.	MI9 E&E 1658 Pilot, Whitley. Orleans Leaflet Raid 3/11/43. Engine trouble. Crew baled out over France.
'The Skipper'	Temp Squadron Leader Cyril W. Passy RAF 138 Squadron	Barn in the Pyrenees mountains.	MI9 E&E 1630, 1631, 1601, 1606, 1607, US E&E *various*, ORS Report K106. Pilot, Halifax. Report as per Madgett, Ward & Rabson.

ADDITIONAL AUTHOR NOTES

Part One

Chapter 5 – A lone German motor cyclist was unusual in rural areas due to the absence of petrol traffic.

Chapters 9 & 10 – 'Denise' had received a telegram from Louis Joseph Smolders, Chief of the Belgian Secret Army in Olen. The message stated Denise's uncle was very sick and his presence there was requested. This was a coded message alerting him that the Secret Army had knowledge of an Allied airman in hiding. Denise met Smolders and was briefed before cycling over 20km to the village of Voortkapel where he interrogated Morley at Maurice's house.

Chapters 11 & 12 – Known locally at the time as Sasse Bridge, it was approached via Sluizenweg and is the Sluis Olen waterworks bridge.

Chapter 13 – The soldiers in the truck were possibly Luftwaffe Feldgendarmerie (Military Police) searching for Allied airmen.

Chapter 15 – Marcel's cigarettes may have come from SOE agent François Beckers, one of two operating in the area. Beckers had social contact with some of the German military who were unaware of his activities.

Chapters 19 & 22 – The traitor mentioned by Marcel and then by Henri Maca was Prosper de Zitter.

Chapter 24 – The tram station was a former depot on Avenue de Tervueren, Woluwe-Saint Pierre, Brussels, opposite Woluwe Park. It was relatively close to the Macas' apartment on Avenue Val d'Or and is now the Brussels Museum of Urban Transport.

Chapter 24 – It is highly unlikely 'The Gunman' would have had a firearm. In the poor light and tension of the moment, the 'barrel of a revolver' may have been a section of a tool or machine part. Helpers in the Comet Escape Line did not carry guns.

Chapters 26–29 – See 1–3 below★

Chapter 28 – Morley's adopted name for Rachel was the correct one. This may have been prompted by him hearing it in the farmhouse or the policeman's home.

Part Two

★**Chapters 1–3** – The high numbers of evaders making the border crossing from Rumes to Bachy and then walking to Cysoing the following morning went against normal Comet protocols. No more than four evaders usually crossed in one operation. The E&E reports, plus written and verbal accounts do not match up with this on the night Morley crossed with the others. Evaders were understandably not always accurate with their recollections, but some reports and accounts remained consistently detailed throughout. They corroborated or suggested the larger numbers making the crossing on that evening. Official documents (especially the US stenographer's handwritten notes made during the debrief interviews), plus written and verbal accounts, indicate that nine evaders and an SOE agent may have crossed from Rumes to Bachy. This is likely to have taken place in two staggered groups but there may have been some variations to the written account in this book. During my second meeting with Henriette 'Monique' Hanotte, I asked about the large numbers and she recalled that night well. George Ward said in his audio tape 'I remember that house; there were quite a few of us there. There was quite a party. I wouldn't call it a dinner party, but I seem to remember ten to fifteen people.'

In George Watt's book *The Comet Connection*, he may have confused the Paris apartment scene with the house in Bachy which Ward and other evaders refer to. Watt reports that the Paris apartment was crawling with people, where there were four or five Allied flyers in addition to H. C. Johnson, himself and the two other evaders who had been with them. There were also family members and the two guides present. He also mentions Harold

Pope specifically. H. C. Johnson's US E&E report states that after being taken to a church in Paris, he was guided along with Watt by a little woman in black to a building with winding stairs, went up six flights and met Pope and a young chap from a Lancaster (Morley). In Watt's own E&E report, he confirms that after meeting H. C. Johnson at Rumes rail station, his account of events was exactly the same as Johnson's. Morley's personal memories and parts of his E&E report match the sequence of events. Those four men were the only evaders in the Paris apartment at the time. Watt and Johnson left with Madame Black later that evening to have their photographs taken.

Chapters 7–8 – Morley and Pope remained in the apartment for just over a fortnight. Other evaders around that period reported similar lengthy stays in the capital. This was a substantial length of time for a large escape line to hold so many of its charges inside safe houses in a city. It would also restrict movement of any personnel waiting further down the line. Morley was told there had been arrests. From official documents, there seems to be no record of this until the collapse of the Comet Escape Line in early January 1944. One reason for the delay may have been explained in 'The Chief', Jacques Le Grelle's interviews after the war. Comet encountered problems because places on the Paris to Bordeaux train had to be reserved fifteen days in advance of the journey. The traveller's identity card was required to purchase a ticket and their name was then written on the ticket. At that time a traveller's details might not be known to Comet Paris section, which then caused additional work for the organisation's false document section. Another obstacle was the identity and document checks regularly carried out on this specific journey. Comet often had good intelligence on the dates and times when these would occur which was of great assistance in planning journeys to Bordeaux, but they could be subject to change. Surprise inspections were carried out at stations, specific stopping points on the line and on trains.

Organising and producing the volume of forged documents and

then dovetailing them to fifteen days in advance required forensic planning, but could still fall victim to a change in circumstances or even error. This may explain how Harold Pope had H. C. Johnson's picture on one or possibly more of his documents. Pope never told Morley the full extent of what happened. Because of the trail of events which followed, Morley never asked him. H. C. Johnson does say in his E&E report that his picture was used by Pope. As those two men did not meet again after the first evening at the Paris apartment until the British Embassy in Madrid, it must have been discussed between them there. Even if Comet's intelligence around identity checks was deemed solid, it does seem strange that they would still take such a big risk with Pope travelling south, knowing that his face did not match the photograph on one or all of his documents.

The evaders had no knowledge of Comet's intelligence or their workings. Similarly, apart from information given by their helpers, few evaders were aware of the organisation and parameters of German controls: i.e. Geheime Feldpolizei (Secret Police), Feldgendarmerie (Ordinary Military Police), Abwehr (German Military-Intelligence Service) and Geheime Staatspolizei (Gestapo). Morley's interpretation largely sees the Gestapo at the fore. His limited knowledge of the organisation and his own fears may have played a part in this thinking. The reality was that the initial players were often Geheime Feldpolizei, Feldgendarmerie and Abwehr before any Gestapo involvement.

Chapter 7 – The bombing raid was a heavy attack on ball-bearing factories in Paris carried out on 26 November 1943 by B17s of the 8th American Air Force.

Part Three

Chapter 1 – The German Alpine patrol was garrisoned next to Estebenborda Farm, close to the crossing point into Spain.

Part Four

Chapter 7 – The mate's reference to 'the crowd' is Merchant Navy slang for 'crew'.

Misc

Operational Research Section Report K115 on the loss of aircraft Lancaster 111 No JB121 'U' of 467 Squadron, suggests the aircraft may have been shot down by an enemy night fighter. Morley's view was always that the aircraft was damaged by a single flak shell. He maintained that the aircraft was under fire from the ground and a blinding flash and powerful explosion occurred underneath, causing the aircraft to lift violently. This is confirmed in the narrative of reports K115 (Morley) and K115A (Garvey) and is not consistent with the effects after being hit from an attack by an enemy fighter.

Some MI9 & US E&E evader reports contained anomalies on dates and the exact continuity of events. This was understandable given the evader's circumstances, but with further research it could often be resolved by cross checks and corroboration with other files, documents and publications (US E&E files generally included the stenographer's handwritten notes made at the actual interview which proved invaluable).

Evaders could also be economical with information in order to keep the identity of helpers and their locations secret. In contrast, the brevity of some MI9 reports may have been down to evaders reaching a point after their ordeal where they just wanted closure, and for the ones resident in Great Britain an authorisation to go home to their families.

BIBLIOGRAPHY

A Dictionary of RAF Slang, Eric Partridge (Michael Joseph Ltd 2016)

A Leap in the Dark, James Arthur Davies (Leo Cooper 1994)

A Quiet Woman's War, William Etherington (Mousehold Press 2002)

A Yank in Bomber Command, Robert S. Raymond (Pacifica Press 1988)

Agent for the Resistance, Herman Bodson (Texas A&M University Press 2002)

Air Raid Precautions (Tempus Publishing Ltd 2007)

Aircraft Recognition (Penguin 2006)

Aircrew, Bruce Lewis (Cassell Military Paperbacks 2001)

Airmen On the Run, Laurence Meynell (Oldhams Press Ltd)

Bale Out, Alfie Martin (Colourprint Books 2005)

Believed Safe, Bill Furniss-Roe (William Kimber London 1987)

Bomber Boys, Mel Rolfe (Grub Street 2004)

Bomber Boys: The RAF Offensive of 1943, Kevin Wilson (Weidenfeld & Nicolson 2005)

Bomber Command Losses of the Second World War; 1943, W. R. Chorley (Midland Counties Publications 1996)

Bomber Crew, James Taylor & Martin Davidson (Hodder 2005)

Bomber Flight Berlin, Mike Rossiter (Corgi Books 2011)

Bombs Away, Martin W. Bowman (Pen and Sword Books 2010)

Child at War, Mark Bles (Warner Books 1999)

Come Walk With Me, John H. J. Dix (Unpublished memoir)

Dangerous Landing, Henry Ord Robertson (Patrick Stephens 1988)

Diary of a Bomb Aimer, Campbell Muirhead (Pen and Sword Books 2009)

Downed Allied Airmen and Evasion of Capture, Herman Bodson (McFarland & Co 2005)

Enemy Coast Ahead, Guy Gibson (Crecy Publishing 2004)

Escape and Evasion, Ian Dear (History Press 2010)

Escape Or Die, Paul Brickhill (Cassell Military Paperbacks 2003)

Escape to Freedom, Tony Johnson (Leo Cooper 2002)

Evader, Denys Teare (Crecy Publishing 2008)

Flying for Freedom, Tony Redding (Cerberus Publishing Ltd 2005)

Flying in Walking Out, Edward Sniders (Leo Cooper 1999)

Flying Into Hell, Mel Rolfe (Grub Street 2004)

Follow the Man With the Pitcher, Kenneth Skidmore (Countyvise Ltd 1999)

Footprints on the Sands of Time, Oliver Clutton-Brock (Grub Street 2003)

Free to Fight Again, Alan W. Cooper (William Kimber 1988)
German Invasion Plans for the British Isles 1940 (Bodleian Library 2007)
Ghosts of Targets Past, Philip Gray (Grub Street 1995)
Halifax Down, Tom Wingham (Grub Street 2009)
Home Guard Manual 1941 (Tempus Publishing Ltd 2007)
Home Run, Richard Townsend Bickers (Leo Cooper 1992)
In the Footsteps of a Flying Boot, Art Horning (Carlton Press New York 1994)
Inferno: The Devastation of Hamburg, 1943, Keith Lowe (Penguin 2007)
Inside the Gestapo, Helene Moszkiewiez (The Bodley Head Ltd 1987)
Journeys Into Night, Don Charlwood (Hudson Hawthorn 1991)
Lancaster, Leo McKinstry (John Murray Publishers 2009)
Lancaster, M. Garbett & B. Goulding (The Promotional Reprint Ltd 1994)
Lancaster Down, Steve Darlow (Grub Street 2012)
Lancaster Target, Jack Currie (Crecy Publishing Ltd 2008)
Les Parisiennes, Anne Sebba (Weidenfeld & Nicolson 2016)
Life, Luck and a Lancaster, Christine Butterworth (Hensham Books 2013)
Lone Evader, Sergeant Ted Coates (Australian Military History Publications 1998)
Lost Voices of the Royal Air Force, Max Arthur (Hodder 2005)
Luck and a Lancaster, Harry Yates (Airlife Publishing 1999)
Men of Air, Kevin Wilson (Phoenix 2008)
MI9 Escape and Evasion 1939–1945, M. R. D. Foot & J. M. Langley (The Bodley Head 1979)
Mission Marathon, Rémy (Librairie Académique Perrin Paris 1974)
Night After Night, Max Lambert (Harper Collins 2007)
On the Wings of the Morning, Vincent Holyoak (Local History Press 1995)
One of Those Days, J. M. Elliott (Unpublished memoir)
Only Birds and Fools, J. Norman Ashton (Airlife Publishing 1999)
Paths to Freedom, Bob Kellow (Bob Cromar Printing, Winnipeg 1992)
RAF Evaders, Oliver Clutton-Brock (Grub Street 2009)
RAF Swanton Morley: A Brief History, Janine Harrington (Prontaprint 2013)
Rear Gunner Pathfinders, Ron Smith (Crecy Publishing Ltd 2008)
Réseau Comete, Rémy (Librairie Académique Perrin Paris 1967)
Resistance, Agnes Humbert (Bloomsbury 2008)
Safe Houses Are Dangerous, Helen Long (William Kimber 1985)
Secret Sunday, Donald Darling (William Kimber 1975)
Shot Down and on the Run, Graham Pitchfork (National Archives, Kew 2003)
Silent Heroes, Sherri Greene Ottis (University Press of Kentucky 2001)
SOE in the Low Countries, M. R. D. Foot (St. Ermin's 2001)

Survivor, Roy E. Hill (Roy E. Hill 2004)

Tail Gunner, Chan Chandler (Airlife Publishing Ltd 2002)

Tested By Bomb and Flame, Austin J. Ruddy (Halsgrove 2014)

The Bomber Command War Diaries, M. Middlebrook & C. Everitt (Midland Publishing 1976)

The Comet Connection, George Watt (University Press of Kentucky 1999)

The Dark Side of the Sky, Harry Levy (The London Press 2007)

The Eighth Passenger, Miles Tripp (Wordsworth Editions 2002)

The Escape Factory, Lloyd R. Shoemaker (St Martins Paperbacks 1990)

The Escape Line, Megan Koreman (Oxford University Press 2018)

The Escape Room, Airey Neave (Doubleday & Co. New York 1970)

The Freedom Line, Peter Eisner (Perennial 2005)

The Great Escape, Paul Brickhill (Faber & Faber 1970)

The Pilot Walked Home, Dennis Hornsey (Collins Clear-Type Press 1946)

The Quest for Freedom, Yvonne De Ridder Files (The Narrative Press 1991)

The Raid on Munster Germany October 10 1943 and My Escape from German Occupied Europe, John K. Justice (Unpublished memoir)

They Fought Alone, Maurice Buckmaster (Biteback Publishing 2014)

Ticket to Freedom, H. J. Spiller (William Kimber 1988)

To the Last Round, Austin J. Ruddy (Breedon Books Publishing 2007)

War Pilot of Orange, Bob Vanderstok (Pictorial Histories Publishing 1987)

War Under the Wire, William Ash (Bantam Press 2005)

Wartime Leicester, Ben Beazley (Sutton Publishing 2004)

We Flew, We Fell, We Lived, Philip Lagrandeur (Vanwell Publishing, Ontario 2006)

When Paris Went Dark, Ronald C. Rosbottom (Little, Brown & Co. New York)